JOHN P. SWIFT

John Swift

AN IRISH DISSIDENT

John P Swift

Gill and Macmillan

Published in Ireland by
Gill and Macmillan Ltd
Goldenbridge
Dublin 8
with associated companies in
Auckland, Delhi, Gaborone, Hamburg, Harare,
Hong Kong, Johannesburg, Kuala Lumpur, Lagos, London,
Manzini, Melbourne, Mexico City, Nairobi,
New York, Singapore, Tokyo
© John P. Swift 1991
0 7171 1870 3
Index compiled by Helen Litton
Print origination by Seton Music Graphics Ltd, Bantry, Co. Cork
Printed by Criterion Press, Dublin

To Adrienne

Contents

Acknowledgments

For their assistance in researching this book, I am grateful to the staffs of the following institutions: the Central Statistics Office, the National Archives, the National Library of Ireland, the Registrar of Friendly Societies, University College, Dublin, Archives, the General Register Office (Births, Deaths and Marriages), Department of Health, the Public Libraries in Dundalk, Co. Louth and Dundrum, Co. Dublin, the Communist Party of Ireland, the Labour Party, the Workers' Party, the Irish Congress of Trade Unions, the Dublin Council of Trade Unions, the Bakery and Food Workers' Amalgamated Union, the Irish Labour History Society, the National College of Industrial Relations, St Joseph's Young Priests' Society, the Catholic Press and Information Office and the Clerk of St Patrick's Cathedral, Dundalk.

I would also like to thank the following individuals for their valuable assistance: Marion Boushell, Peter Cassells, Fergal Costello, Owen Curran, Joe Deasy, John de Courcy Ireland, Johnny Devlin, Stephen Doyle, Eric Fleming, Des Geraghty, Michael Halpenny, Ken Hannigan, Seamus Helferty, George Jeffares, John Kane, Ray Kavanagh, Jean Kennedy, Barbara Keogh, George Lawlor, Kay MacKeogh, Luke MacKeogh, Cathal MacLiam, Don McLave, Angela McQuillan, Patrick Mooney, Tom Morrissey, SJ, Fiona Murray, Donal Nevin, Carmel O'Connor, John O'Dowd, Michael O'Halloran, Michael O'Regan, Manus O'Riordan, Michael O'Riordan, Bob Purdie, Pat Rabbitte, TD, Patrick Shanley, Andée Sheehy Skeffington, Noel Ward and Sarah Ward Perkins.

I am especially indebted to Francis Devine, Marie Mac-Sweeney and Marie Woods for reading several drafts of my manuscript and making numerous helpful suggestions. Any omissions or errors are, of course, entirely my own. Marie MacSweeney also produced the final typed version of the manuscript and I am grateful to her for that.

I am greatly indebted, too, to my late parents, John and Harriet Swift; and to my sister and brother, Alice Robinson and Grosvenor Swift, for responding to my interminable round of questions. My father's lucid and slightly understated descriptions and analysis of events and personalities were an invaluable contribution to the book.

Finally, I wish to thank my wife, Adrienne, and my sons, David, Justin, John, Neville and Robert, for enduring the disruption to family life while I was writing this work. Adrienne also read several drafts of the text, making many useful suggestions, and for that, too, I thank her.

John P. Swift
Dublin, March 1991

Abbreviations

AEU	Amalgamated Engineering Union
AFL—CIO	American Federation of Labour—Congress of Industrial Organisations
AGM	Annual General Meeting
ASW	Amalgamated Society of Woodcutters
ATGWU	Amalgamated Transport and General Workers' Union
BFWAU	Bakery and Food Workers' Amalgamated Union
CIA	Central Intelligence Agency
CIU	Congress of Irish Unions
CPI	Communist Party of Ireland
CSEU	Civil Service Executive Union
CSO	Central Statistics Office
CYM	Connolly Youth Movement
DCTU	Dublin Council of Trade Unions
DTUC	Dublin Trades Union Council
EEPTU	Electrical, Electronic, Telecommunications and Plumbing Union
FWUI	Federated Workers' Union of Ireland
GPMU	Graphical, Paper and Media Union
IAAM	Irish Anti-Apartheid Movement
IBCAWAU	Irish Bakers' Confectioners' and Allied Workers' Amalgamated Union
IBNAU	Irish Bakers' National Amalgamated Union
ICTU	Irish Congress of Trade Unions
ILHS	Irish Labour History Society
ILO	International Labour Organisation
INTO	Irish National Teachers' Organisation
ITGWU	Irish Transport and General Workers' Union
ITUC	Irish Trade Union Congress
IUF	International Union of Food and Allied Workers' Associations
IWL	Irish Worker League (Larkin's)
IWL	Irish Workers' League (forerunner of IWP and CPI)
IWP	Irish Workers' Party

MPGWU	Marine Port and General Workers' Union
NATO	North Atlantic Treaty Organisation
NCIR	National College of Industrial Relations
NEC	National Executive Committee or Council
NICRA	Northern Ireland Civil Rights Association
OBU	One Big Union
PUTUO	Provisional United Trade Union Organisation
RMC	Resident Management Committee
SIPTU	Services Industrial Professional and Technical Union
TUC	Trades Union Congress
UCATT	Union of Construction Allied Trades and Technicians
WFTU	World Federation of Trade Unions
WUI	Workers' Union of Ireland

Sweet Music and Swift's Bread

In the first week of July 1988, John Swift's activities included attending, as a guest, the four-day annual conference of the Irish Congress of Trade Unions, organising and participating in formal discussions on the Soviet trade unions, picketing Bewley's Grafton Street shop and café where a strike was in progress over the closure of the firm's bakery, and rebuking the striking bakers for their feeble picketing. Also within that not untypical week, John Swift read a book as well as a daily newspaper. To engage in these pursuits involved him in several journeys by bus and not a little walking. What is remarkable about all of this is that he was then approaching his ninety-second birthday. These activities of Swift's were indicative, not only of his passionate and life-long interest in the international labour movement, but his extraordinary zest for life, perhaps his most striking characteristic.

John Swift was born in Dundalk, Co. Louth, in 1896, the year James Connolly first came to Ireland, and only two years after the founding of what is now the Irish Congress of Trade Unions. Some seventeen years were to elapse before the 1913 Dublin Lock-Out would occur, while the Bolshevik Revolution, heralding the first socialist state, was a further four years away. Verdi, Brahms and Johann Strauss II were among famous composers who were still living at the time of Swift's birth.

Not a great deal is known about Swift's ancestry. The common presumption that the name Swift is of Anglo-Irish origin is only partly true. A branch of a Yorkshire family of that name settled in Dublin and Kilkenny in the early seventeenth century. A member of a junior branch of that family was Jonathan Swift, the famous author and Dean of St Patrick's Cathedral, Dublin. Not of English origin, however, are the Swifts of County Mayo, their name deriving from a mistranslation of the anglicised form of the Gaelic Ó Fuada, also known as Foody in English.[1] Whether Swift's roots were English or Irish is unclear. What is certain is that all his known ancestors were of Catholic extraction.

Laurence Swift, John's grandfather, was the youngest of four sons of Patrick and Alice Swift who were tenant farmers at Antylstown, Donaghmore, near Stackallen, Co. Meath. On 4 February 1854 Laurence Swift married Mary Anne Rice in St Patrick's Cathedral, Dundalk. It was also in Dundalk that the first three of their four children were born. Yet Laurence Swift, a baker by trade, worked in Dublin throughout his adult life. For more than twenty years, in the mid-1800s, he was a member of the Little Britain Street Bakers' Society,[2] one of several rival bakers' unions in Dublin at that time. For the last few years of his life, Laurence Swift was a partner in John Allen's bakery at 85 North King Street, Dublin. At the time of his death, in April 1862, at the age of 50, Laurence Swift's address was 5 North King Street. He was buried in Dublin's Glasnevin Cemetery in a grave owned and occupied by his former business partner, John Allen, who had predeceased him. Allen's widow, Maria, was buried there later. Not interred there, however, was Mary Swift, Laurence's widow. Seemingly, after her husband's death, she returned to Dundalk where she died on 10 October 1907, at the age of 74. She was buried in St Patrick's Cemetery, Dundalk.

Patrick Swift, John's father, the third child of Laurence and Mary Swift, was born in Dundalk on 8 September 1858. Having served an apprenticeship as a baker in H. F. & J. M'Cann, Church Street, Dundalk, he worked in that firm until 1890. Patrick Swift was a member of the Dundalk Bakers' Society (the Dundalk Bakers' Union) and its president in 1890.[3] In June of that year he was a leader of a significant bakers' strike in the town. Working conditions in the bakery trade were extremely bad then in many parts of the country, particularly in Dundalk. A year earlier, in 1889, delegates from Belfast, Dublin, Dundalk and Newry had assembled in Dublin to establish the National Federal Bakers' Union.[4] The first delegate meeting of this body was held the following year in Belfast. Dundalk was among the twenty-one branches represented at that gathering. After deciding the objectives of the organisation, the meeting heard reports from delegates of pay and working conditions in various parts of the

country. The union's record of that meeting reveals that the worst
conditions were reported by the Dundalk delegate, Mr Morris:

> . . . In M'Cann's shop [where Patrick Swift was employed]
> men were paid 24/- per week; the foreman getting 28/-.
> The hours were 90 to 102—night work (Cries of shame).
> In Mrs. M'Ginnity's wages are 24/- for underhands (jour-
> neymen), and 30/- for the foreman. The hours are 115 per
> week (Shame). They go into M'Cann's at 2 o'clock on
> Sunday and come out at 11 on Monday. In McGinnity's it is
> 1 o'clock on Sunday—the men going home at 11 and
> coming back at one—two hours at home every day (cries
> of shame and hisses). In Kiernan's there were 7 men, 2
> being jobbers (casuals). Wages 24/- for underhands and
> £2. for the foreman. Hours 90 in the week. In Kidd's place
> there were 6 men, one jobber. Wages 24/- to 30/-. These
> men came in on Sunday morning at 7 o'clock, worked all
> day, and on Saturday after their work is done they have
> got to deliver and collect accounts before they are paid. If
> they didn't they wouldn't be kept. ('A voice—It's good
> enough for those who do it')[5]

Some of Mr Morris's statements did not go unchallenged.
M'Cann's, for example, observed:

> . . . He [Mr Morris] states 90 to 102 hours per week is the
> time the men have to work. He would be more accurate if
> he stated 72 to 90, because if the men be in 90 hours they
> have not to work all that time. During the time the bread is
> baking in the oven they can take a little relaxation . . . ![6]

At that time the Dublin tablehands (journeymen) were working
a sixty-six to 70-hour week for 34/-, with foremen being paid
43/-. In Newry, not far from Dundalk, the average weekly wage
of journeymen was 35/-.[7] Prices of commodities in Dundalk
during this period included 2*d* for a 2 lb loaf of bread,[8] 1/- to 2/6
per pound of tea,[9] 7½*d* per lb of bacon[10] and 2*d* for a local
weekly newspaper.[11] A dozen bottles of stout cost 1/6 to 1/9,[12]
while a gallon of whiskey could be bought for a £1.[13]

On 14 June 1890, a month after the union's delegate meeting,
the Dundalk bakers went on strike in support of the following
demands: 'That 30/- be paid to underhands, and 36/- to foremen

for a week of 66 hours (including one and a half hours for meals). Week to commence at 6 a.m. on Monday mornings. Overtime to be paid for at the rate of 9*d* per hour; no night work or Sunday work; and that they will not be required to work with non-union men or to serve [sell] any bread.'[14] According to a contemporary report, the strike involving some fifty members in seven firms[15] was a resounding success: '. . . The employers acceded to substantially all the demands of the men. Sunday and night work, as well as bread serving to be abolished; the men are to work 66 hours in the week, instead of an indefinite number as heretofore, non-union men are to be disemployed; and an increase of 3/- per week in the wages given. . .'[16]

Having referred to the success of the Dundalk bakers and others, the Federal Union, in its executive report for the quarter ending 30 June 1890, added:

> In conclusion, we wish to draw your attention to the soul-stirring lines written by Patrick Swift, President, Dundalk Bakers, on obtaining their freedom:

> > Awake! Arise to freedom's call!
> > You men who over toil,
> > And cast aside that yoke of gall
> > Which long did round you coil.
> > Your hours of labour now shall be
> > But ten in twenty four—
> > Get ready, then—stand up like men,
> > And we'll be slaves no more!

> > The Union and the early grave
> > Has been the end too long
> > Of many a weary brother slave
> > Who sank beneath his wrong;
> > Whilst others, too, have passed away
> > Ere manhood days were o'er,
> > And sank beneath the tyrant's sway
> > To be their slaves no more!

> > And when the Sunday morning dawns,
> > And bells ring out for prayer,
> > The Baker cannot go to Church—
> > He has no time to spare.

> What matter if his soul be lost?
>   The work must go before!—
> We'll put that down whate'er it cost,
>   And be their slaves no more!
>
> Let all who have the cause at heart
>   Like brothers, then, unite;
> Let each man act a manly part
>   With all his soul and might;
> And go together hand in hand,
>   Combined from shore to shore—
> Our rights demand and by them stand,
>   And be their slaves no more.[17]

Reports that the strike had been successful proved to be premature, at least in M'Cann's where the employer reneged on the settlement terms. Moreover, as a consequence of leading the strike in that firm, Swift and two others, John Cooper and James Reilly, were locked out or dismissed.[18]

An oblique reference to this was made by Murray Davis, General Secretary of the Federal Union, at a public meeting held in Dundalk on a second and prolonged bakers' strike which occurred a year after the original one. This extract from his speech on that occasion is taken from the *Dundalk Democrat* of 20 June 1891:

> . . . It was said in Dundalk that night that there were not proper and able enough men to be got in Dundalk to do the work required; but this was not true. He had been pointed out two or three men who were in that particular employment at the time of the last strike, and had since to leave it. These men were honest, industrious, hard-working fellows, and the best proof of it was that they were now doing well in business for themselves . . .

This was undoubtedly a reference to Swift and his two colleagues who, having been unable to secure alternative employment, had established their own bakery business, Swift, Reilly & Co., at 83 Clanbrassil Street, Dundalk's principal thoroughfare. Their bakery opened on 13 February 1891, eight months after the strike.[19] So successful was this undertaking that the premises had to be extended the following year.[20] Two years later again, however, having failed to convince his partners to mechanise, Reilly left the firm to set up his own bakery at 58 Clanbrassil Street.[21] The original business then became known as Swift and Cooper.[22]

Swift & Cooper's premises extended from a shop at the front in Clanbrassil Street to a confectionery bakery at the rear, backing on to the wall of Lord Roden's demesne. Immediately behind the shop was an office where Patrick worked; beyond that a bread bakery, and beyond that again stores in which ingredients were stocked. Goods were transported through the premises on a buggy than ran on a railed passageway. The firm's horse-drawn vans, serving parts of Counties Louth, Cavan, Down and Monaghan, were loaded outside the shop. At its height, some twenty persons were employed in the business, ten being bakers or confectioners, eight van drivers, with the remainder working in the shop.

On 1 February 1894, at the age of thirty-five, Patrick Swift married Alice Deane in St Patrick's Cathedral, Dundalk. The combination of surnames must have been a source of some amusement! At about the same time, Patrick's business partner, John Cooper, wedded Alice's sister, Mary Deane. For a few years after their marriage Patrick and Alice lived over their bakery at 83 Clanbrassil Street (now 'Musik Tapes') and it was there, on 26 August 1896, that their first child, Laurence John (John) Swift was born.[23] Mary Elizabeth Swift, the second child, born on 11 April 1898, died after two days. The third, Mary Bridget Swift, known as May, was born on 29 May 1903 and on 16 June the following year, Patrick (Paddy) James Swift, the youngest, was born. On the day following his birth, 27 August 1896, John Swift was baptised into the Catholic Church in St Patrick's Cathedral, Dundalk.

John Swift had no recollection of living in the house of his birth. When he was still an infant his parents moved their home, but not their business, to 77 Clanbrassil Street (now 'Modern Fashions'), a few doors away from their bakery. Their new rented dwelling was part of a large premises comprising a house and draper's shop. Apart from the shop on the ground floor, managed initially by a Miss M. A. Watters and later by the Misses Murphy and Jones, the remainder of the building was divided into two separate living quarters. One of these was the home of the people who ran the shop, while the other was occupied by the Swifts and their business partners, the Coopers. The Swift family included John's grandmother, Mary Swift. She had childhood memories of the Famine and of attending the funeral of Daniel O'Connell in Dublin in 1847. John was eleven when she died in 1907. Behind the Swifts' new home was a yard, a coach house, stables and, beyond that again, a garden.

At the age of about four, Swift was sent to the Sisters of Mercy's kindergarten. It was known as the Grande School, to distinguish it from a national school on the same site, but beyond a wall, run by the same order of nuns for the children of less privileged families. Staffed mainly by nuns, the kindergarten was part of a junior and secondary girls' school where the daughters of middle-class families were trained to become 'young ladies'. Swift's tuition comprised elementary singing, the sewing of pictures on to cardboard and some prayers. Occasionally, in the presence of their parents, the children would perform little plays such as *Who Killed Cock Robin*.

There were two orders of religious Brothers in the town, the Irish Christian Brothers and the De La Salle Brothers. Pupils of the former were from families socially better off than those who sent their boys to the latter. Those of an even higher social stratum enrolled their sons in the local Marist College. When he was seven, Swift left the kindergarten to attend the Irish Christian Brothers' school. In this fee-paying junior and secondary school for boys, classes or forms were known as *books*.

While a pupil in the third or fourth book, Swift and others were involved in operating a black market of goods stolen from the various businesses of their parents. Sweets, chocolates, tin soldiers, cigarettes, tobacco and snuff were among the items pilfered. The boys bartered or sold their commodities to one another. With fresh cakes daily, Swift was in a strong position in the market place! The Brothers would turn a blind eye to these practices, perhaps hoping that their pupils might learn something about commerce. Occasionally, the more popular Brothers would be given a cake or some snuff or tobacco. It was through pilfering cakes from his parents' business that Swift acquired a smattering of the bakery trade. As retribution for his misdemeanours, the foreman coerced him into assisting in the confectionery bakery.

Irish was an optional subject in the fourth book. Although neither of Swift's parents had a knowledge of Irish they encouraged him to study the subject. However, as most of the Irish taught in the school took the form of prayers, he soon lost interest in the language. It was also while a pupil of the fourth book that Brother Ford tested him for the school choir. At that time Swift had a bad stammer. As therapy for this, Brother Ford would bring him to the piano after school and play a single note repetitively in regular rhythm. To the same rhythm Swift would read some poetry. With assistance from his mother, this technique was practised at home and, in time, the impediment disappeared. Possessing a good soprano voice, he joined the school choir in which he was often selected by the choirmaster to lead the sopranos or to sing solo. One of the pieces he enjoyed performing at that time was 'The Huntsmen's Chorus' from Weber's opera, *Der Freischütz.*

The choir also sang in St Patrick's Cathedral and St Nicholas's Chapel in the town. A favourite pastime of the boys was to parody the words of the hymns and other church music. Swift was one of a group who served Mass and Benediction, duties requiring some knowledge of Latin which was taught in the school. The boys would make fun of the litany during Benediction. An instance of this in the cathedral caused quite a stir. In the responses, instead of singing *Ora pro nobis* (Pray for us), they chanted: 'Oh Hurrah for Swift's Hovis!' This, of course, was a reference to Swift's father's agency for 'Hovis' bread. If this particular mischief went unnoticed by the cathedral's German organist, Herr Heuermann, whose knowledge of Latin and English was rather limited, there were others present who were more observant. The incident created a scandal that went beyond the cathedral and the school.

There was a rather vicious Brother in charge of the fifth book. A common practice of his was to hurl a thick strap at an offender with the command to bring it forward for a lashing of the hands. Science classes began in that book. In one of the lessons on electricity, the class would stand in a circle holding hands. By means of an electrical generator, the Brother in charge would put one of the pupils in contact with the electricity. This, of course, would be transmitted to the others and everyone in the circle would receive a mild shock. With electricity being quite a novelty at that time, Dundalk then being lit by gas, this was considered a wonderful thing by the boys.

Swift's father took a keen interest in his son's education, particularly science, which he regarded as undermining the whole basis of theology. A great Darwinian, he regarded the Book of Genesis as nonsense. On returning from school, Swift would be asked by his father what science he had been taught. His father would laugh on hearing, as he invariably did, that it was purely physical science. He found it incomprehensible that such knowledge could be imparted without reference to any intellectual implications that might emanate from scientific discoveries.

In the course of his school-days Swift witnessed some sectarian incidents which were to influence him profoundly. Returning from their Sunday evening service in St Nicholas's Chapel, Swift and the other Catholic altar boys would meet pupils of the Protestant college leaving their church. Armed with sacks containing their soutanes and surplices, sometimes augmented with stones, the Catholic boys would provoke a fight with the Protestants and serious injuries would often be sustained. About such incidents, Swift observed: 'I felt revulsion from these fracas and withheld from joining in them.'[24] No less repugnant to him was the sectarianism he witnessed when he was, for a short period, a pupil of the De La Salle Brothers. There, a Jewish boy who did not participate in the religious class was persecuted by other pupils. John's family was not unaffected by sectarianism in the town. He recalled that, when his aunt, Sarah Deane, a Catholic, married a Protestant from Lurgan, Co. Armagh, some of her local co-religionists were 'less than kind'. As a consequence of this, her husband, David Millar, an employee of the post office in Dundalk, transferred to Manchester and the couple left the town.[25]

Of his school-days which he enjoyed, Swift said: 'When I left the Brothers . . . I could read and write fairly well, had some knowledge of elementary chemistry and physics and knew enough Latin and French to whet a taste for foreign languages.'[26] He could have added that, for composition, he won prizes of holy pictures! As for the Brothers who taught him, Swift had this to say: ' . . . Though they had colleagues vicious strappers, who should never have been teachers, many of the Brothers were kindly but deprived hard-working men . . .'[27]

During Swift's childhood, Dundalk had a population of approximately 13,000.[28] The mode of transport was horse drawn and motor cars were rare. With the gramophone only beginning to appear and there being no radio, only live music could be heard. There was no scarcity of musical activity in the town. Among artists who appeared there in the early years of this century were John McCormack, the famous tenor,[29] the singer and song writer, Percy French,[30] Dr Ormond's Celebrated Viennese Ladies' Orchestra,[31] and the Elster-Grime Grand Opera Company.[32] On their third Irish tour in 1905, John Philip Sousa and his band performed in the town hall. Admission prices for *The March King's* concert were 5/- and 4/- for reserved seats and 2/- and 1/- for unreserved.[33]

Local amateur talent contributed much to the musical life of the town. In the Emmet, the Grattan and the O'Mahony, Dundalk boasted three first-rate bands. Of the three, the Emmet was the most popular. Dressed in the white breeches and green swallow tail coats of the United Irishmen, the Emmets were an impressive spectacle to behold. Featuring prominently in their repertoire were selections from the operas, *The Bohemian Girl* and *Maritana* by Balfe and Wallace respectively. The Dundalk Orchestral Society had its own orchestra of some fifty-five members,[34] among whom were one of the M'Canns of the bakery firm, and Swifts' general practitioner, Dr Flood. Each year the orchestra gave two public performances, playing such works as Rossini's overtures *Semiramide* and *William Tell*; Schubert's *Rosamunde*, 'The Grand March' from *Tannhäuser* by Wagner and excerpts from Gounod's *Faust*. Conducting the orchestra was the local professional and versatile musician, Tom V. Parkes. Possessing a fine tenor voice, Parkes was also an accomplished organist, pianist and violinist.

Musical evenings in people's homes were very common at that time. Swift's home was no exception and a wide variety of musicians performed in their parlour. On more formal occasions these could include the likes of the aforementioned Dr Flood or Tom Parkes. But Patrick Swift would meet musicians in the street and bring them home. This proved quite a problem for John's mother for, although some were obvious ragamuffins, Patrick would insist that they be treated like gentlemen. Some of these street musicians had talent. A German band of five or six played stringed instruments. Their rendition of *Waves of the Danube* was John's first hearing of Ivanovitch's popular waltz. It was believed later that the band members were spies preparing for World War I. Another musical visitor to Swift's home was a one-man band. On his back he carried a large drum, with a drumstick strapped to his right arm. Cymbals on top of the drum were operated from above by a wire attachment running down his back to the heel of one of his boots. By moving his arm and his foot, he could play the drum and cymbals as an accompaniment to his main instrument, the melodeon.

During Swift's childhood, people created much of their own entertainment. Nicknames were common and the town was full of characters. John's family was not without its share of colourful figures. One who certainly fell into this category was his father, who had a great interest in literature and music. As well as being an elecutionist who liked reciting verse, including some he composed, he was an accomplished raconteur. Endowed with a good baritone voice, he could also play the harp and violin.

Patrick had a circle of friends whom he met fairly regularly in Connolly's pub at 15 Clanbrassil Street (now the Lorne Hotel). In the snug at the front of that hostelry they would entertain themselves discussing philosophical subjects, telling amusing stories or conferring nicknames on other local characters. Sometimes Patrick and his friends would visit Toberona (John's Well) on the Castletown Road, where Swift's head yardman, Pat Quigley, and his wife lived. There, after a few drinks, the repartee and banter would resume. Toberona acquired the legend that gifts of eloquence would be bestowed on those drinking its waters. Later, perhaps back in Connolly's snug, when one of the friends would tell a tall tale, another would retort: 'Tell that in Toberona!'

Patrick used to visit Dublin to order ingredients for the bakery. He would stay in Jury's Hotel in College Green. On such occasions and on others in Dundalk, he would drink excessively and be confined to bed, sometimes suffering from hallucinations. While recuperating, he would pace up and down his bedroom and would not eat. On his recovery, he would go to the other extreme, becoming quite intolerant of alcohol and advising others of its evil. Some of his friends would coax him back to the drink and he would eventually make his return to Connolly's. John would be given a few pence by his mother to look for his father, who, more often than not, could be found in the snug of his favourite haunt on the opposite side of the street. There, from one of Patrick's coterie, John would receive 3*d* to keep secret his father's whereabouts.

Patrick's political position depended on whether he was sober or drunk. When sober, he was a Parnellite, a fact attested to by his membership of the United Irish League. In 1890, Patrick's nationalism had found expression in his support for the release of Irish political prisoners in Britain.[35] Under the influence of drink, however, he would espouse Fenianism. Patrick had a socialist outlook, though this was of a rather sentimental nature and never developed much beyond that.

Although a nominal Catholic and a regular attender at High Mass, Patrick was a rationalist. Love of music was his primary motive for attending Mass. Outside the Church, there were few opportunities then to hear music by the great composers of the eighteenth and nineteenth centuries. But Patrick had another reason for going to Mass. He feared that his business would suffer if he was not seen regularly at chapel. Among Patrick's collection of books were several works by the evolutionists, Thomas Huxley and Charles Darwin, including Darwin's *Origin of Species*. Such books were obtained from the Rationalist Press Association in London and kept in a private bookcase in his bedroom.

Alice Swift, the eldest of six children of John and Bridget Deane who lived and ran a pub at 1 Linenhall Street, Dundalk (now The Leinster Inn), differed greatly from her husband. A Catholic, though not a pious one, she had been educated in the Sisters of Mercy's Grande School. Although her parents were Parnellites, she was uninterested in politics. A little taller than average, Alice had good taste in clothes and enjoyed dressing in the latest fashions. She also liked wearing expensive jewellery, often changing it several times a day. When not worn, the jewellery would be hidden behind volumes of *Lives of the Saints* in a bookcase in the parlour where the respectable books such as Shakespeare, Burns and Dickens were kept. According to John, Alice was 'a rather proud woman'. Many of her friends were members of the Women's National Health Association, which was patronised by Lady Aberdeen, wife of the Lord Lieutenant. The welfare of sufferers of tuberculosis which had been endemic since the Famine was the main concern of the association. Alice was on the fringe of this organisation but was probably not a member. She was afraid to join such bodies because of her husband's objections to associations with people he regarded as pro-British snobs.

John's uncle and aunt, John and Mary Cooper, were simple but kindly people. John was very fond of them. Like Patrick, John Cooper supported the Irish Parliamentary Party and had been a member of the United Irish League. A native of Castle-bellingham, Co. Louth, he was general supervisor of the bakery. Though the Swifts and the Coopers were relatives and business partners, and lived in the same house, seldom did they mix. Many of Alice's friends were unaware of the Coopers' existence. Unlike the Coopers, Alice had a taste for the high social life.

The fact that Mary Cooper kept hens in the backyard was a major source of annoyance to Alice who could not tolerate the presence of the poultry and the mess they created close to the house. She discussed the problem with the head yardman who suggested that the yard be concreted. This was done and after a period of time the hens stayed away.

Seldom were John's parents without one or two servants, very often the daughters of employees in the bakery. There was usually a good relationship between the Swifts and their servants. The family and servants ate together, slept in the same quarters and, generally, the servants were regarded as part of the family. Such arrangements between families and servants were quite common then in Dundalk.

In this period before the Social Welfare Acts there was the Poor Law under which the destitute were given outdoor relief, usually in the form of grocery vouchers. For the more acute cases, there was the workhouse, also known as the union. Administering the Poor Law were the Poor Law Guardians, most of whom were local business people. One of them was John's great uncle, Michael Deane, who owned a pub in the town. Now run by Michael's granddaughter, Agnes Meade, the pub, at 64 Bridge Street, has changed little in appearance and still bears his name.

As many Poor Law Guardians sought election on a low rates policy, the Poor Law was run as economically as possible. One means of controlling costs was to persuade the better-off families in the town to adopt a beggar. Alice and Mary each had a beggar calling regularly to them. Michael Deane had influenced Mary to adopt hers, a cripple known locally as 'The Clappers' Byrne, who played the bones and danced. Mary's beggar would call to the back door to be given some food or money. Alice's beggar was a woman of middle-class background who had fallen on hard times. Like some of the other local businessmen's wives, Alice would give the beggar clothes. Her beggar became quite adept at exploiting the snobbery of these women. Dressed in a coat or dress received from one, she would identify the donor to another. Not to be outdone, the second woman would often provide garments equalling or surpassing those given by her rival. It seems that the clothes were later sold in Drogheda in a shop run by the beggar's sister.

John Swift, an uncle of John's and known to him as Uncle Johnny, was an occasional guest of the family. While he was a Catholic, his wife, Frances (Fanny), was a member of the Church of Ireland. Conforming to a common custom of the time, sons of that marriage were raised in their father's faith while daughters were brought up in the religion of their mother. A loyalist and member of the Royal Irish Constabulary, Uncle Johnny disagreed strongly in politics with his brother, Patrick, and many were the political rows between them when he stayed with the family. After his retirement in 1906, Uncle Johnny settled near Dundalk. He worked on one of the bakery vans and sometimes brought John on the run to the Castlebellingham district.

During his childhood, John spent some holidays with his parents in Manchester. They stayed with Alice's sister, Sarah Millar, and her husband, David. Other travels of John's youth included trips with his mother to Belfast where they visited her sister, Margaret White, and her husband, Henry, a tailor. Occasionally, John accompanied his parents to Dublin.

Swift and Cooper's business went bankrupt around 1909. John was twelve or thirteen at the time and still at school. He was shocked to learn of this turn of events from posters in the town giving notice of the sale of vehicles and other assets of the firm. The main cause of the bankruptcy was competition from Belfast bakeries which had mechanised. Swift and Cooper's resistance to mechanisation derived from Patrick's confidence and pride in the traditional hand-craft method of baking. Patrick's drink problem may have been a contributory factor in the downfall of the business. Following the bankruptcy, the family moved to a small rented premises in Bridge Street where they lived for several months on the proceeds of the sale of their furniture, before opening a small bakery and shop in the same premises. From there, John delivered bread and cakes to relatives and friends of the family.

When he was fifteen, John left school to commence work as a junior clerk in the firm of Dr Michael C. Moynagh, solicitors, in Roden Place. His mother had arranged this through her cousin, Johnny Watters, the firm's head law clerk. Much of John's time was spent copying legal documents in pen and ink. The typewriter was then only beginning to appear and the firm's clients and, indeed, some judges, were not always prepared to accept typewritten documents. Conscious that, as Crown Solicitor for County Louth, Moynagh would be involved in political prosecutions, Patrick had reservations about his son working for the firm. In fact, no such cases arose while John was there. Nevertheless Patrick would have preferred if John had worked in the bakery trade.

Michael Moynagh had two sons working in the firm, Frank, a barrister, and Stephen, a solicitor. John was not long in Moynagh's when Stephen Moynagh left his father's business to open his own legal practice in Francis Street. He took with him some of his father's employees, including John. John worked on Saturday mornings and had the duty of closing the premises at one o'clock. His wages of 2/6 a week were due for payment at that time. Very often, at this stage, his boss, Stephen Moynagh, would return from the Commercial Club, a drinking society of the upper classes, of which he was a member. Putting his hand in his pocket for John's wages, he would frequently say: 'Oh, I am sorry, Swift, I have no change. I will pay you next week.' John would have to wait a week, sometimes more, for his wages. John enjoyed legal work and what he described as 'the logic of the law'. All his life, he retained an interest in legal matters, particularly in cases of libel and slander.

The small bakery which Patrick ran in Bridge Street was insufficient to sustain the family and, in the winter of 1912/1913, when John was sixteen, the Swifts left Dundalk for Dublin.[36]

Eyes and Ears Only for Larkin

The Swift family settled in the Clanbrassil Street area of Dublin. Their first lodgings were in a house in Lombard Street West. This had been arranged through John Cooper, whose cousins, the McQuillans, occupied a second flat in the same house. The Coopers were already living in Dublin, in Christchurch Place. With no children of their own, they had virtually adopted John's sister, May, and she was living with them.

John Swift commenced work immediately as an apprentice in Jacob's biscuit factory, in Bishop Street. His father had arranged this through a friend in Dundalk in the mistaken belief that the baking of biscuits was similar to that of bread and cakes. Bored by the mechanised process of biscuit production, Swift left the firm after only a few weeks. Later in 1913, he secured work as a confectioner in Galbraith's bakery, a branch of a Drogheda firm located at 17/29 Vicar Street, an obscure thoroughfare off Thomas Street. He was employed on day work as an improver, a stage between that of an apprentice and a journeyman. Abused by employers, this intermediate step was abolished later by the union. Seldom were bakers considered sufficiently improved to command the full journeyman's rate!

At that time there was widespread unemployment in the Dublin bakery trade. As a result, Swift's father was unable to get permanent work. Two years earlier, in 1911, the Bridge Street Bakers' Society, Dublin's principal bakers' union, had collapsed following a disastrous strike against mechanisation.[1] Although re-established at Ormond Quay a year later,[2] the union was still impotent.

The employment of unionised bakers in the capital city is normally regulated by the Dublin Bakers' Union. It is to the union that unemployed members report daily for casual work or jobbing. They are sent in rotation to bakeries as replacements for absent colleagues or to augment staff during peak production periods. In this way a baker may get work for a day, a few days or a week and, occasionally a permanent job may ensue. But with the collapse of the Dublin Bakers' Union in 1911 the control of casual employment passed from the union to the employers. Consequently, unemployed bakers seeking work were referred to the employers' house of call in Middle Abbey Street,[3] to be selected, arbitrarily, for casual employment. This, of course, was repugnant to union members accustomed to securing work through their union. While the house of call never provided Swift with employment, it may have been the source of some casual work secured by his father.

Within months of the Swifts' arrival in the city there occurred the 1913 Lock-Out. It commenced as a strike on 26 August (Swift's seventeenth birthday), when tramworkers, members of the Irish Transport and General Workers' Union (ITGWU), abandoned their vehicles in the streets of Dublin. This followed the sacking by their employer, the Dublin United Tramway Company, of 200 of their number who had refused to leave the union. It was a response, too, to their employer's demand that, in the event of the union calling a strike, they would remain at work.

William Martin Murphy, the company's principal shareholder, had other major business interests in Ireland and abroad. His Irish business empire embraced such notable establishments as Independent Newspapers, Eason's, the booksellers and news-agents, and the Imperial Hotel (now Clery's department store).

The strike spread rapidly to the Independent and Eason's and was supported in sympathetic action by ITGWU members else-where. Less than a fortnight after the dispute began, more than 400 firms, members of the Employers' Federation, demanded that their employees sign the following undertaking renouncing the union:

> I hereby undertake to carry out all instructions given to me by or on behalf of my employers, and further I agree to immediately resign my membership of the Irish Transport & General Workers Union (if a member) and I further undertake that I will not join or in any way support this union.

It was when employees refused to sign this undertaking that the strike evolved into a Lock-Out.

Some 20,000 workers were directly involved in the dispute. When their dependents are added, this figure rises to approximately 100,000, then more than a third of Dublin's population. Bitterness and violence were features of the Lock-Out, which saw the break-up of strike meetings by police and the imprisonment of strikers and union leaders. While blacklegs were afforded police protection, strikers were viciously baton charged by the police. Two Dublin workers were batoned to death.

Lasting for six months, the dispute caused considerable hardship for thousands of Dublin families. Grinding poverty was prevalent in most districts of the city. Mitigating the situation somewhat was the charity of the St Vincent de Paul Society, complemented by the ITGWU's Lock-Out fund. From workers throughout the world came donations to the union's fund totalling some £150,000[4] (approximately £6 m. in 1991 values). There was an inconclusive ending to the dispute, with strikers drifting back to work. Many were obliged to sign the employers' infamous document repudiating the union.[5]

If the outcome is interpreted as a battle lost to the employers, then surely the union won the war! Within a mere seven years of the commencement of the Lock-Out, membership of the ITGWU had increased from approximately 30,000 to 130,000.[6] Perhaps more important, the events of 1913 were to inspire generations of Irish workers to join trade unions. More than seventy-five years after the event, the 1913 Lock-Out remains the most significant dispute in the history of the Irish trade union movement.

The Bakers' Union was not involved in the Lock-Out. For one thing, most Dublin bakeries were either non-union or only partly organised. Numerically and financially weak following its demise in 1911, and rebirth a year later, the union was still struggling to survive.[7] Nevertheless, individual members of the union donated 6*d* weekly to the Lock-Out fund of their ITGWU colleagues.[8]

Although not then a trade union member, Swift was greatly interested in the events of 1913, and particularly in the leader of the Lock-Out, James Larkin. Swift described Larkin as a big, powerful man, over six feet tall, and broad, with a large, almost lion-like head, protruding cheek bones, a large angular nose and large mouth.[9] But it was for his oratory that Swift most vividly recalled Larkin:

> He [James Larkin] was a very impressive speaker. In fact, I have never heard an orator to equal or surpass Larkin. It is not very often you hear oratory that impresses you with its sincerity. It is very often forced, a kind of falseness, theatrical if you like. But, with Larkin, it was quite natural and spontaneous. When he would appear to be annoyed, he would really be annoyed . . . He had a great sense of social justice, and injustice, of course, and it was very easy for him to get annoyed, and it was most convincing.[10]

Swift followed Larkin's meetings around the city. These were often spontaneous affairs for Larkin would stop at a street corner and start an impromptu meeting. He was always sure of an audience and crowds would gather quickly to hear him speak. Swift was present at many of his great meetings in Beresford Place and College Green. On those occasions the platform would be shared by other ITGWU leaders such as Connolly, O'Brien, P. T. Daly and Foran. Yet, due to the powerful presence and oratory of Larkin, Swift was oblivious of these other speakers. For that reason, too, he had no recollection of ever seeing James Connolly.[11]

During the 1913 Lock-Out, the Swifts were living in their second Dublin dwelling, a tenement house located at the junction of Clanbrassil Street and Daniel Street. It was a three-storey building consisting of a small grocery shop at street level, above which were two floors occupied by three tenants. The Swifts' accommodation on the second floor comprised two rooms. One of these at the back of the building was the bedroom of John's parents. The second room at the front served as a combined kitchen, dining and living area during the day and the bedroom of John and his brother, Paddy, at night. The mattress on which they slept would be placed on the floor at night, and in the morning it would be lifted and stored in their parents' bedroom. With no running water in this fairly typical Dublin tenement, tenants were obliged to share the only available toilet situated in the yard at the back of the house. Water for other domestic purposes was drawn from a tap in the yard.

In this period of the Lock-Out there was acute poverty in that part of the city. For much of the time Swift's father was unemployed, with the result that the family was almost destitute. They received help from a widow who lived in a flat above them. She ran a stall in the Iveagh Market. Most residents in the neighbourhood were receiving grocery vouchers from the Society of St Vincent de Paul or ITGWU food parcels, some of the latter having found their way into the black market. Swift's parents were reluctant recipients of the society's charity. With Alice the reluctance was a matter of pride. She was finding it difficult to adjust to the family's impoverishment. While Patrick could cope better with that, he disliked being dependent on the Catholic Church and, of course, the St Vincent de Paul Society was run by that Church.

Just as the Lock-Out was drawing to an end in early 1914, Swift joined the Irish Volunteers. He was seventeen. Paddy Birch and Joe Flynn, two of his friends from Galbraith's bakery, enrolled at the same time. The Irish Volunteers had been formed in November 1913 as a response to the founding a year earlier of the Ulster Volunteers. Resistance to Home Rule in Ireland, particularly in Ulster, was the object of the latter body. On the night of the inaugural meeting of the Irish Volunteers in Dublin's Rotunda, Swift had been among the overflowing crowd that had assembled in Sackville Street (now O'Connell Street). Patriotic call was the primary motivation in his decision to enlist. A subsidiary consideration related to his interest in physical culture. Having been members of a physical culture club in Marrowbone Lane, he and his companions from Galbraith's liked the drill, regarding it as a kind of exercise.

A house belonging to the Dublin Total Abstinence League and Workmen's Club, at 41 York Street, Dublin, was the headquarters of Swift's company of the Volunteers. They would drill there in the evening after work, while on Saturday afternoons the four companies comprising the Third Battalion, in which Swift and his friends were enrolled, would assemble and drill at Larkfield, Kimmage. This activity involved the handling of arms (imitation wooden guns!), keeping in step, marching up and down and forming in fours.

An officer of the Third Battalion was the then practically unknown Eamon de Valera. Neither Swift nor his friends were impressed by this future Taoiseach and President of Ireland:

He [Eamon de Valera] was a man we didn't care much about. He was very severe drilling, giving the orders in Irish and none of us knew Irish. He would never make free, was always grim, and we would make fun of him. He would come from Blackrock on a bicycle and, at that time, he was very thin and very tall, and he would have his full uniform on him sitting on the bike, and it looked so funny, he looked so grim on this bicycle, frowning.[12]

On Sundays all battalions would participate in route marches. The Third would assemble in Terenure and march in columns of four to the vicinity of the Three Rock or Kilmashogue mountains south of Dublin. On these particular expeditions there would also be manoeuvres.

Volunteers had to buy their own haversack, leather belt and bandoleer at a total cost of 5/-. They also contributed 3*d* weekly to a savings fund for their uniforms. The uniform which consisted of a tunic, breeches, peaked cap, puttees and boots, could be bought for about thirty shillings. A Volunteer was expected to supply his own gun and ammunition. Swift never reached the stage where he could afford either. No such difficulties were experienced by the officer and rank and file Volunteers of the upper classes. They invariably appeared in full uniform with gun and ammunition.

The outbreak of World War I, in August 1914, had a profound effect on the Volunteers. A month later the British Parliament passed the Government of Ireland Act, but with two conditions. These were that the legislation would not be enacted until after the end of the war, and then only after the British Government had had an opportunity to make special arrangements for Ulster.[13] In order to secure Britain's good will to activate Home Rule after the war, John Redmond, the Irish Parliamentary Party Leader, offered the services of the Volunteers to assist Britain's war effort.

There followed an immediate split in the Volunteers, the vast majority, approximately 170,000,[14] forming the National Volunteers under Redmond's leadership. Of the remaining 11,000,[15] most were republicans and members of Sinn Féin. They remained in membership of the Irish Volunteers. Thousands of Redmondites joined the British Army. According to Swift, a contributory factor in that was unemployment. In order to boost recruitment to the British Army, Britain took steps to run down industry and create unemployment.

By the time that the split occurred Swift had become somewhat disillusioned with the Volunteers. With the ever present prospect of conflict between the Irish and Ulster Volunteers, civil war seemed almost inevitable. He was fearful of that. He was dissatisfied, too, with the lack of discussion on social and political questions. Talks given by the officers were limited to such themes as national hatred of Britain, glorification of Irish history that was anti-British, and eulogising the heroes of Irish history. Debate on what kind of Ireland was being fought for was discouraged. From the limited discussions that Swift and his friends conducted, it was clear that the Ireland to which the officers aspired was based on the papal encyclicals, particularly Leo XIII's *Rerum Novarum*. Condemning socialism, it recommended as a solution to class war the establishment of corporations similar to the medieval guilds.

Having been a regular and avid reader of Larkin's socialist weekly, the *Irish Worker*, to which Connolly also contributed, and an enthusiastic follower of Larkin's campaign, Swift had become interested in socialism. He was beginning to feel uncomfortable with the Volunteers' obsession with nationalism. In addition to that, and in common with many others, he was demoralised by the split. To follow the recruiting officers and join the British Army had no appeal for him. At the same time, he was uncomfortable with the militant nationalists and their lack of social policies. Disillusioned and frustrated by this situation, Swift drifted out of the Volunteers in the summer of 1915. He was then nineteen years old.[16]

A Bit of Rhetoric

About a month prior to his nineteenth birthday, in August 1915, Swift was the victim of a highly dangerous practical joke. It was planned and executed by the foreman in Galbraith's bakery, Willie Brady, who instructed him to wash his hands before bringing a quantity of puff paste to a work bench. Swift's hands were still moist, as were his feet from the damp floor, when he attempted to lift the paste. Instantly, amid a loud blast and smoke, he was hurled against the dough mixing machine and rendered unconscious. A live electric wire concealed in the paste had stuck in one of his hands.

On regaining consciousness, he was taken to the Poor Law dispensary in Meath Street where he was examined by an elderly doctor. He was in a bad state, trembling and generally disorientated. As treatment for this condition, the doctor prescribed doses of bromide before sending him home.

During the following weeks, Swift's health deteriorated and he was confined to bed with nausea, tremors in his limbs and depression, symptoms diagnosed by the doctor as epilepsy. Though this diagnosis proved to be unfounded, it may simply have been a ploy to secure Swift's admission to hospital.

At that time the National Health Insurance had little provision for hospital treatment and patients other than those with private means had recourse to one or other of the city's two Poor House hospitals, the North Dublin Union and the South Dublin Union. It was to the latter that Swift was admitted on 25 August.[1] Situated on the site of the present St James's Hospital extending from James's Street to Rialto, the South Dublin Union was then a forbidding prison-like institution of grey buildings surrounded by high grey walls.

Much of the nursing care was dispensed by permanent inmates, able-bodied paupers drawn from the destitute unemployed.

Apart from several epileptics, most of the twenty or so patients sharing Swift's ward had physical deformities. A few were mentally handicapped. The majority were young people in their twenties or thirties. When not in bed, Swift and his fellow patients were at liberty to potter around the yard-like enclosure at the rear of the ward. From there could be seen the institution's work rooms, producing the grey homespun worn by pauper inmates and patients alike. The authorities ensured that the institution was as self supporting as possible!

Still suffering from tremors, depression and general inertia, Swift was inclined to stay in bed worrying about his condition. On his almost daily visits to the ward, Dr Cremin, the medical superintendent, would encourage him to get up and occupy himself. Taking this advice, Swift made a gradual recovery and on 9 October,[2] more than six weeks after his admission, he was discharged from hospital. Expediting his recuperation was the knowledge that his illness had been of a psychosomatic nature.[3]

Six months following Swift's discharge from the South Dublin Union there occurred the Easter Rising of 1916. That event, planned by a small group of leaders of the Irish Volunteers and the Irish Citizen Army, took the citizens and, indeed, the rank and file participants completely by surprise. On the afternoon of 24 April, Easter Monday, the day the rebellion commenced, Swift went to see a film in the De Luxe cinema in Camden Street. Everything appeared to be normal when he entered the cinema but, when he emerged after a couple of hours or so, he found a squad of British soldiers spread across the street between the cinema and Gorevan's drapery shop on the opposite side. Lying prone on the street, the soldiers were aiming their rifles in the direction of Jacob's biscuit factory which, unknown to Swift then, had been occupied by a group of insurgents. With no shots being fired, Swift and some others who gathered outside the cinema thought that the military presence was a practice session. However, it would have been unusual to see soldiers practising in the streets. Not until he returned home did he discover there had been a rebellion.

In the days that followed, people continued to go about the city, though they were sometimes impeded by the military. On one of his rambles, Swift got as far as Sackville Street. It was there that he saw insurgents' rifles pointing through the block-aded windows of the GPO, principal stronghold of the rebellion. On reaching North King Street on another occasion, he found it barricaded with household furniture. Poorly armed with some rifles and long-handled pikes, Volunteers were positioned behind the barricades prepared, apparently, to resist the military.

This situation prevailed for about a week before the Rising was crushed by British forces. During that period, the business of the city was greatly disrupted. With most shops remaining closed many basic commodities became scarce. The Swift family was obliged to do some home baking after managing to obtain a supply of flour. According to Swift, the general reaction to the rebellion was one of hostility, particularly among those whose relatives were fighting for Britain in World War I. With the expectation of Home Rule after the war, the insurgents were widely perceived as traitors, sabotaging Home Rule and, con-sequently letting Britain off the hook. Initially, Swift took a more sympathetic, perhaps romantic, view of the insurrection. At the same time it appeared to him to be entirely nationalist in character, with no socialist overtones. Only after the rebellion did it become generally known that a socialist element had been involved in the person of James Connolly. Although Swift was familiar with Connolly's writings in the *Irish Worker*, these had limited political import, being confined mainly to immediate issues such as the 1913 Lock-Out. It was a considerable period of time after the rebellion before Swift became acquainted with Connolly's socialist teachings, when they were published by the ITGWU and others.

The executions of Connolly and the other 1916 leaders deeply shocked and angered Swift. Analysing this later, however, he concluded that it represented little more than anti-Britishness. He assessed the rebellion as an ill-conceived and suicidal adven-ture. He considered the occupation of buildings by the insurgents a particularly imprudent strategy, a viewpoint surely vindicated by the swift suppression of the uprising. He described the Pro-clamation as 'a bit of rhetoric; a bourgeois document, obviously copied from the Declaration of the French Revolution'. That Connolly, undoubtedly Ireland's greatest socialist theorist, would sacrifice his life for such a cause, in which he had no apparent influence, was incomprehensible to Swift.

Notwithstanding his critical evaluation of the rebellion, Swift derived satisfaction from certain consequences of that event:

> Although the 1916 Insurrection, with the subsequent struggle against British occupation, didn't achieve a socialist state or anything like it, it did some of the preliminary work to that in establishing certain independence of Britain which could be developed later into a socialist state. This view is justified, I believe, in view of the subsequent failure of Britain to develop into anything like even giving the prospect of a socialist state. As I see Britain today [1986] although it has vacated a lot of its colonies, in essence, it is as imperialist as it ever was. One has only to look at the manner in which it supports its parasitical monarchy. I'm sure they support that as an appendage of the imperial might they once exercised. It is a symbol of that and, although they may not have the substance of empire in having power over colonies abroad, still they cherish the symbol of that which is the British monarchy. So, it has been worth sacrifice and trouble to achieve independence from that, and 1916 has justified itself in that respect.[4]

Meanwhile, the Swift family had left their tenement to live in a new dwelling at 13 Clanbrassil Terrace, off Clanbrassil Street. Their greatly improved accommodation comprised the upstairs flat of the two-storey house, with two bedrooms at the front and a kitchen cum living-room and a toilet at the back. Neighbours at number seven of the same terrace were the Coopers and May Swift.

The upturn in the family's fortunes was not unrelated to the fact that Swift's father had secured a permanent job in Peter Kennedy's bakery in Patrick Street. Swift, too, had been employed almost continuously since leaving hospital the previous October. For a couple of weeks that month he had worked as a confectioner in Rathmines bakery, 22 Upper Rathmines Road. That position had been offered to him by the proprietor, Matthew Campbell, who had formerly been manager in Galbraith's. Only two employees, a forewoman and Swift, were employed in the Rathmines confectionery bakery. When it became evident that, due to a clash of temperament, they could not get on together, he resigned his position.

Later, in October 1915, immediately prior to Hallowe'en, Swift sought and secured work in another Dublin bakery, Johnston, Mooney & O'Brien's. He was employed in their Ballsbridge plant baking rough confectionery such as bracks, crumpets, scones and soda farls. Still considered as an improver, he was paid a wage of £1 a week. Conditions were rather primitive in the confectionery department, an old underground bake-house known as the grain hole. With the combination of coal- and coke-fired ovens and bad ventilation, the discharge of smoke and sulphurous heat was almost intolerable. To make matters worse, it was night work, with no prescribed working hours. The six-night week, including Sunday, could amount to well over fifty hours. Such factors, perhaps, influenced him to join the Bakers' Union before the end of 1915. Only a handful of the hundred or so bakers in the firm were organised. Swift remained an employee of the Ballsbridge bakery until Easter 1916 when the Rising prevented him travelling to work.

Unhappy with the arduous working conditions in Johnston, Mooney & O'Brien's, Swift had already resolved to seek day work, baking better class confectionery. He was fortunate, therefore, through a newspaper advertisement, to obtain such work in Bewley's bakery in Westmoreland Street. Bewley's specialised in high-class confectionery which they sold in their café and shop on the same premises. Swift commenced employment in this establishment after the rebellion. Once again, he was regarded as an improver, with a wage of £1 per week.

Each afternoon, in Bewley's, flour would be brought to the bakery from the floor above in preparation for the following morning's work. While colleagues of Swift's would drag these ten-stone sacks down the fairly long wooden stairway, he would carry this weight on his back, throwing it from his shoulders on to the wooden block floor. One sack landed with force dislodging part of the ceiling of the café below. Swift was summoned to the café immediately, where, amid the ensuing pandemonium, he found Ernest Bewley, the owner, apologising to several 'elderly ladies' who had been covered with dust. He was reprimanded by Bewley in the presence of these customers.

For his union activities in Bewley's, Swift was to be more severely disciplined. Before working for that establishment, which was then unorganised, he had had to obtain sanction from the union. That had been forthcoming when he volunteered to recruit the firm's employees. But, as Bewley's staff was not disposed to join the union, his recruiting efforts were in vain. Worse still, for his endeavours on behalf of the union, he was sacked by Fred Andrews, the English foreman. This occurred, Swift believed, without Ernest Bewley's knowledge.[5]

Following his dismissal, Swift's name was entered on the union's *slate* or idle list in November 1916.[6] So great, however, was the scarcity of work in the trade, that the union encouraged its younger members to emigrate, leaving for older and married workers whatever work was available. As an inducement, commutation, or emigration grants were provided by the union.

For a month or two Swift subsisted on his meagre earnings from casual work augmented with the dole. However, with World War I in progress, officials were present at labour exchanges offering work to aid Britain's war effort. Refusal of reasonable offers would result in the cessation of dole payments. Those accepting work were guaranteed exemption from conscription which had been introduced in Britain through the Military Services Act, 1916.

It was in such circumstances that Swift and Michael Clarke, a confectioner acquaintance from Galbraith's, were offered outdoor building work in Kilwinning, near Kilmarnock, Ayrshire, in Scotland. Reluctant to become a financial burden on his parents, Swift decided to accept the job. After being granted thirty shillings by the union[7] for his boat fare and expenses to Glasgow, he travelled to Kilmarnock in the company of Clarke in January 1917.

Accustomed to working in warm bakeries, Swift found the outdoor building work more than he could endure. After developing severe bronchitis, he returned home around St Patrick's Day and went back on the slate and the dole. Towards the end of May, at the Lower Gardiner Street labour exchange, Swift and some twenty others accepted offers of employment in a lead works in London.

4

Marching to Verdi

It was on 3 June 1917, following an overnight journey from Dublin, that Swift's party arrived in London.[1] They stayed in a lodging house on Bow Road in the east end of the city. It was owned by their new employer, a Dutch company called Einthoven, which manufactured lead for munitions factories. Each morning Swift and the others travelled by tube to the lead works in the Thames docks at Rotherhithe. Ore brought there by boat was fed in large lumps into big blast furnaces of enormous temperatures. On emerging from the furnace base as liquid fire, it was poured into moulds. After being left for several days to cool and harden, the metal was then mixed in furnaces with other substances.

For several reasons, the lead works was a most unpleasant working environment. The main one, perhaps, was the bad atmosphere that existed between the Irish and British workers. It was only a year since the Easter Rising and there was a very strong anti-Irish prejudice at what was considered an insurrection against Britain at war. Moreover, with the firm's young British workers conscripted, those remaining, some the fathers of the young conscripts, resented the Irish. In response to the sneers and boycotts of their British workmates, Swift and McDonald, a Dublin colleague, would ridicule them and their British empire.

Another problem in the place concerned the onerous working conditions. In the intense heat generated by the furnaces, the work, all done by hand, was quite exhausting. Working hours averaged about twelve daily, seven days a week, and included some shift and night duties. A major grievance of the Irish was their inability to attend Sunday Mass. But this was hardly a sacrifice for Swift! Four years earlier, he had ceased participating in Catholic observances and he no longer considered himself a

Catholic. Nevertheless, the Irish complained to the management several times about this and other grievances. The management was anti-Irish and unresponsive. Exasperated, Swift and McDonald led a strike which was supported by about half of their Irish colleagues.

Tribunals composed of civilians from the civil service and local authorities had been established to administer the Conscription Act, particularly in industry. These tribunals had authority to determine the merits or demerits of exemption applications. For leading the strike, Swift and McDonald were brought before such a tribunal and charged under the Defence of the Realm Act with causing a work stoppage in an undertaking of national importance. Having heard the case, the chairman stated that the grievances would be examined and Swift and McDonald could return to work. They were each fined a week's wages of two pounds and were warned that any repetition of their action would result in their being handed over directly to the military authorities.

Despite repeated representations to the management of the lead works, nothing was done to resolve the grievances. Infuriated by this, Swift and his Dublin colleague resolved not to work under such conditions and subsequently refused to accept orders from a foreman. Unwilling, seemingly, to jeopardise their exemptions from conscription, the remaining Irish withheld support. To avoid the certainty of being handed over to the military, Swift and McDonald parted company and went on the run.

Since his lodgings were the property of the lead works firm, Swift had to seek a new abode. In either Lewisham or New Cross, he secured accommodation in a Rowton lodging house. For one shilling a night he had a small, clean cubicle to himself. A hearty breakfast was available for six pence. Named after Baron Rowton, the English aristocrat, philanthropist and director of Guinness's brewery, Rowton houses were similar in purpose to Dublin's Iveagh Hostel. With the military police or Red Caps looking for anyone without exemption papers, particularly deserters and absentees without leave, Swift had to move lodgings frequently. An Irish cripple working in the Rowton House became friendly with Swift and helped him to evade arrest. Apart from informing him of the nights when Red Caps were likely to call, he would recommend alternative accommodation. This, of course, meant that Swift was constantly on the move, seldom staying more than two consecutive nights in the same place.

Agents of companies seeking workers often visited these lodging houses. In this way, Swift got a job as a carpenter's mate, building aeroplane hangars in Eltham, Kent, outside London. He was not questioned about his position by the management. Their priority was to get the work done as quickly as possible and thus qualify for government bonuses. Air warfare had started by this time and London was being bombed by the Germans. For this aspect of the conflict, the British had been unprepared and consequently there was a special urgency to produce aeroplanes.

During this period the opera season was on in Drury Lane under Sir Thomas Beecham. Swift was a frequent patron on Saturday nights, though he sometimes went instead to one of the Queen's Hall concerts. One Saturday night, having attended a performance of Mussorgsky's opera, *Boris Godunof,* Swift returned to the Rowton house. A couple of hours later he was awakened by Red Caps demanding to see his exemption papers. Bereft of these documents, he and a number of deserters were taken to a police station in either Lewisham or New Cross. Detained in separate cells until Monday morning, they were then taken individually to a civilian court and brought before a magistrate. To the charge of being an absentee under the Military Service Act, Swift had no defence. He was informed that he would be handed over to a military escort. Two Red Caps accompanied him to the Duke of York Schools, Chelsea, headquarters of the London Irish Rifles Regiment. A young officer there ordered him to put on a military uniform. Refusing, Swift declared that as a republican and a socialist he would neither obey military orders nor soldier for Britain. The consequences of that, he was told, would be a court martial and a long term of imprisonment. Having reiterated his position, he was informed that he would be dealt with at the regiment's training depot in Winchester. In the course of this exchange, the officer informed Swift that they were doing him a favour by putting him into an Irish regiment. Not once did Swift encounter an Irishman in that body.

Following an escorted train journey to Winchester, Swift was taken to the regiment's training quarters and placed in a guard-room cell. Another prisoner in the same cell was wearing an army uniform, but in a slovenly manner and obviously with some reluctance. This man, an English conscientious objector, having already served a prison sentence for his stand, was awaiting a court martial. Interested in ascertaining his objections, Swift discovered that his companion was a Tolstoyian anarchist. This meant nothing to Swift then but his cell-mate explained his belief that governments make and enforce laws and the enforcement of laws is tyrannical and immoral. Swift later considered this 'a ridiculous doctrine'. Swift was brought before a senior officer who advised him to wear the uniform and indicated that a refusal would lead to imprisonment. Disregarding this warning, Swift was informed that he would be remanded to a court martial. Later, back in his cell, he was visited by another officer, a lawyer, offering him a defence at the court martial. The offer was declined. Leaving aside the fact that there was no defence, Swift had no confidence in being defended by the army and wanted to be independent of them.

At the court martial held a few days later, Swift was flanked by two soldiers with fixed bayonets. During the proceedings, he stood facing three officers 'sitting like statues' at a table. The only other person present was a fourth officer, the adjutant. Addressing Swift as 'Private Swift, number . . .', the chairman, a captain, put the charge which, of course, was admitted. Observing that Swift had had no work in Ireland and that Britain had brought him over and given him employment, the captain asked him did he not feel under an obligation to serve Britain against her enemies. Replying to this, Swift declared that he did not feel under the slightest obligation. He was in Britain, he said, because of unemployment in Ireland caused by British misrule. The proceedings were terminated immediately. Before being escorted back to his cell, he was informed that the court's decisions would be promulgated in due course. The promulgation ceremony took place within a week. Under the escort of two soldiers with fixed bayonets, Swift was marched to the centre of a field where the entire regiment of about a thousand soldiers was assembled in large square formation. Accompanied by several colleague officers, some on horseback, the regimental commander rode to the centre of the field. When a bugler had sounded the signal for the proceedings to commence, the adjutant read aloud the findings of the court martial: 'Private

Swift, number . . . was tried by court martial on . . . on a charge of disobeying a lawful military command, was found guilty of charge and the court sentenced him to two years' imprisonment with hard labour.'

This elaborate ceremony was staged with the purpose of putting fear into the other soldiers. But it seemed farcical to Swift then as a high proportion of the battalion were conscripts being prepared for the slaughter of war. Many of them would willingly have changed places with him.

About a week after the promulgation, again under the escort of two Red Caps, Swift was brought by train to London and was imprisoned in solitary confinement in Wormwood Scrubs. As one would expect, the diet in that establishment was pretty meagre. Breakfast consisted of skilly (thin porridge), one square of bread and a mug of tea or cocoa. Soup and potatoes, sometimes supplemented with boiled fatty meat, was the usual fare for lunch. For tea, there was bread, margarine and cheese, with the same beverage as breakfast. Meals were served through an aperture in the centre of the cell door which could be opened from the outside. Through this opening would be passed a leather-like tray laid with a knife and spoon of similar material and a rubber mug and plate. The authorities took every precaution to prevent prisoners committing suicide. Other measures included the removal of prisoners' boot laces and the braces of their trousers.

Several planks laid on struts on the floor at night served as Swift's bed. On these were placed a hard, almost leather-like, three-piece mattress and some bed clothes. Each morning after breakfast, a warder ordered Swift to remove everything from the cell, including a stool, a small table and the bed and bedclothes. These were stored in recesses outside the cell door and were not brought back until evening. Except for a slop bucket, the cell was completely cleared during the day.

The thick walls of the dimly-lit cell ensured that Swift could hear no sound. His only break from that environment was the time spent each morning emptying his slop bucket and washing himself. As a result, it was not long before he became affected by this isolation. He would pace up and down the cell in his heavy prison boots making as much noise as possible. He would do this to the point of exhaustion before sitting down on the bare flags of the cell floor. Weak on account of the inadequate diet, he tired easily. His general health had disimproved while working in the lead works and he suffered much from coughing and bronchitis.

Swift's musical interest served an unusual purpose before landing him in further trouble. To break the silence, he whistled a lot. He was very fond of opera at that time, particularly Verdi, and he would whistle such tunes as the marches from *Il Trovatore*. An old Cockney warder cautioned him several times to cease whistling as it could be heard outside and was against the regulations. But due to his solitude, Swift's whistling was compulsive. When brought before the Deputy Governor, he was charged with whistling Irish rebel songs! Unknown to Swift then, some prisoners of the 1916 Rebellion were serving sentences in the gaol. Among that group was Joe O'Neill, a prominent member of the Irish Bakers' Union who later worked in Peter Kennedy's bakery in Parnell Street, Dublin. For his transgression, Swift was sentenced to three days' bread and water.

After about a month in Wormwood Scrubs Swift was transferred to Wandsworth Prison. No longer in solitary confinement, he was obliged to participate in organised activities. Each morning, he and the other prisoners were taken to a yard for exercise, where, under the close supervision of warders, they walked for an hour in one of three large concentric circles. To prevent any communication between them, prisoners were at a distance from each other. Any prisoner showing signs of catching up on a colleague was liable to a three-day sentence of bread and water. Despite the restrictions, they still managed to communicate a little with each other.

During his first week or so in Wandsworth, Swift worked for a couple of hours each afternoon in his cell sewing leather attachments to post office mail bags. After a fortnight he continued doing the same work, but in a large work-room, with about a hundred other prisoners. Here again, communication between prisoners was forbidden. Yet, despite the close supervision of warders and being separated from each other, the prisoners were able to hold brief conversations. Swift discovered that the authorities did not distinguish between conscientious objectors and criminal prisoners. Usually, the latter were serving sentences for robbery and acts of violence. Swift discovered, too, that, unlike himself, most conscientious objectors were Quakers and pacifists. He was not sympathetic to them. At that time he could not understand their position and thought they were evading military service. But he found out afterwards that many of these men were very brave. As a result of the harsh treatment they received, several committed suicide while others went insane. A number who refused to wear uniforms were forcibly disrobed and left in cold cells where some of them died.

Once a month conscientious objectors and criminal prisoners were allowed a visitor and to send and receive a letter. As a precaution against conspiracies, letters were censored by the prison authorities. Throughout his incarceration, Swift was denied these rights and, despite extensive enquiries, he never received any explanation for this discriminatory treatment.

Unaware of their son's whereabouts, Swift's parents arranged to have enquiries made in the British parliament through Alfie Byrne, MP for the Harbour Division of Dublin. A popular political figure in Dublin, Byrne was later to serve many terms as the city's Lord Mayor. On four occasions, between 24 October and 19 December 1917, the matter was raised in Westminster, where Byrne sought Swift's discharge from prison. Thus, in the House of Commons on 4 December 1917, Byrne asked Mr Macpherson, the Under-Secretary of State for War:

> If it was the intention of the Government to punish Irishmen because of their religion; if they are aware of the treatment of John Swift, an Irishman, who through unemployment in Ireland was compelled to leave his home in order to earn his living, and after a few weeks in Great Britain was conscripted, although all the time in Great Britain he was engaged in work of national importance; if he is aware that this man was engaged for seven days a week in a lead factory, and was refused permission to attend church on Sunday, and owing to his efforts to do so was fined £2 and afterwards dismissed; if he is aware that after his dismissal from the lead factory this man found work at building aeroplane sheds in Kent, when, at the instigation of his oppressors in the lead factory, he was arrested as an absentee and conscripted; if he is aware that he is now doing two years in an English prison for refusing

to soldier, which he would not be asked to do only for his loyalty to his religion, and if he will order his discharge?[2]

On 12 December, in another bid to secure Swift's release, Byrne asked the Prime Minister:

If, in order to show how the military authorities respect the laws of exemption in the Military Service Act, he will issue instructions to the Censor to allow the particulars of the John Swift case to be sent to His Holiness the Pope . . .[3]

There is more than a little irony in the case pleaded by Byrne given that Swift had long since abandoned Catholicism. Admittedly, he had attended Mass in Wormwood Scrubs but that had been purely to get a break from his cell. Nothing came of Alfie Byrne's representations. He was simply fobbed off by various government ministers including the Home Secretary, who, almost two months after the matter was first raised, declared that he had been unable to trace Swift's case.[4]

It was in the prison workroom, in November 1917, that Swift first learnt that the Bolshevik Revolution had occurred. He regarded that event, leading as it did to the creation of the first and most significant socialist state, as the most momentous political development in modern history. Information on the revolution reached the prisoners through an issue of the London *Times* given to a conscientious objector by a visitor. Whatever their opinion of the revolution, the conscientious objectors were generally heartened by the event, believing it could possibly shorten the war. Among the prisoners associated with Swift, news of the events in Petrograd led to jubilation and rejoicing. A criminal prisoner who considered himself to be a kind of ventriloquist started whistling the air of what Swift later recognised as *The Red Flag*. This labour song was written by an Irishman, James Connell, whose brother was a member of the Bridge Street Bakers' Society, a forerunner of the present Dublin No. 1 Branch of the Bakers' Union.[5] With his well-established reputation for whistling, Swift was among those blamed for this infringement of prison regulations. He and some others were taken from the workroom and returned to their cells.

A day or two later, Swift was escorted to a cell in the military wing of the prison. That evening he was visited by an officer and two Red Caps carrying a military uniform. This 'typical British officer, full of arrogance' ordered him to remove his prison garb and put on the uniform. When he refused, the Red Caps were instructed to remove his prison garments forcibly. In resisting, he was upended on to the floor, sustaining an injury when the back of his head struck a flagstone. On their departure, the military police took the prison clothing but left the uniform.

It was November and very cold in that unheated cell. Swift was suffering badly from his bronchitis. Covering himself as best he could with the uniform, he lay down in a corner of the cell and tried to sleep. The cell light, normally switched off around eight o'clock at night, was left on, and he was aware that the authorities were keeping an eye on him through the spy hole in the door. His illness quickly developed into a fever with severe bouts of coughing. Eventually a military doctor gave him a medical examination. Having rejected the doctor's advice to don the uniform, he was put on a stretcher and given an injection which put him to sleep.

On awakening, he discovered he was in what constituted the prison hospital, a series of cells entered by a passage at the back. He also found that while under the effects of the drug, the authorities had partially dressed him in military uniform. He was visited by another doctor, an Englishman, whose father had attended Portora Royal School, Enniskillen, Co. Fermanagh, where Oscar Wilde had received part of his education. An admirer of Wilde's writings, the doctor would quote some of the author's poetry to Swift. But, as Swift explained, the doctor's friendly attitude was not reciprocated.

> At that time, I was quite ignorant of Oscar Wilde and heard his name as a term of opprobrium. If homosexuality was being discussed, there would be talk of Oscar Wilde. I had experience of homosexuality when I was going to school, when adult men tried homosexuality on me, and I had a very strong feeling against it. I took a turn against this man on that account because I found as I became more familiar with him I suspected that he was a homosexual.[6]

Meanwhile, the Military Service Act had been amended, making it possible for conscientious objectors to volunteer for non-combatant duties. The doctor advised him to take advantage of this provision. He informed Swift that he had seen many conscientious objectors subjected to the kind of treatment he had been experiencing, and warned him that on his discharge from hospital he would be returned to a cold cell where he would probably suffer a relapse. Swift had been told about this kind of thing while in Winchester. His anarchist cell-mate there had advised him to wear the uniform and to take a stand on an alternative form of protest.

After a week in hospital Swift was brought to another cell, this time a heated one, where he was interviewed by a sergeant. Enlarging on advice already given by the doctor, the sergeant, 'a civil kind of man', cited examples of non-combatant duties such as ambulance work in the medical service, agricultural work, road making and baking. Swift volunteered to bake, but not, as he explained, without a great deal of soul-searching:

> Now I didn't do this without a terrible struggle with myself, because, when you take up a position of principle like that you will fight very hard to hold on to it. But the alternative was going back to that cell and freezing to death. There would be two things to be considered in that. You wouldn't want to die, that would be a natural thing; even if you did die, they wouldn't give a damn! Then, with regard to ideology, you wouldn't want to give in to them. There could be an amendment to that—why not best them, and that was what I did. But it was a terrible struggle.[7]

It was not long before Swift regretted his decision. He began to oppose the authorities in different ways, doing things reluctantly and showing resentment. After refusing to drill, he was left in his cell without food or liquids. He attempted to rationalise his position, questioning himself as to what difference there was in consenting to work in the lead works and agreeing to bake. In both instances a compromise was involved. After concluding that there was no difference in principle, he agreed to drill, and this became his main activity for the remaining weeks of his detention in the military wing of Wandsworth. He had experience of that while serving in the Irish Volunteers and did not find it irksome. It was certainly preferable to sewing mail bags or being confined in a cell.

Before the end of 1917, Swift was transferred to Aldershot Prison, a military establishment known as the 'Glass House', which accommodated the worst type of military offenders, including some sentenced for acts of violence and murder. Also imprisoned in Aldershot were many deserters. Discipline was extremely rigorous, the most common form of punishment being pack drill which was administered for such breaches of discipline as persistently disobeying orders. An offender, packed with a heavy load, including blankets and iron rations, and armed with a rifle, was brought to the barracks square to parade. In quick succession, the drill sergeant barked out the commands: 'Right turn! Left turn! Quick march! Halt! Present arms! Shoulder arms! Ground arms!' This could continue for some hours until the prisoner became exhausted and humiliated.

There was no shortage of work to occupy the prisoners at Aldershot. Swift was usually on fatigues. Sometimes this was sanitary work, emptying slop buckets and cleaning field toilets. On other occasions he worked in the stores. Not only was that more pleasant, but it provided opportunities to steal some extra food.

Swift was acquainted with two prisoners who were Jews. Having committed robberies, they had been imprisoned for breaching military law. It was their ambition, after the war, to form a business selling army surplus. Many prisoners sentenced for stealing were not inherent robbers, but stole army property simply to avoid being sent to the Front. Some would later volunteer for the war just to escape the disciplinary regime of Aldershot.

Presumably as practice for what lay ahead, Swift and some of his colleagues were put on the rifle range digging trenches. In charge of this operation was a rather severe and unpopular corporal. One day a row developed between the corporal and one of Swift's mates. For intervening in support of his colleague, Swift found himself back in his cell.

In that wing of the prison it was expected that there would shortly be a draft to a war zone. Within a few days Swift was drafted. He was brought to the prison parade ground where many others were already assembled. In a brief morale address, the commanding officer exhorted them to uphold the honour of the British Army! Under the escort of two military policemen, a group of five or six that included Swift and his two Jewish colleagues were driven by lorry to either Dover or Folkestone. For the duration of the journey they were handcuffed in pairs. After being escorted on to a boat, they were separated from hundreds of other soldiers in uniform who had come from various locations. Neither they nor Swift knew their destination.[8]

Cloud of Hell

When Swift and his fellow prisoners arrived at a French port, probably Calais, they were brought by lorry to Étaples. It was a small seaside resort some twenty or thirty miles south of Calais, and principal British infantry base in France during the war. There, they were taken to a military barracks and placed in guard room cells, where a senior officer interviewed them separately. He had a file on Swift and referred to his reluctant consent to bake for the army. The officer informed him that he would be employed as a cook, not as a baker.

Swift had feared he would be re-imprisoned or faced with an ultimatum of obeying military orders or being shot. Now, suddenly and unexpectedly, after being incarcerated for approximately six months, he found himself relatively free. Naturally he was surprised and delighted with this development. After being put on soldier's pay, he was sent to a cookery school in Wimireux, a small coastal town near Boulogne, where he was trained as a cook for officers. This enabled him to eat almost as well as they did, a change he welcomed very much after the frugal prison diet. Officers ate well, and considerably better than ordinary soldiers. Swift spent three weeks there and found it a pleasant experience. Daily classes finished by early evening and trainees were then free to engage in leisure pursuits. Local pubs were the usual attraction for soldiers, though they were also known to patronise brothels. In most French towns of any size there was a brothel. While in Étaples, Swift had seen a queue outside what he thought was a pub, and had been surprised and shocked to find it was a brothel, with soldiers chatting and smoking outside, treating the matter quite casually.

About the end of January 1918, having completed the cookery course, Swift was sent towards the Line, to a small town near

Bethune, from where reinforcements were assigned to their units. He was posted to the Second Fifth Battalion of the King's Own Royal Lancasters, a unit of the 55th Division, then based on the Western Front between Arras and Dulens in north-eastern France.

The foremost parts of the Front (or Line), comprised three parallel lines, a front, support and reserve. The first two were about a quarter of a mile apart, while closer to half a mile separated the support and reserve lines. All three were joined by connecting trenches. Timber struts, raised about six inches above the bottom of the trench, served as a floor. Cooking, eating and sleeping quarters were in dug-outs beneath the trenches, sometimes up to fifty feet below ground level. Some of these dug-outs were quite elaborate, with ceilings, walls and floors of timber. This special trench work was carried out by sappers, many of whom were miners in civilian life.

Patrols, composed of four to six privates, led by a corporal, were sent from the front line on various assignments. Normally, these tasks were rotated but, as Swift was usually in the reserve line cooking for officers, he was less frequently selected than others. One of the patrols' tasks was to look for casualties in the area between the trenches, and it was on such a search party that Swift came across this poignant scene:

> We found four or five dead soldiers sitting together, and I don't think there was a mark on any of them. They were not disfigured, and there was no expression, even of terror, on their immobile faces. They looked just like statues, and you would think they were asleep. Their clothes were not torn and the only sign of injuries was fresh blood splattered on nearby primroses.

The dead were army servicemen who had been constructing trenches when they were killed by an explosion during a bombardment. The authorities knew they were dead through stationary observation balloons which constantly photographed no-man's-land and the surrounding area to check for casualties, shell damage and, of course, movements in the enemy's position.

In order to obtain information on the Germans, particularly their precise position, patrols were sent into no-man's-land. These risky exercises, carried out at night, were dreaded by the soldiers. When selecting men for this task, the sergeant or corporal would joke about it, saying: 'I want four volunteers for tonight's patrol', and would point at four soldiers, adding, 'You and you and you and you!' To guard against surprise attacks, the Germans sent up flares over no-man's-land and beyond, which would light up the whole area. The British did the same towards the German lines. On the only night that Swift was present on such a mission, a German flare landed near his patrol creating a huge flame. Lying nearby was a petrol tin of the type used for bringing water to the trenches. Believing it contained water, Swift threw the tin on to the flames. It turned out to be petrol and caused an enormous blaze. The Germans immediately started a bombardment, and the patrol had to beat a hasty retreat. On his return to base, Swift was questioned closely about the incident by an officer.

An even greater fear of the soldiers, and one Swift was fortunate to escape, was selection for a raiding party. Their highly dangerous assignment was to cross no-man's-land at night, enter the enemy's trenches and capture one or two German soldiers. Normally, this was carried out before an attack to obtain information about the enemy.

Soldiers served twelve- to fourteen-day stints in the trenches, taking turns in each of the three lines. This was followed by a week in a rest camp usually three or four miles behind the reserve lines. Departure from the trenches was a ceremonial occasion. Troops leaving the Front assembled behind the reserve line and, led by the Commanding Officer on horseback, were played back to camp by a band. The same band entertained soldiers during their break from duty. Soldiers also occupied themselves with sports activities like boxing and football. Often the camps were close to a French village where troops could drink and chat in pubs. They were also permitted to write home once a month on official stationery supplied by the army. Like the monthly one they could receive, the letter was censored by an officer. This was done openly as a security precaution.

Strange as it may seem, troops often felt safer in the trenches than in rest camps. The latter, usually under canvas, were particularly vulnerable to the frequent enemy air raids, and with the combined uproar of guns defending the camp and enemy bombs being dropped, sleep was often impossible.

The army had a range of punishments for dealing with war zone breaches of discipline, the severity of disciplinary action being determined chiefly by the gravity of the offence. For instance, soldiers found guilty of serious disciplinary breaches such as disobeying orders or inciting to mutiny, particularly during fighting, would be court martialled and shot. Less serious offences, like refusing to empty a slop bucket, would be noted and dealt with later because, in the Line, the soldiers' services were required to be always on hand. However, before leaving for a rest camp, the offender would be brought before a summary court martial to be charged. Usually he would be sentenced to Field Punishment Number One, which entailed being tied to an object like a post or a tree. Swift once observed two soldiers tied to the posts of a boxing ring. A variation of this was the crucifixion punishment where the victim would be tied to an object in the crucified position, but with his feet on the ground. Whatever form it took, this punishment was always administered in a public place in the camp where the victim could be seen by passing colleagues. But, as they took little notice of it, this attempt to humiliate the prisoner was ineffective. If the punishment had any value, it was the boredom it inflicted on the detainee.

During Swift's first two weeks at the Front there was practically no fighting. That changed dramatically, however, on Holy Thursday, 21 March 1918, when the Germans launched a major offensive. It commenced about five o'clock in the morning, just before daybreak, with a sudden general bombardment for miles along the Front. Swift was in the reserve line dug-out when it started and he and the other troops in the three lines were awakened and ordered to prepare for action. When they were accoutred and stood to, those in the support and reserve lines went to the connecting trenches where they were ordered to the front line.

When an attack started, it was concentrated on the front line with mortar, bomb and artillery shell fire. When it was thought that sufficient damage had been done there, the attack moved to the second line to hinder reinforcements. After that, the same fire power was directed towards the third line. This was known as a barrage or, if very severe and concentrated, drum fire.

When Swift arrived at the front line it was still being bombed. He and the others were ordered to stand to, to mount the fire step, a raised part of the trench which placed soldiers in the firing position. Lance Corporal Price, a Welshman, was in the trench issuing orders. Popular with the men, he had just been speaking to Swift when a small shell exploded in that part of the trench. Price was killed instantly, having been hit on the head by a fragment of the shell. Swift was more fortunate, suffering relatively minor injuries to his arm and hand.

Not until the bombardment abated did Swift receive first aid in the trench. Having satisfied a senior officer that his injuries warranted further treatment, he was ordered to go to the casualty clearing station situated in a sunken road behind the reserve line. Due to the heavy bombing and shelling still in progress, it took him several hours to travel this short distance. Parts of the trench were blocked by the bombardment, and at times he had to climb out and look for the continuation of the trench. Also impeding his progress were the other wounded making the same journey. When he eventually reached the exit he was stopped by Military Police armed with revolvers. They questioned everyone leaving the trenches. Deserters, many of whom would panic during the fighting, would be ordered to return to the Line. If they refused they would be shot instantly. Swift was permitted to proceed to the casualty clearing station, a large treatment area under canvas. Casualties were extremely heavy that day and he had to wait a long time while more urgent cases were treated. Many of the seriously injured required the immediate amputation of limbs. All this time, large numbers of dying and dead were being brought in on stretchers. After receiving treatment, Swift was brought on the first available lorry to Boulogne, and then to a camp hospital in Busshy, a townland in a rural part of northern France. He remained there for about two months until 18 May 1918. This prolonged hospital stay had more to do with his poor general state of health than with his wounds.

While in Busshy, Swift learnt something of the methods employed by soldiers evading war. They had two principal means of prolonging their illness to avoid being sent back to the Front. One was to put iodine from their first-aid kit on a cigarette and inhale the smoke. Apparently, a few whiffs of that increased their temperatures and they would be certified unfit for service. A second method was probably more dangerous. They ate the strings of cordite from the cartridge of a bullet! This led to days of vomiting, high temperatures and lack of appetite. Though nearly dying, they opted to suffer rather than go back to the Line.

During his recuperation in the hospital, Swift kept a small notebook which has survived. It contains much information on how he occupied his time. He attended many lectures by speakers from British and American universities on subjects as diverse as Shakespeare and other notable British writers, Christian ethics and philosophy, and economics. He also read a lot, including at least nineteen volumes of poetry and prose by renowned British authors. Poetry was then a particular interest of his, and he wrote a great deal of verse during the two months he spent in Busshy. This example is taken from the opening lines of his poem, *A Cloud of Hell:*

A Cloud of Hell

T'was such a scene as surely would delight
The hearts of Satan, and th'infernal crew;
Where men fell dazed or dead in gory fight,
To soak the fire swept soil in bloody dew.
Where bodies lay, dismembered and unknown,
Some not dead, but mute with battle crash,
Some left with voice, in agony to groan,
Or curse their God, their land, their bleeding flesh.
And from above the murdering spirits fly,
As though the hosts of heaven were the foe;
Foul hell seemed elevated to the sky,
Showering its fury on the earth below.

By the time Swift was discharged from Busshy hospital, the Germans were in retreat, having broken through earlier for several miles towards Paris. The Americans had since entered the war, a development viewed rather sceptically by Swift: 'The Americans entered the war when it was nearly over, in the same way as they entered the Second World War, and made plenty of money from both wars.'

Swift rejoined his battalion which was pursuing the Germans. He found that an enemy retreat could be more dangerous than its advance as the retreating army could choose where to stop and, naturally, would do so in the most defensive positions available. This could leave the pursuing army more vulnerable to attack. For a brief period, the battalion was based near Arras, a town Swift was glad to visit. His interest stemmed from it being the native town of Robespierre, a leading figure of the French Revolution. The retreat continued through a number of French and Belgian towns until 11 November 1918, a day Swift received two important items of news.

Early that morning, the battalion had arrived at a place near the town of Ath in western Belgium. There being no Line, the troops took up a position with as much cover as they could muster. They were ordered to parade in a nearby field and had no idea what they were about to hear. The Commanding Officer arrived on horseback and announced that an armistice had been arranged with the enemy, and that a cease-fire would come into effect at eleven o'clock that morning. Swift described the reaction to that:

> Well, of course, the men went mad! They broke up throwing their weapons away, and the Military Police had to be called to restore order. Even then some of the men lost control. A few became reckless, wandering around and, with the Germans nearby, they were killed. I remember one man in particular, Moloney, with whom I was friendly. He was of Irish descent, but had a strong English accent. He looked after sanitation, constructing field lavatories, and he was killed just a few hours after the announcement.

Swift's second news item came in a telegram from home informing him that his mother was seriously ill. His immediate application for leave was granted three days later after the army had checked the authenticity of the telegram with the Dublin police, who had visited Swift's home to confirm that the facts were as stated. When Swift finally arrived home he found that his mother was dead and buried. A diabetic, she died in the South Dublin Union hospital on 15 November 1918, at the age of 57.[1] A contributory cause of her death was the severe flu epidemic that year which caused thousands to die.

Swift could have deserted then, but this did not appeal to him. After a few days at home, he returned to the Front in Belgium where the German retreat was still in progress. He continued to work as an officers' cook in the reserve line. Occasionally, his accommodation and working conditions were rather better than one might expect in war. Officers took possession of the best house they could find. They had no compunction about that. The residents would just have to leave to make way for the officers and their staff. Cooking facilities in a lot of these houses were of a high standard, a matter of much interest to Swift. When the battalion eventually reached Brussels, a hotel was commandeered to accommodate the officers and their staff. It was situated in a picturesque place besides a park on Chaussée Waterloo. They spent several months there, including Christmas 1918. Swift went regularly to the opera in Brussels and it was during that visit that he first saw Gounod's *Faust.*

In the spring of 1919 the battalion was sent to the army of occupation in Germany. They passed through Cologne on their way to Euskirchen, a small town where Swift had minor surgery to his hand. After that, they continued to advance down the Rhine Valley where they spent some months. Swift availed of this time to acquire some knowledge of the German language, having already acquired a smattering of French. They remained in Germany until about November 1919 when they were informed that the entire battalion would be moving immediately, not, as Swift expected, to the battalion's headquarters in Preston, but to the Curragh, Co. Kildare, in Ireland, for demobilisation.[2]

A Skeleton in the Cupboard

Following his demobilisation in the winter of 1919, Swift, then twenty-three years of age, returned to his Clanbrassil Terrace home. His application to rejoin the Bakers' Union was deferred on account of the high level of unemployment in the trade. For that reason, too, he secured little constant work during the ensuing few years. However, for part of this period he held a permanent position in the Army and Navy Canteens, a civilian organisation providing catering services for the armed forces. Having accepted an offer to bake for that establishment, he was employed initially at the Curragh and later in Belfast. He was still based in Belfast when he resigned from the organisation in 1923. On returning to Dublin, he reapplied for membership of the Bakers' Union, but with unemployment still rampant in that industry, his application was again unsuccessful.

There had been much political upheaval in Ireland during his two-year absence abroad. Even before his departure, the executions of the 1916 leaders had transformed Irish public opinion and expectations of Home Rule had been superseded by demands for national independence from Britain. A manifestation of this development was the 1918 general election which saw the rout of the Irish Parliamentary Party by Sinn Féin.

There followed the War of Independence or the Black and Tan War. In the course of that struggle, Swift met and became friendly with Seán Harrington, an IRA officer. He had first come into contact with Harrington through two of his aunts, Mary Cooper and Margaret White. Following the deaths of their husbands around 1920, Margaret White had left Belfast to live with her sister, Mary Cooper, at 7 Clanbrassil Terrace, a few doors away from the Swifts. In his capacity as an insurance agent, Harrington was a regular visitor to the aunts' flat. Regarding him as a faithful son of the Catholic Church, they cherished hopes that he might prevail upon their nephew to return to the faith. Alas, the aunts were to be disappointed, for not only did Harrington fail in this mission but, under Swift's influence, he too became a free-thinker.

It was in the early 1920s that Swift and Harrington founded the Dublin Philosophical Society. The society was concerned with what its members regarded as fundamental matters of science and philosophy. Contemporary political questions were not debated and this suited the more conservative members who were not eager to discuss such topics. Astronomy, human and animal anatomy and Darwin's theories of the origin of species were among the subjects discussed under the society's auspices. A human skeleton enlightened the study of anatomy. It had been given to Swift by Willie Turner, a technician in Trinity College and a member of the society. On Saturday evenings the society organised visits to Dunsink Observatory.

Meetings of the society were held in Seán Harrington's top-floor flat in Camden Row. Often during the sessions there were IRA attacks on police and military in the vicinity of the flat. Such was the frequency of these assaults that the thoroughfares between Camden Street and Jacob's biscuit factory at Bishop Street became known as the *Dardanelles*. Though a diligent member of the society, Harrington was frequently absent on the run owing to his IRA involvement. As a result of these disruptions the Dublin Philosophical Society did not endure for long. It was not formally wound up but simply ceased to exist. Possibly through his study of philosophy, Harrington, while remaining a staunch republican, later left the IRA. As for the skeleton, Swift brought it home where it was received unenthusiastically by his father. That was mild, however, compared with the hysteria it caused some years later when kept in a cupboard in the Bakers' Union's premises. All was well until the day Mrs Slevin, the caretaker, opened the cupboard, saw the skeleton and nearly died on the spot!

The signing of the Treaty in December 1921 brought to an end the War of Independence. Early the following year the Civil War began. It was during that conflict that Swift became friends with another IRA member, his first cousin, Paddy White. Well liked by Swift and others for his engaging personality, White had worked in the west of Ireland before coming to live with his mother and aunt in Clanbrassil Terrace. An adventurous type, White brought arms home during the day and overhauled them in his bedroom. Had the authorities found him in possession of these weapons, he would probably have been shot. In the draconian measures that had been introduced by the Cosgrave Government, unauthorised persons found possessing arms or ammunition were liable to execution. Nor was this an idle threat for, during the Civil War, seventy-seven republican prisoners were to be executed as reprisals for violent actions by the Irregulars.

Paddy White disappeared to some hideout at night. Though not in the IRA or sympathetic to that organisation, his brother, Harry, had been arrested and interned in the Curragh on suspicion of being a member. Consequently, their mother and aunt were alone in their flat at night. Feeling some sympathy for them, Swift volunteered to sleep in their flat. He did this against the advice of his father who was concerned for his son's safety. Concealed ingeniously in the aunts' flat was an arsenal of weapons. Bullets were hidden behind a picture of the Sacred Heart above John's bed! Under a heap of coal in the back yard was concealed a cache of arms. The aunts themselves retired to bed with guns tied around their bodies under their night-dresses!

The house had a certain notoriety on account of Paddy White's IRA activities. On one of the nights when Swift was staying there, a party of Free State soldiers raided the place. They were led by Commandant Bolster who had acquired a reputation for ill-treating prisoners. Swift admitted them to the house after they had nearly knocked down the hall door. They enquired about Paddy White's whereabouts but Swift was neither willing nor able to assist them. Following an unproductive search of the flat they took him away in a truck to Wellington Barracks (now Griffith Barracks) on the South Circular Road. There, he was fortunate to be brought before an officer with whom he was acquainted and whose father was a member of the Bakers' Union. Having satisfied his superiors that Swift had no IRA connections, the officer informed him that he was free to leave.

As he explained, Swift discerned little difference between the Civil War protagonists:

My sympathies were with Eamon de Valera, what they called the Irregulars. I was not greatly touched by this struggle, however. I had matured more in my political views and had become definitely socialist. While my sympathies were with the republicans, I did not expect a great deal from them. I regarded them as slightly to the left of the Treatyites. The difference between them was not sufficient to induce me to join them or to participate.[1]

It was also in that period of the early 1920s, through his interest in music, that Swift formed a friendship with Vincent Hyland. They first met quite casually at a public concert in St Stephen's Green. An accomplished amateur flautist, Hyland was greatly interested in music and he and Swift attended many musical events together. Both were unemployed although Hyland had no connection with the bakery trade. After learning that work was available in Paris, they left Dublin to seek employment in that city. Swift had acquired a taste for French life during the war and he and Hyland were anxious to improve their elementary French, particularly the spoken language.

In Paris, they worked as builders' labourers on the construction of what was to become the elegant department store, Au Printemps (in the springtime), situated in the centre of the city on Boulevard Haussmann. They lodged about two miles away in Clichy, a suburb not far from Montmartre. On their day off, on Sunday, they enjoyed visiting some of the city's numerous museums, art galleries and exhibitions. No less interesting to them were their rambles in Père Lachaise Cemetery, the final resting place of such celebrities as Rossini, Chopin and Oscar Wilde. Swift's sojourn in Paris was curtailed, however, after he became ill with vertigo. That occurred when the building on which he was working reached the third or fourth storey. His attempts to overcome this condition were ineffective and he became so ill that he had to be hospitalised. The hospital to which he was admitted was a British institution catering primarily for invalided and wounded British soldiers who had settled in France after the war. Swift spent several weeks there before returning to Ireland. He had been in Paris for four months.

Back in Dublin he immediately reapplied for membership of the Bakers' Union but was not accepted until 1924. He was not long on the slate when Bewley's sent for a confectioner to replace one on leave. Suitably qualified for the firm's specialised work, Swift was selected for the task. In the intervening period since his dismissal from Bewley's in 1916, the Westmoreland Street bakery had been fully unionised. Even the foreman who had fired him for attempting to organise the union had become a member, albeit a reluctant one.

Swift was only a few days there when the owner, Ernest Bewley, offered him a permanent job with the firm. Bewley made it known that he was aware Swift had been a conscientious objector and had met some of his Quaker co-religionists in English gaols. How Bewley discovered this Swift is not sure but he recalled that, while awaiting his court martial in Winchester, he was visited by a representative of the Anti-Conscription Fellowship who was a Quaker. This was perhaps the source of Bewley's information. Before accepting the offer of work Swift informed Bewley that his objections to soldiering for Britain had been based on his republican and socialist convictions and not on Quaker or pacifist grounds. Bewley was unperturbed about that. Whatever practical reasons he had for accepting the job, Swift freely acknowledged that a consideration was ill-feeling towards the foreman who had sacked him earlier and who had since been obliged to join the union.

A year or so following his return to Bewley's, on 15 February 1926, Swift's father died of Parkinson's disease, at the age of sixty-seven.[2] Fourteen years earlier, after moving to Dublin, Patrick had settled down reasonably well and had overcome his drinking problem. After surviving on casual work as a baker for a few years, he had secured a permanent post in Peter Kennedy's bakery in Patrick Street where he was employed up to his final illness. By 1916 he had rejoined the Bakers' Union. Swift recalled his father and his uncle, John Cooper, who had also re-enrolled in the union, resolving to support imminent strikes in their respective bakeries. Perhaps through shame or pride Patrick never returned to his native Dundalk.

While Patrick was interred with his wife in Glasnevin Cemetery, he died and was buried without a religious ceremony. Swift elucidates on the circumstances of that:

> Before his death I asked him if he would like to have a priest because my aunts were very active about this and

were very concerned that he would die without some recognition of the Church. So, thinking that possibly he himself would like to have some religious attention before he died, I asked him one day and he shook his head very decisively. At that time he couldn't speak and, not only that, he couldn't write and it was quite an ordeal. He wasn't disposed that way at all. For all my time in Dublin with him he never showed any interest in going to church.[3]

A rare enough occurrence now, a non-religious death and burial in Ireland in 1926 was virtually unique. Swift was thirty when his father died.[4] No influence on John was greater than that of his father. It was Patrick who introduced John to the worlds of science, philosophy, politics, music and literature, subjects that were to be of absorbing interest to John all his life.

Praise God for All!

It was late in 1915, when he was nineteen, that Swift first joined the Bakers' Union.[1] At that time the organisation was known as the Irish Bakers' National Amalgamated Union (IBNAU).[2] While a national union of bakers has existed intermittently since the early 1870s,[3] several of its constituent local unions are of much earlier origin. These would include Waterford, Limerick and Cork where local unions have existed, respectively, at least since 1822, 1837 and 1860.[4] Probably older still is the present Dublin No. 1 Branch which seems to have originated as a Society of Bakers in Boot Lane (now East Arran Street), Dublin, on 14 May 1789.[5] Consequently, the Dublin No. 1 Branch would appear to be not only the oldest local bakers' union, but one of the most ancient unions in Ireland.

The Boot Lane organisation was established 'for the support of the Sick and Burial of Deceased of Sd [said] Society'.[6] From 1806 onwards the admission fee for new applicants was £1. 12s. 6d, while formerly lapsed or expelled members rejoining paid half that amount.[7] Twice during the 1840s the society moved premises, first, in 1843, to 1 Audoen's Arch, High Street, former meeting place of several of the city's trade and merchant guilds, including the Bakers' Guild,[8] and then, in 1846, to 8 Upper Bridge Street.[9] In the period between 1860 and 1887, four smaller rival bakers' societies, New Row West,[10] Wood Quay,[11] Little Britain Street[12] and Werburgh Street,[13] were incorporated into the Bridge Street body. 'The adoption by the Dublin trade unions of the arms, mottoes, saints and dates of origin of the old Dublin Guilds is more interesting as a trait of Irish character than as any proof of historic continuity.'[14] While few would dispute this assertion of Beatrice and Sydney Webb, it would be wrong to assume that the adoption by these early unions of the trappings of the guilds represented merely an expression of sentimentality. In fact, these pioneering unions had more compelling reasons for retaining such traditions. During the late eighteenth and much of the nineteenth centuries, combination laws were in force in Ireland. Under this legislation, workers were prohibited from combining to raise wages, shorten working hours or restrict the numbers of apprentices. Unions had to contend, too, with the conspiracy laws under which combinations were regarded as conspiracies. Penalties for infringing anti-combination legislation were severe and included imprisonment and transportation, the latter carrying a minimum sentence of seven years. Many Irish workers were penalised for combination offences.[15] Recorded in the crime returns of the Dublin Metropolitan district for the period 1843 to 1849, for example, are thirty-seven convictions for offences connected with combinations or conspiracies to raise the rate of wages. To circumvent this repressive legislation, most of the early unions, including the bakers, disguised their true purpose by adopting the arms, mottoes, saints, dates of origin and sometimes even the names of the medieval guilds. The alternative title of the Little Britain Street Bakers' Society, for instance, was the Guild of Saints Clement and Anne. Moreover, the society's president and trustees were known, respectively, by the guild titles of master and wardens. Trustees were also known by the alternative guild title of stewards.[16]

All the early Dublin bakers' unions were known as societies or associations. Their arms and mottoes were adopted from the Dublin Bakers' Guild which was instituted in 1478.[17] From Swift's secular perspective it would be difficult to conceive a more inappropriate motto than the Bakers' Union's *Praise God for All.* To minimise its impact when, in the 1940s, it was being inscribed in the union's new hall, Swift translated it into Latin.

Even after it became lawful in 1871 for workers to organise for the purpose of engaging in disputes concerning wages and working conditions, the societies were tardy in shedding the customs and trappings of the guilds. That was evident in 1875 when the Bridge Street Bakers' Society adopted new rules that had been certified originally in 1834. Inclusion in the revised text of the organisation's alternative titles, Friendly Brothers of St Anne and Dublin Operative Bakers' Friendly Society, and of other provisions evocative of the guilds, demonstrated the caution with which unions emerged from a century of suppression. The first 1875 rule, for example, stated: 'That this society has for its objects in general the glory of God, the honour of our most gracious Sovereign, [Queen Victoria!] and the good of our neighbour, but in particular the well-being of its members . . .'! No less redolent of the guilds was Rule 18 in the revised document: 'That the society shall provide three large linen sheets and tablecloths, six candle-sticks, a snuffers and a snuffer's tray, and such other articles as they may deem necessary for the decent laying-out of the dead . . .'[18] The influence of the guilds was evident, too, in the apprentices' indentures. Today's apprentices might find it sobering to consider the plight of their Bridge Street precursors whose indenture laid down that an apprentice '. . . His Master faithfully shall serve, his Secrets keep, his lawful Commands everywhere gladly do . . . He shall not commit Fornication nor contract Matrimony within the said Term . . . He shall not play at cards, Dice Tables . . . He shall not haunt or use Taverns, Ale-houses or Play-houses nor absent himself from his Master's Service Day or Night unlawfully . . .'[19] Not until 1935, following the introduction of a new indenture form, were apprentice bakers finally freed from these rigorous conditions.[20]

The Bridge Street bakers had some traditions of their own. To meet the additional weekend demand for bakery products, a double night's work would be produced on Friday night. Casuals would be recruited from the idle list to assist with the extra workload and the men with constant work would provide them with food for the night. They would also give them sixpence: fourpence for a whiskey and twopence for a pint of stout.[21]

A long-standing custom of the present Dublin No. 1 Branch that possibly originated in the guilds is the disbursement of *goose* money to retired members. Swift was among the recipients of this annual pre-Christmas gratuity, which, in the mid-1980s, varied from £10 to £30.

An older tradition than goose money and probably the most ancient custom of all was that of sons following their fathers into the trade. One reason for this was pride: fathers would encourage their sons to follow them into the trade. A more significant factor was the not infrequent restriction of the trade to bakers' sons. Such exclusiveness was designed, of course, to protect bakers' sons from the scourge of unemployment. Employers generally welcomed the practice, believing it would produce employees with a special interest in the trade.[22] The custom was not confined to bakers but was prevalent in many trades, for instance, printing[23] and bricklaying, although the bricklayers' union also accepted journeymen's nephews.[24]

As a consequence of this tradition, it was common to find generations of families in particular trade unions. In that regard, Swift's family would be fairly typical. As has already been noted, Laurence Swift, Swift's grandfather, was a member of the Little Britain Street Bakers' Society for twenty-one years. That was from 1838 to 1859[25] when union dues were $3\frac{1}{2}d$[26] and wages about £1 per week.[27] Although Swift's father was president of the Dundalk Bakers' Society in 1890,[28] it is not known when he first joined that organisation. Through the combination of running his own bakery business in Dundalk and being subsequently unemployed in Dublin, Patrick Swift was not a member of the Bakers' Union from 1891 to 1916. It was in the latter year that he joined the IBNAU's Dublin branch,[29] remaining a member up to his final illness in the mid-1920s. Other relatives of Swift's who were members of the Bakers' Union include his brother, Paddy, and his second son, Grosvenor. From about 1920 until his death in 1960, Paddy Swift was a member of the Dublin No. 1 Branch of the Irish Bakers' Confectioners' and Allied Workers' Amalgamated Union (now the Bakery and Food Workers' Amalgamated Union). Having enrolled in that branch in 1965, Grosvenor remained a member for some twenty years before establishing his own confectionery business in Dublin.

1911 was a disastrous year for the Bridge Street Bakers' Society. For the first time draw plate ovens and other mechanical aids were being introduced in the Dublin bakeries. Up to then bakers' wages had been based on payment per batch and not on the number of hours worked. To reap the benefits of the new machinery, the employers proposed the introduction of time-based payments. This the society resisted and a strike involving some 300 bakers ensued. By engaging non-union men mainly from the provinces and establishing a house of call, to where bakers seeking work were referred, the employers neutralised the strike. As a result, after a fortnight's payments of dispute benefit, the society's funds of £300 were depleted and the strike and the society collapsed.[30]

One year after this débâcle, members of the society and others regrouped to form a new organisation, the National Amalgamated Bakers' and Confectioners' Trade Union of Ireland.[31] The new body became known as the Dublin Branch of the Irish Bakers' National Amalgamated Union in 1913,[32] retaining that title until 1918 when it was renamed the Irish Bakers' Confectioners' and Allied Workers' Amalgamated Union (IBCAWAU/ Bakers' Union).[33] In 1912, the Dublin branch and later the national union were located at 22 Upper Ormond Quay. Then, in 1920, both bodies moved premises to 37 Lower Gardiner Street,[34] present address of the union's Dublin No. 1 and No. 2 Branches.

The new Dublin union declared as its primary objects: 'To gain recognition by employers, increase wages and abolish night baking'.[35] Strengthened by its early merger with the only remaining bakers' society in Dublin, the Metropolitan, the union set about organising all categories of skilled and unskilled workers in the trade.[36] At the same time, as Swift recalled, bakers barely tolerated their more highly skilled confectioner colleagues, often describing them contemptuously as *candymen*.[37] In Cork City, that friction between confectioners and bakers has prevailed to the present day, evidenced by their membership of separate union branches.

In the early years of the Dublin branch's existence, the table-hand's weekly rate was £1. 14s. and night baking was universal. A week's idle money or unemployment benefit amounted to one night's pay plus four shillings. In addition to paying union contributions of 3 pence for every night worked, members were levied 2 pence weekly for a funeral fund and a further 2 pence to support the Dublin Labour Party and Trades Council.[38]

Within the first decade of its existence, the branch recorded substantial progress. This was manifest as early as 1915 when the branch purchased its Ormond Quay premises.[39] It was in the area of pay and conditions, however, that the most tangible progress was made. Between 1914 and 1920, the period in which both Swift and his father enrolled in the union, the tablehand's weekly rate increased from £1. 14s. to £4. 14s.[40] That remained the wage until 1926. Thus, in the decade ending in 1924, the tablehand's rate rose by 176 per cent, more than double the 85 per cent increase in the consumer price index for that period.[41] Other union gains at that time included the introduction of one week's paid holidays, a reduction in the weekly working hours from approximately sixty to forty-six, and the virtual abolition of Sunday and night work. Moreover, control of the employment of casual labour reverted to the union when the employers' house of call became redundant.[42] Significant as these successes unquestionably were, recognition by the employers was arguably a more important victory for the union.

Many of the gains by the Bakers' Union were common to other trade unions. For example, between 1913 and 1920, the Dublin Typographical Provident Society, an antecedent of the present Irish Print Union, secured for its members weekly increases of £2. 17s. 6d. By 1912, the printers had negotiated the introduction of the forty-eight hour week. Apparently the printers met stronger employer opposition to their claims than did their baker colleagues. While the gains of the bakers during the 1910s were achieved without recourse to industrial action[43] to secure their rights, the printers were obliged to strike on no fewer than four occasions for a total of thirty weeks.[44]

These achievements of the unions, Swift believed, were aided by British Government policy during the war. Anxious to avoid labour disputes that might lead to economic disruption, the government, through its arbitrators, was prepared to make significant concessions to the unions.[45]

Shortly after joining the Bakers' Union in 1915, Swift attended his first general meeting of members. It was held in the old Trades Hall in Capel Street which was then the headquarters of the united Irish Trade Union Congress and Labour Party, and the Dublin Trades Union Council. There was much trouble then at meetings of the Bakers' Union over how to deal with the scabs who had broken the 1911 strike. Eventually the scabs were permitted to rejoin the union. Supporting that development, the majority of members, including Swift, took the view that if the union was to be consolidated it would have to embrace all bakers. That led to quite a disturbance at meetings as many members were utterly opposed to the scabs and did not want them in the union. Resentment over this issue lasted for generations, manifesting itself at meetings in such comments as: 'He scabbed it' or 'His father scabbed it' or 'His grandfather scabbed it.'[46]

Through unemployment and emigration, Swift was not a member of the Bakers' Union between 1917 and 1924. By the time he rejoined in 1924, many of the Dublin bakeries had been organised. Consequently, there had been a considerable growth in the membership of the branch. Surprisingly, little of this progress is recorded in the union's records. What is chronicled, however, is that in 1917, the year Swift emigrated to work in Britain, branch membership was 180 and funds £370[47] (approximately £14,000 in 1991 values). By 1930, six years after his re-entry to the union, branch membership had risen to more than 800.[48] Four years later again, in 1934, branch funds stood at the remarkable sum of £29,000[49] (approximately £1 million in 1991 values).

Not by Bread Alone

When Bewley's opened a new branch at 78 Grafton Street, in 1927, Swift and two others, the foreman and an apprentice, were transferred there from the firm's Westmoreland Street bakery. Swift was appointed deputy foreman, and foreman a few years later when his old adversary, Fred Andrews, left the firm. An apprentice during Swift's term as foreman was Alfred Bewley, son of the firm's owner, Ernest Bewley.

Earlier that same year, shortly before he was 31, Swift was elected to his first union position when Bewley's Westmoreland Street bakers and confectioners chose him as their represent-ative.[1] He held a similar position on behalf of his Grafton Street colleagues in 1928[2] and 1929.[3] Carrying the title, *Committee Man*, this part-time post equated with that of shop steward in most other trade unions. Committee men from all the organised Dublin bakeries comprised the management committee of the union's Dublin branch. Swift was, therefore, also a member of the branch's management committee from 1927 to 1929. There was then an unwritten union rule that a foreman was ineligible for membership of the branch's management and executive committees. It was not applied in Swift's case, probably because Bewley's was a relatively small bakery. An advantage of working in Bewley's was the firm's co-operative attitude to local union representatives discharging their duties.

With the formation in 1928 of a second Dublin branch of the Bakers' Union to cater for general workers, shop assistants, clerks and van sales personnel, the original organisation of bakers and confectioners became known as the union's Dublin No. 1 Branch.[4] Considering the impressive achievements of the latter body, from its inception in 1912 to the time Swift rejoined in the mid-1920s, it might be assumed that the members were reasonably content with the leadership. For most of this period the principal leaders were Denis Cullen, Frank Moran and Christopher Noonan, respectively, President, Treasurer and Secretary. The secretary-ship was a full-time post while the presidency and treasurership were honorary, part-time positions. However, Cullen and Moran were also full-time officials through holding the national union offices of General Secretary and Organiser respectively. The members were, undoubtedly, appreciative of the work of these leaders in rebuilding the branch after the collapse of the Bridge Street Society in 1911, and negotiating the much improved wages and working conditions in the intervening period.

Yet, within a year or so of Swift's re-entry to the branch, the leadership was under pressure, particularly from the younger members. There was discontentment about several issues, the most emotive being a reduction in wages which occurred in 1926 when the tablehands' rate fell by nine shillings per week.[5] Four years earlier, the printers had suffered a cut of eight shillings weekly.[6] These reductions were general and followed the unusual development of a decrease in the consumer price index, which, between 1925 and 1933, fell from 189.75 to 151.[7] Economic problems experienced by the Cosgrave govern-ment preceded these wage reductions. Although the cuts were opposed by Swift and some of his young branch colleagues, most union leaders maintained that the economy could not sustain higher wages and the movement was too weak to fight the issue. Also of concern to Swift and his associates was a branch decision granting the President and Treasurer dividends from the branch's investments.[8]

Possibly the greatest grievance of the young activists, however, was their leaders' inertness in confronting the problem of non-union bakeries. Frequently operating in primitive premises, these establishments constituted a threat to the superior conditions that obtained in unionised bakeries. There was a feeling that the leadership had become negligent and was not fighting the non-union issue with sufficient vigour.

In 1927, in an attempt to remedy this situation, a small group of young bakers under Swift's leadership had a resolution adopted by the branch establishing a subcommittee. Known as the Disputes Committee, the subcommittee had a membership of about ten, among whom were Johnny Byrne, Michael Conroy,

Walter Duffy, Paddy Hogan and their chairman, Swift. In an intensive campaign, the disputes committee organised the picketing of non-union bakeries and the canvassing of shops and institutions to boycott their products. There was strong branch support for this action, with 270 members responding to an appeal for volunteers.[9] It was common for bakers to turn out up to six nights weekly after work to lend assistance. Since the union had no members employed by these firms, technically there was no dispute between the parties. Consequently, the picketing by the branch was illegal. Some of those involved in the action were members of the IRA or had recently left that organisation. Two of them blew up Garry's non-union bakery which was located in a lane close to the Royal College of Surgeons in Ireland on St Stephen's Green. The two members were disowned by the branch executive which was then strongly anti-IRA and sympathetic to the Cosgrave government. One of the members, Tom Nolan, was sentenced to two years' imprisonment. Swift often visited him in Mountjoy Gaol. The disputes committee organised collections in the bakeries for Nolan's wife. Generally, the campaign was most successful, with virtually all non-union bakeries being organised or being put out of business. The committee's achievements generated a new enthusiasm among members of the branch.

Shortly after its founding, the disputes committee established the Bakery Trade's Social Club. The club's chairman was Swift, while secretaries over the years of its existence included Billy Monks and John Moran, the last mentioned being the son of Frank Moran, national union organiser. As will be seen, the social club's objectives were much wider than the title would suggest. Essentially, it catered for the social, cultural and educational interests of the union members and their families.

Inter-bakery soccer competitions were an early venture in the club's extensive range of activities. There were at least six teams in Dublin, and apprentices of that city competed with each other and with colleagues in Belfast, Cork, Limerick and Waterford. Among other undertakings were a cycling club for young members and their families, general knowledge question times, lectures on trade education and classes in first aid. The last mentioned was important as safety and public health legislation were less advanced then than now. A hospital visiting committee was formed whose members paid weekly visits and brought gifts to sick and disabled branch colleagues. Excursions to seaside resorts in the Dublin area were run by the club. Open to members, their families and their friends, these outings, usually by train, would commence in the early afternoon, finishing late at night after an evening meal and dance.

Funds for the club's activities were raised through raffle ticket sales in the bakeries and dances run on Saturday nights in the Ierne Ballroom, 12 Parnell Square East. Small dance bands were common then and a popular one at the club's dances was *The Pembroke Orpheus*. It was composed almost entirely of bakers, several of whom were members of a family called Johnson who worked in Boland's bakery in Grand Canal Street.

Swift's interests were in more serious cultural activities. From the profits of raffles and dances were funded a choir and an orchestra of union members and their relations. To encourage this, professional tuition in singing and instrument playing was sponsored by the club. The choirmaster of Whitefriar Street Catholic Church, Mr Power, was engaged to train the union choir. He was less than enthusiastic when, at Swift's instigation, the choir gave renditions of *The Red Flag*. A later teacher of the choir was Leo Maguire, baritone with the Dublin Grand Opera Society and composer of such popular ditties as *The Gypsy Rover* and *The Dublin Saunter*. He was probably better known as the presenter of the Saturday afternoon sponsored radio programme for Walton's music shops, and especially for his concluding catch-phrase: 'If you feel like singing, do sing an Irish song!'

Tuition for the orchestra's string, brass, reed and percussion sections was provided in the Municipal School of Music (now the College of Music), in Chatham Row.[10] The first teacher, Mr May, was a professional violinist and member of the family of that name who, up to the early 1970s, ran a music shop at 130 St Stephen's Green West. In the decade or so before its closure, the shop's well-stocked sheet music department often had the appearance of chaos. With insufficient space to store all the music in the firm's attractive wooden cabinets, the overflow would be stacked in such unlikely places as the stairs leading to the upper floors of the premises. Yet, despite its chaotic appearance, the staff, and particularly Mr May himself, never seemed to experience the slightest difficulty satisfying a customer.

Rehearsals of the choir and orchestra were held in the union's Lower Gardiner Street premises. Famous opera choruses, Moore's melodies and some songs composed by Swift were among compositions sung by the choir. Included in the orchestra's repertoire were excerpts from Balfe's *The Bohemian Girl* and Wallace's *Maritana*; *The Coriolanus Overture* by Beethoven and Schubert's *Marche Militaire*. The choir and orchestra, each of some twenty members, were sufficiently accomplished to perform not only at social functions of the union but public concerts held in the Father Mathew Hall in Church Street and Rathmines Town Hall.

It was not long, however, before the orchestra began to lose some of its key instrumentalists. They became semi-professional, baking during the day and playing in jazz bands at night. This had a detrimental effect on the orchestra which, like the choir, performed on an amateur basis and, after a few years, it had to be disbanded. The choir was more resilient, surviving intermittently for many years. Periodically, it would lapse, only to reassemble for some social event in the union. The last formal performance by the choir was in May 1967 when it combined with the ITGWU's choir to entertain delegates attending the fifteenth congress of the International Union of Food and Allied Workers' Associations in Liberty Hall, Dublin. On that occasion, the programme, selected by Swift, included one of his favourite pieces of music, *The Chorus of the Hebrew Slaves*, from Verdi's opera *Nabucco*. Swift's songs, 'When Friends Have Met' and 'Our Hands to Our Brothers' were broadcast on RTE radio on 24 March 1985 when remnants of the choir sang in a *Donncha on Sunday* (Donncha Ó Dulaing) programme marking the Golden Jubilee of the Dublin Bakery School.

There was much discussion on social and political theory in the early 1930s. Under the social club's auspices, public lectures and discussions were organised on such topics as socialism, Soviet communism, Irish republicanism, Italian and Portuguese corporatism and German national socialism. Lectures on corporatism/fascism were held purely to criticise and expose these right-wing theories. Among the club's lecturers were Tom Johnson, leader of the Labour Party, and two prominent priests, the Jesuit, Fr Edward Coyne, who defended private property, and Fr Michael O'Flanagan, supporter of the Spanish republican cause. The speaker on Italian corporatism, Count Tomacelli, was Mussolini's ambassador to Ireland. A section of the audience expressed resentment at such a lecture being held under trade union auspices and Swift, who presided at the meeting, had to appeal for tolerance. The attendance included Hanna Sheehy Skeffington[11] and, according to Swift's account, she made a devastating criticism of Mussolini's version of corporatism.[12]

Satisfied that the threat of Italian corporatism had been exposed, the club decided to confront Nazism. Some advocates of Hitler's national socialism were then in Trinity College as exchange students from German universities. Swift undertook to look for a real Nazi from this group. He visited the college where he met Martin Plass, a student of English literature from Berlin University. A member of Hitler's storm-troopers, Plass agreed to lecture in the union's premises on the German Labour Front, the Nazi's corporate alternative to the banned trade unions. But aware, apparently, of international trade union hostility to Hitlerism, the German Minister to Ireland prohibited the lecture at the last moment.

There is no evidence of objections by branch members to the club's lectures on Italian corporatism or the attempted one on the German Labour Front. The omission is notable since members did express fears that the club was communistic. At a general meeting of the branch held on 22 January 1933, Denis Cullen, the President, replying to a remark by a member about communism, stated that eighteen months earlier a lecture had been given under the club's auspices to which strong exception had been taken by the members. The president went on to say that Swift had undertaken, when spoken to on the matter, not to allow any lecture to be given without first notifying the executive committee. In an obvious reference to Swift and some of his associates, the president stated that communism was inimical to trade unionism and that the union was considered too aristocratic and too wealthy by some members advocating communism.[13] The following year, 1934, responding to taunts about communism, Swift stated that he had no connection with the Communist Party and had never attended any of its meetings.[14] The Communist Party of Ireland had only been re-formed the previous year. Actually, for reasons that will be considered later, Swift was then a member of the Labour Party, having joined in 1927.

The communist question arose again at a branch general meeting in 1936. A member, T. Delaney, said that there were whispers that the social club stood for communism. The basis of his concern was that members of the club's cycling section had been given cards with the title *Labour Youth Corps*! Replying to this, Swift said it was the younger members comprising the cycling section who had agreed to call themselves a Labour League Corps. He said there was nothing communistic about it, nor about any of the lectures which had been given. 'The Club', he said, 'stood for the policy of the Irish Labour Party.' Swift's reply did not reassure everybody. Mr T. Liddy mentioned that lecturers had been brought from Trinity College. When Swift explained that the lecturers in question were Labour Party members, another member, F. O'Brien, declared that it was well known that one of the largest communistic cells in the country existed in Trinity College and he feared the social club was drifting to the left!

Some of these attacks on the club, and by implication on its leading members, including Swift, originated outside the union. This is clear from F. Gillespie's statement at the same meeting. Referring to a forthcoming lecture, he said that Catholic clergymen had taken exception to some of the speakers![15] Perhaps there were more sinister reasons behind the allegations about communism. There was certainly strong Catholic influence in the union from the 1930s to, at least, the 1950s.

The Bakery Trade's Journal, another project that originated in the social club, was published for three years by the club before being adopted as the official organ of the union. This undertaking was financed by revenue from bakery trade advertisements and profits from the club's fund-raising activities. The union's 1938 national delegate meeting decided that union members should be levied and supplied with copies. Excluding the years 1937 and 1938, when it appeared monthly, the journal was a quarterly publication from its first edition at the beginning of 1936 to 1947, when it ceased publication. Swift was editor throughout this period, and he wrote, anonymously, a great deal of the journal's contents, including a regular feature article under the pseudonym *Bolivar's Half-Hour*.[16] Aimed primarily at members of the union, the *Bakery Trade's Journal* dealt with matters of trade union interest, news of the bakery school, trade exhibitions and political questions, for example, fascism.

A major concern of the social club was the lack of any formal technical training in the bakery trade in Ireland. Such education was possible only rarely when an employer bore the cost of sending an operative to a British course. Following a recommendation by the club, the Dublin No. 1 Branch decided to establish its own bakery school and technical classes. A small bakery equipped with the minimum requirements was installed in modified stables at the rear of the union's premises, 37 Lower Gardiner Street.

With no tradition of bakery trade education in Ireland, the branch was obliged to advertise for a teacher in a British trade journal. An application from a Welshman, Sam Anthony,[17] particularly impressed the executive committee. He had just graduated from Birmingham Bakery School and was most enthusiastic about this unique trade union experiment. He accepted the job on an overman's rate of pay, somewhat less than he might have expected to earn as a teacher in a British educational institution. The school opened in 1935 and there were no difficulties filling its evening classes. Volunteers were sought by the branch, and there was a good response, mainly from adult members anxious to improve their knowledge of the trade. It was not long before younger members and apprentices also started attending. In the late 1930s, the social club, with assistance from the union, succeeded in interesting other branches in the promotion of trade education in their areas and this led to the founding of the Belfast Bakery School and of classes in Limerick and Drogheda.

The work of bakery school students was exhibited at the Royal Dublin Society's Spring Shows in 1936 and 1937. The second exhibition came to the notice of some members of the City of Dublin Vocational Education Committee (VEC). So impressed were they with the display that the VEC later offered to take over the running of the school. Initially the branch was wary of this, but reservations had to be balanced against the considerable financial burden of running the school, a matter of particular concern to Swift who was then Branch Treasurer. After undertaking to employ Sam Anthony and to confine apprenticeship classes to union members, the VEC's offer was eventually accepted. There was also agreement to establish an advisory committee comprising union, employer and VEC representatives, to manage the school. There was no conflict between the three organisations represented on the school's advisory committee as all members were united in their common objects to raise standards and promote the interests of the industry. It is widely accepted in the trade that the school has raised standards of hygiene and quality. Swift was chairman of the advisory committee from its inception in 1937 until his retirement from union office thirty years later, when he was made an honorary member for life.

A major aim of the branch was to make it compulsory for apprentices to attend the school. They secured the employers' agreement on this. At first, apprentices attended classes after work but, since 1954, the courses have been run on a day-release basis. The period of apprenticeship was four years. An apprentice failing the first year's examination would forgo an increment in pay and would have to repeat the examination. A second failure would result in the apprentice having to leave the trade.

Bakery exhibitions, initiated and primarily organised by the social club, were a development of the bakery school. Having arranged an exhibition of students' work in the union's premises in 1937, the club, with union assistance, organised a national bakery exhibition the following year. This was held at the same venue and in conjunction with the union's biennial national delegate meeting. A feature of this exhibition was a section devoted to anti-fascist propaganda, with labour and anti-war literature on sale. A year later, in 1939, a second and much larger national exhibition was held in the Engineers' Hall, opposite the Mansion House in Dawson Street. It was formally opened by Seán Lemass, Minister for Industry and Commerce. John O'Dowd, a former secretary of the Irish Labour History Society and author of a history of the Dublin Bakery School, has evaluated the union's achievement up to 1939:

> The 1939 Exhibition constituted a remarkable achievement for the Bakers' Union; in four short years it had begun its own bakery school and held its own exhibitions of bakery craft. It had seen the school develop into a part of the City of Dublin VEC which was the principal provider of technical education in Dublin while at the same time bringing the exhibition from being a section of the annual Spring Show into being a national exhibition in its own right.[18]

Owing to the shortage of necessary ingredients, it was not possible to hold exhibitions during the war or early post-war years. Some years after the war, the union participated in an international bakery exhibition in Holland, where a display of bakery products sponsored by the union won first prize. International bakery exhibitions, promoted by the club in association with the union, were held in the Mansion House, Dublin, in 1949, 1951 and 1953. The 1951 event, opened by the Taoiseach, John Costello, included displays and competitions of products of union members from ten European countries and the US. A new feature was introduced at the 1953 exhibition when apprentices from Ireland, England, Scotland and Wales participated in working competitions. These international contacts by the union were facilitated by the establishment of a joint committee of English/Welsh, Scottish and Irish bakery workers' unions, and the Irish union's affiliation in 1939 to the International Federation of Food and Drink Workers. The initiative for such international links originated in the social club.

As for Swift's motives for seeking the establishment of a bakery school, these extended beyond personal and union interest. He was still employed as a foreman in Bewley's when the school opened in 1935, and was anxious to acquire some scientific knowledge of the ingredients of bakery products. As a trade unionist soon to become a full-time national union official, he wanted to ensure that technical education was available to union members. He believed that if members were educated in the trade, it would enhance union claims for improved wages and working conditions. Swift and the other founders also conceived the school serving the community by setting standards in ingredients, workmanship and hygiene. Now fully integrated into the VEC's College of Technology, Lower Kevin Street, the National Bakery School of Ireland, as it is presently known, has developed greatly since the 1930s. Still managed by an advisory committee of union, employer and VEC representatives, the school currently employs some twelve teachers.

The social club had yet to undertake its most ambitious and controversial enterprise, the procurement of new union premises. As we shall see, it was this project more than any other that was to bring Swift into conflict with Catholic actionists in the Bakers' Union.[19]

Meanwhile, in 1935, following interference in the bakery by a manager, Noel Poynton, Swift resigned from Bewley's. Originally employed as a shop assistant, Poynton had been promoted to a managerial post after marrying Sylvia Bewley, an office employee and daughter of the firm's owner. At that time the union's presence in Bewley's was confined to the bakeries. The firm's shops and cafés, usually managed by elderly women hostile to the union, were unorganised. This was an important reason why bakery workers resented interference from those quarters. Besides, there had been a tradition of independence in the bakery for many years.

Swift's action was in breach of union rules, as members intending to resign from their jobs had first to obtain the authority of the union. That was logical where the union controlled the recruitment of staff. With no suitable replacement available to the union to fill this specialised post, the two principal union officers visited Bewley's and instructed Swift to withdraw his notice. Reluctantly, Swift attempted to comply with this direction but Bewley's would not accept that, and he found himself in a rather embarrassing position. He went back on the slate and was sent to Johnston Mooney and O'Brien's bakery at 7/8 South Leinster Street where, after being employed for a short period as a casual, he secured a permanent job.

By the mid-1930s, Swift was a member of the executive committee of the Dublin No. 1 Branch, comprising the positions of president, treasurer and two trustees. These part-time offices were usually filled by elections held at annual general meetings of the branch. Swift first contested a trusteeship in 1930 and, in a poll of more than 800, was defeated by a mere five votes.[20] He suffered a heavier defeat the following year[21] and, in 1933, though he topped the poll, the President overruled the result on the basis that he had only received about 25 per cent of the total vote.[22] He was defeated in a second ballot that year.[23] The 1934 election results are not recorded, but at a special general meeting held on 24 November 1935, it was mentioned that Swift had resigned the trusteeship.[24] Evidently he was elected a Trustee in 1934 or 1935. It was also at that meeting of 24 November 1935 that Swift was nominated as Treasurer,[25] a post he secured though this is not minuted in the branch's records. It is surprising that Swift was not elected earlier to the executive committee.

Impeding his progress were allegations of communism against himself and the social club.

It is clear from election results that, in the early 1930s, branch general meetings were extremely well attended. The turnout of over 800 [26] at two of these meetings suggests that virtually the entire branch membership was present. This differs significantly from the situation today where unions often experience problems of low attendances which would justify an investigation by the trade union movement.

At a national delegate meeting of the Bakers' Union that commenced on his fortieth birthday, 26 August 1936, Swift was elected to the full-time position of National Organiser. His election by the narrow margin of eighteen to sixteen votes was facilitated by the absence of two prominent Dublin delegates who, during the ballot, were in a County Wicklow pub prematurely celebrating his defeat! [27]

Quest for Knowledge

It has been recorded that Michael McInerney,[1] a former political correspondent of the *Irish Times*, described Swift as one of the cleverest men he had the privilege of knowing.[2] He is also reported as saying that Swift's writing was one of the finest examples of English prose to appear in that paper's feature pages.[3] Whatever validity there may be in McInerney's opinions, most of Swift's acquaintances would have acknowledged that he possessed an intellectual and analytical mind. He also had a wide command of English and could write, not only with clarity and brevity, but with the wit and style one expects to find in literature.

These attributes were useful to Swift in his continuous quest for knowledge. His life-long interest in reading further expanded his education. He read a great deal, particularly following his return from Paris in the early 1920s, and it was principally through reading that he educated himself in such subjects as science, philosophy, economics, literature and the arts.

The period beginning in the mid-1920s was not the easiest time to acquire books on free-thought, an area of special interest to Swift. He was fortunate, therefore, to meet Paddy Stephenson,[4] a librarian in Kevin Street Public Library and later Chief Librarian of Dublin City, who was able to furnish his reading requirements. It appears that, because Stephenson had been a member of the Fianna and in the GPO during the 1916 Rebellion, the authorities were not zealous checking books he ordered for his free-thinking reader. Unlike his son, Sam Stephenson, the controversial architect, Paddy Stephenson was a socialist and he and Swift became close friends.

In furthering his learning in the late 1920s and early 1930s, Swift came into contact with a number of intellectuals. Among this group were several students with whom he became friends. There was David Ruddstein of the Royal College of Surgeons in Ireland and Max Freedman, Jacob (Jack) Weingreen and Philip Robinson of Trinity College, Dublin. The first three were members of a large Jewish community in the Clanbrassil Street area, where Swift also resided. Ruddstein, Freedman and Robinson subsequently graduated in medicine while Weingreen became Professor of Hebrew, and a Fellow of Trinity College.

In the 1930s, medical students of TCD were obliged to study zoology. Through his friendship with Willie Turner, an employee of the college whom he had met in the Dublin Philosophical Society, Swift was able to pursue his interest in Darwinism by attending some of Professor Bronte Gatenby's zoology lectures in Trinity.

During the early 1930s Swift was introduced to Robert Hannan who had entered Trinity as a divinity student with the intention of becoming a Church of Ireland clergyman. However, after coming under the influence of Professor Henry Macran, the celebrated Kantian and Hegelian, he decided instead to study philosophy. Hannan's parents, 'both narrow Protestants', disapproved of Robert's association with Swift, blaming him wrongly when their son abandoned divinity. Hannan went on to take a degree in philosophy. Before meeting Hannan Swift had studied philosophy informally and, among other philosophers, had read Locke, Hume, Kant, Hegel and Marx. He was greatly impressed by Hannan who had 'a very fine mind'. Furthermore, Hannan was naturally disposed to discussing philosophical questions almost to the exclusion of anything else. Swift and Hannan became friends and, over a period of years, Hannan visited Swift's home every Saturday. There, after tea, they discussed philosophy into the early hours of the morning. In this way, Swift learnt much from Hannan and he acknowledged that Hannan's influence on him was considerable. Hannan later chose a career in education, teaching for a time in the Jewish Stratford College in Rathgar.

It was also around the early 1930s that Swift held his first discussions with communists. They were James Larkin, Jun., son of Larkin, Sen. and Johnny Nolan. Swift was already acquainted with Larkin, having met him at meetings of a joint union bakery committee comprising the Bakers' Union, the ITGWU and the

WUI. He distinctly remembered Larkin and Nolan being present at a meeting in Weingreen's rooms in Trinity when reading his philosophical paper, *Social Principles*. It was criticised by Larkin for not conforming to Marxist dogma.

Swift and Larkin, Jun. were later colleagues in the Dublin Trades Union Council and on the executive of the Irish Trade Union Congress. Differing greatly from his flamboyant father, Larkin, Jun. was a rather cautious and shy type. Unlike his father, who always spoke extempore, the younger Larkin had a passion for debating and analysing issues, sometimes to the point of boring his associates. Nevertheless, Swift was impressed by Larkin, Jun., finding him an intelligent and able colleague who was committed to the political as well as the industrial objectives of the labour movement.

Johnny Nolan, a man of cultural and political interests, was a life-long member of the Communist Party of Ireland. Apart from managing the Party's bookshop, New Books, from the 1940s to the 1980s, Nolan was, for many years, National Treasurer of the Party. Mainly through Swift's periodic visits to New Books, he and Swift developed a friendly relationship which was to last until Nolan's death in 1988.[5]

During the late 1920s, prior to his encounters with Larkin, Jun. and Nolan, Swift had discovered another centre of learning. That was the Contemporary Club, an oasis of free-thought and expression in an illiberal and very intolerant society. Founded in 1885 by Professor Charles Oldham of University College, Dublin,[6] its early members included the writers George Russell (AE) and William B. Yeats, Francis Sheehy Skeffington, the pacifist, and O'Leary-Curtis, an associate of Arthur Griffith in founding Sinn Féin. Incidentally, O'Leary-Curtis, it appears, was reputed to be mean. His reputation was the subject of this rhyme which Swift recalled:

> I met O'Leary-Curtis
> And he took me by the hand.
> He asked me how was Ireland
> And who was going to stand.

The lines, of course, are a parody on 'The Wearing of the Green', a ballad that was popular in the early decades of this century.

The Contemporary Club ran weekly discussions in Lincoln Chambers, Lincoln Place. These would commence at eight o'clock on Saturday evening, continuing into the early hours of Sunday morning. Suspicions that these late sessions had more to do with the consumption of alcohol than serious debate may be discounted since tea was the only beverage served. A member or occasionally a guest speaker would give an address or lead a discussion on some subject related to free-thought or expression. Among guests Swift remembered hearing were the author, Beverly Nichols, and the Fine Gael politician, Richard Mulcahy.

During Swift's period as a member, the president was a senator, Dr Robert Rowlette of Mercer's Hospital. One of the secretaries was Harry Nicholls, a senior official of Dublin Corporation. He was conspicuous as a Protestant who had served as an officer in the Irish Volunteers and had participated in the 1916 Rebellion. Among other members in those years were C. S. (Todd) Andrews, later prominently associated with such semi-state organisations as Córas Iompair Éireann (CIE) and Bord na Móna; Walter Brown, owner of a Dublin flour mill; Owen Sheehy Skeffington, son of Francis and Hanna, lecturer in French literature and language in TCD, and later a senator representing that college; and Seán Keating, the artist, husband of socialist, Mai Keating, who attended some of the meetings. Justin Keating, the former Labour Party Minister for Industry and Commerce, is the son of Seán and Mai Keating. Although membership of the Contemporary Club was confined to men, women relatives and friends of members could attend and participate in debates every fourth Saturday. The club embraced people of diverse political opinions. Members of Cumann na nGaedhael, later Fine Gael, and Fianna Fáil were to be found there. Socialists were scarce, however, among its predominantly middle-class membership. Liberal-minded people with no party political affiliations formed the majority. Swift remained a member of the Contemporary Club until the 1940s when it ceased to exist. He had no difficulty identifying with Dr Todd Andrews' explanation for its demise: 'It was finally extinguished by the zealots of censorship, religious triumphalism and the dominance of materialism in the national ethos.'[7]

The acquisition of knowledge, particularly of the academic kind, was not regarded by Swift as an end in itself. He perceived it as an instrument to not only develop his full potential but facilitate his more effective participation in society. This latter consideration was manifest as early as the mid-1920s when he initiated and became Chairman of the Bakers' Union Disputes Committee. It was evident again in 1927 when he joined the Labour Party.[8] His decision to enroll was prompted by his membership of the Bakers' Union. The first of two general elections that year was held in June. Denis Cullen, the Union's General Secretary, was a Labour candidate and the union appealed to its young members to assist with the campaign. Responding to this, Swift enrolled as a member in the campaign headquarters, the Dublin Trades Union Council's premises, 44 Lower Gardiner Street. It was also there during that campaign that he first met Tom Johnson, the Party's General Secretary. Initially he was unimpressed by Johnson, resenting the fact that he was an Englishman. He revised this assessment, however, as he became better acquainted with Johnson in the late 1930s and early 1940s. Although Johnson's socialism was of the English Fabian Society variety and quite different from Swift's Soviet model this did not prevent them from developing a friendship. Swift was impressed by Johnson's important contribution to the Democratic Programme of the First Dáil and, in the 1930s, to the provision of improved working-class housing in Dublin. Above all, Swift admired Johnson's integrity and abhorrence of sectarianism. As a reflective person, hesitant in speech, Johnson lacked the charismatic leadership qualities that were so evident in his contemporary, Larkin, Sen. Yet, mainly because of his integrity as a socialist, Swift was later to regard Johnson as the most significant leader of the Labour Party since the foundation of the state.

During that June election, Ronald Mortished, the Assistant Secretary of the Party, was editor of a Labour paper entitled the *Irishman*. Swift was a contributor of articles and verse. He recalled a visit to the campaign headquarters by another Labour candidate, William O'Brien, the ITGWU's General Secretary. Swift was already acquainted with O'Brien through the joint union bakery committee. Observing Swift and Mortished in conversation, O'Brien, with characteristic sarcasm, exclaimed: 'Young Swift, (O'Brien always addressed Swift in that manner) have you nothing better to contribute to the labour movement than poetry?'

In that first election of 1927, Cullen, Johnson and O'Brien were all successful and Labour won 22 seats, an achievement not since surpassed by the Party. Jubilation was to be short lived, however, for in a second election that September, the number of Labour deputies fell to thirteen, with Cullen, Johnson and O'Brien all losing their seats.

Swift, of course, had more profound reasons for joining the Labour Party. He had long since become a convinced socialist. Only eleven years had elapsed since Connolly's execution and he had hopes that Connolly's teachings might be invoked to instil some genuine socialist ideas into the Party. Like other socialists of his generation, he was satisfied that, within a reasonable period of time, the Labour Party would enlist sufficient public support to establish a socialist workers' republic.

From his viewpoint, the Party's short history had been auspicious. Fifteen years earlier, in 1912, Connolly and Larkin had been prominently associated with its founding. The Party's acclamation of the Bolshevik Revolution in the years immediately following that event was another factor that spurred Swift to become a member. Throughout his life Swift admired and defended the Soviet Union. He was impressed by the enormous political, economic, social and cultural advances of that state since the revolution. As examples of these achievements he would cite the elimination of unemployment and all its attendant problems, the provision of a free and comprehensive health service for all citizens and the availability of an equally free and comprehensive educational system for all children irrespective of the financial standing of their parents. When discussing these aspects of Soviet life, Swift would compare the situation there with that of most of the major capitalist countries where unemployment was endemic and health and educational services, where they existed, were constantly threatened by lack of adequate funding.

Swift was convinced that the Soviet trade unions played a central role in that society:

> The greatest achievement of the Soviet system of government has been the development of the trade union movement which is at the very base of their democracy. You must have organs and organisations to sustain

democracy, it is not an abstract thing. The Soviet trade unions penetrate every aspect of social life from the production stages in the enterprise committees in factories and other work places to the planning stages in developing the economy. Only a mass organisation can do that and a very developed form of democracy brings large numbers of people into making decisions and carrying them out.[9]

In contrast to his views on socialism and the Soviet Union, Swift rejected capitalism and the *Free World.* He contended it was free only for the fittest to survive and that those who could manipulate economic and capital values and substances determined the kind of life one could enjoy.

Sensitive to criticism of the Soviet Union, Swift seldom voiced reservations about that state. This raises the question: was Swift's position reconcilable with his advocacy of a society of free expression? He believed that it was. Since the Bolshevik Revolution, he pointed out, beginning with World War I, the USSR had been virtually under siege. As evidence of that, he cited the Civil War and the associated military intervention of the main capitalist powers, including the Americans, the British and the French. There was the subsequent Nazi invasion during World War II, resulting in the destruction of much of the Soviet economy, not to mention the deaths of some 20 million Soviet citizens. In the Cold War that followed, he recalled, the USSR had been the principal target of vilification by the West. Notwithstanding such adversity, Swift noted, the Soviet Union had advanced from being little more than a feudal country in 1917 to that of a socialist superpower by the 1960s. The creation of this first socialist state, involving enormous economic and social changes, was bound, in his view, to meet resistance from powerful vested interests inside and outside the USSR. In order to establish and consolidate socialism in that hostile environment, the Soviet Union was justified, he believed, in temporarily restricting certain democratic rights such as freedom of expression.

Describing himself as a Marxian socialist, Swift regarded Marx as the greatest of all the socialist theoreticians. Although he found some Marxist theories defective, for example, those on value and surplus value, regarding them more as slogans than logical propositions, he subscribed generally to Marxist doctrines on class struggle, property and the dominance of capital in determining the evolution of society. On the question of religion, Swift had no belief in theology. He described himself as a rationalist, being more of an agnostic than an atheist.[10]

Some of Swift's acquaintances assumed, incorrectly, that he was a member of the Communist Party of Ireland. Others simply wondered why he did not join that organisation. That there was confusion about these matters is understandable. The confusion derived from his pro-Soviet views, his visits to the Soviet Union, his prominent position in the Ireland–USSR Society and particularly his participation in Communist Party activities, including articles he wrote for the *Irish Socialist*, the Party's former monthly paper. He was also a fairly regular contributor to the fund of that journal.[11] Moreover, for many years he was on friendly terms with leading Communist Party members, such as Michael O'Riordan and Johnny Nolan in Dublin and Andy Barr and Betty Sinclair in Belfast. He admitted that he had no ideological reservations about the Communist Party and that, in this respect, that Party was closer to his views than Labour. Although never a member of the Communist Party, it mattered not to Swift whether he was described as a socialist or a communist. Indeed, on at least one occasion, on national television, he acknowledged that he was a communist. Enlarging on that, he declared that he supported the system in the Soviet Union and that he thought life was much better there than in Ireland.[12]

Swift's justification for joining Labour rather than the Communist Party was that the former had strong official links with the trade union movement. The union of which he was a member had been affiliated to the Labour Party since the late 1920s. When Swift joined that Party it was part of a single organisation known as the Irish Labour Party and Trade Union Congress. He regarded such associations between the political and industrial wings of the labour movement as essential to the development of socialism.

Ironically, in that first 1927 general election, Larkin, Sen., for whom Swift still had a great admiration, was a successful candidate of the Irish Worker League.[13] Founded by Larkin in 1923, the league later became a constituent of the Communist International.[14] Larkin thus became the first and only communist to be elected to the Dáil. However, as an undischarged bankrupt, arising from a libel action against his paper, the *Irish Worker*, he was prevented from taking his seat. The motion to stop him was moved by the Labour Party.[15] The unsuccessful intervention of Larkin, Jun. as a candidate of the league in the second 1927 general election resulted in the defeat of the Labour Leader, Tom Johnson. Larkin, Sen. had returned to Dublin from America in 1923 after an absence of eight years.[16] The ITGWU to which he returned was vastly different from the one he had left in the aftermath of the 1913 Lock-Out, not least because of a four-fold increase in membership.[17] A dispute developed between Larkin and O'Brien over the leadership of the union resulting in Larkin's removal from his position as General Secretary and his expulsion from the union. That, in turn, led to the establishment in 1924 of a rival organisation, the Workers' Union of Ireland (WUI).[18] At this time Larkin was in Moscow attending a meeting of the Communist International. On his return from the Soviet capital he was appointed General Secretary of the new union. The WUI soon consolidated its position by recruiting thousands of Larkinite members of the ITGWU, particularly in Dublin. The schism was to diminish greatly the effectiveness of the Irish labour movement for many decades.

One of the celebrations marking Larkin's return to Dublin was a public fête held in the grounds of Pearse's St Enda's School in Rathfarnham. Swift and his father were among the large gathering paying tribute and Swift observed with satisfaction that there still appeared to be plenty of fire in Big Jim.

Intellectual Terrorism

The Irish Free State was a virtual theocracy during the 1930s, with Catholic Church influence pervading nearly every aspect of life. All the main political parties acquiesced with the Church by tailoring their policies to comply with Catholic social teaching. Part of that teaching was corporatism, a policy being implemented by several European fascist states. In Ireland the Church was not alone in promoting that ideology. It was, too, the policy of the National Guard, better known as the Blueshirts, and of Fine Gael. Moreover, Fianna Fáil established a commission on what it described, euphemistically, as vocational organisation, but which was practically indistinguishable from corporatism.

Nowhere was Catholic control greater than in education where, in state schools, the Church did not *pay the piper* but still *called the tune*. The authoritarian attitude of the Church left little room for enquiring minds, much less dissent. Few were prepared to challenge Church teachings and those who even questioned encountered intolerance and hostility. An aspect of that period was the proliferation of Catholic Action lay groups. They attracted the zealots who harassed and intimidated those promoting objects at variance with Catholic doctrines. Little wonder 'intellectual terrorism' was Swift's description of the atmosphere of the newly independent, insular state.

In promoting its social and other teachings, the Church had recourse, not only to the clergy, but its many active lay groups. While Church doctrines and activities were disseminated most effectively through the pulpit, they were also widely reported by the Catholic press, notably the *Irish Catholic* and the *Standard*. Such publications nowadays have low sales and little influence, but at that time they held considerable sway. The *Standard*'s circulation alone in 1939 was 50,000 copies per week.[1] The

Church was also well served by the state's broadcasting service, and the national and provincial press, where its activities, and more important, its teachings, were accorded generous and uncritical coverage.

Sexual morality was a major preoccupation of the Church. The 1934 bishops' Lenten pastorals condemned, among other things, suggestive films, jazz and all-night dances. It was the last item, and another one, mixed bathing at the seaside, that most concerned their lordships. A statement on the dances by the Irish bishops, read by Dean Quinn, a parish priest in Dungannon, Co. Tyrone, appeared in the *Irish Catholic* under the enticing heading 'Sensuous Dances and Pagan Dresses'. Noting that during intervals at dances boys and girls would leave the hall 'for rest and fresh air', Dean Quinn commented: 'During these intervals the devil is busy; yes, very busy, as sad experience proves, and on the way home in the small hours of the morning he is busier still.' About the women who wore the offending dresses, Dean Quinn declared that he 'would not call those people ladies, for no lady worthy of the name, and certainly no Catholic lady, would dream of appearing in such a semi-nude condition . . .'[2]

Fr Browne, parish priest of Lixnaw, Co. Kerry, was also worried about the dances. He told the District Justice at Listowel District Court that he could never rest while there were all-night dances in his parish! Opposing applications for renewals of dance-hall licences, he complained of persons who attended dances from other towns, in cars, describing them as 'a pack of scoundrels of the lowest type who were devils incarnate'. In deference to the priest's representations, the District Justice imposed a three-mile limit in respect of persons attending the dance halls.[3]

The bishops were also perturbed by what the *Irish Catholic* described as 'The Campaign of Immodesty at the Seaside'.[4] Expounding on that topic, the Bishop of Galway declared: 'No manly man wants to be bathing with women, and no modest women wants to bathe with men.'[5] In an editorial entitled 'Pagan Standards of Dress and Conduct Imitated by Bathers', the *Standard* defined the problem thus:

A number of bathers parade themselves in the skimpiest and lightest of bathing dresses along the strands, and the neighbouring places. Men and women most lightly clad in swimming costumes, will dance and romp together. They will dress and undress in the open in closest propinquity and in the sea carry on graceless pranks in which men lose all chivalry and women all their gracious dignity. Young men and women with little covering may be seen bathing in open promiscuity.[6]

The *Standard* went on to warn its readers that this scandal, if allowed to develop, would 'be worse than any plague and more dreadful than any armed invasion . . .'!

Religious intolerance was another feature of the 1930s. Ecumenism, heralded by Pope John XXIII, was more than a generation away when the leading Irish Catholic prelate, Cardinal MacRory, Archbishop of Armagh and Primate of All Ireland, declared that the Protestant Church was 'not even part of the Church of Christ'.[7] No doubt the Protestants too had their share of bigots, not all of them in the North where Catholics were being subjected to widespread discrimination.

It was neither Catholic sexual precepts, nor religious bigotry from whatever source, that was absorbing Swift. His concerns were the more momentous matters of the increasing threat of fascism, the growing influence of Catholic sociology and the connection between these two developments. Catholic social teaching was given new impetus, in 1931, with the publication of Pope Pius XI's encyclical, *Quadragesimo Anno*. It commemorated the fortieth anniversary of Pope Leo XIII's encyclical, *Rerum Novarum*. Both documents condemned socialism and, as a solution to class war, recommended the establishment of corporations resembling the medieval guilds. There is a remarkable similarity between these doctrines and the policies adopted by the European fascist states.

Following Mussolini's seizure of power in Italy in 1922, fascism had spread to Portugal under Salazar in 1932 and to Hitler's Germany a year later. A hallmark of these regimes was the suppression of trade unions and the imprisonment and murder of many union activists. Workers were forced to become members of joint workers' and employers' corporations under the control of employers and fascist party officials. It was claimed by the fascist states that those structures resolved the class war.

While not condoning the barbaric methods employed by these dictatorships, the Church allied itself with fascism by associating with its leaders and blessing its armies. Senior Church dignatories abroad, in the company of fascist leaders, went as far as giving the fascist salute.[8] The German bishops went further. In their joint pastoral letter in early 1937, they declared that they would be ready 'to support the Führer in his fight against Bolshevism, and in his other tasks'. They went on to state that they regarded it as their duty 'to support the head of the German Reich in his defensive struggle with all the means at their disposal'.[9]

The Irish hierarchy's response to the 1931 encyclical was to launch a relentless anti-communist campaign. The Soviet Union was a target of special censure, perhaps partly because of the accomplishments of its first five-year plan. Completed in 1933, much was achieved under that programme including the elimination of unemployment. The hierarchy's concern over a perceived danger of communism contrasted with apparent indifference to the main contemporary social problems. Unemployment, for instance, rose dramatically during the first half of that decade, the number out of work increasing from 25,000 to 133,000.[10] There was also a high rate of emigration, with almost 30,000 leaving the country in a single year (1937).[11] Poverty is less easily measured, but many who survived that era testify that destitution was not uncommon and conditions were much worse than those experienced during the recessions of the 1950s and the 1980s. Yet, while the hierarchy persistently denounced communism, they were silent on social deprivation and its causes.

Anti-communism was a common theme of pastoral letters and sermons during much of that decade. Incensed by an example of this heard in the Pro-Cathedral during the 1933 Lenten season, mobs went on the rampage. They attacked Connolly House, headquarters of the Revolutionary Workers' Groups, later to become the Communist Party of Ireland; the Labour Party Workers' College in Eccles Street; and the Marlboro Street offices of the WUI.[12] Connolly House, then situated at 64 Great Strand Street, bore the brunt of the attack, the assault on it lasting for three nights, with large mobs assembling in nearby streets. Included in this rabble were Catholic Action elements, a criminal gangster group known as the *animal gang*, and members of the Army Comrades Association, forerunners of the Blueshirts. Appropriately, when the attack began, those inside the premises (about forty members or supporters of the Revolutionary Workers' Groups), were attending a lecture entitled 'The Danger of War'. During the onslought, windows of the building were smashed and literature and other objects were seized and burnt in the street. The building was then stoned and several attempts were made to set it on fire. Apart from bricks and stones, the assailants' arsenal comprised iron bars, hammers, hatchets, razors and knives. In conjunction with the hostilities there was shouting of slogans like 'Up the Pope!', 'Down with Communism!' and 'Down with Russia!'. During intervals in the offensive the mobs sustained themselves by singing Catholic hymns such as *Faith of our Fathers, God Bless the Pope* and *Hail Glorious Saint Patrick*. The police took no action against the aggressors but warned the occupants to behave themselves!

Some workers, among whom were rank and file members of the IRA, rallied to the support of those under siege. However, the IRA itself, the only organisation capable of taking effective action against the aggressors, remained aloof. Under the leadership of Seán MacBride and Maurice Twomey, the IRA had been drawn into the international anti-communist campaign. Communism was rejected by the IRA and no communist could be a member of that organisation.[13]

The incidents at Connolly House received extensive coverage in the national press. This excerpt from the main story of the *Irish Press* of 30 March 1933 gives a graphic account of the final evening's hostilities:

> What was nothing less than a pitched battle raged in Dublin last night for many hours when a crowd of upwards of 2,000 attempted to destroy Connolly House.
>
> Thirty people were injured, one man being shot in the knee, during the wild scenes which followed. Eventually the building was 'captured' and an effort made to fire it at the rere. The crowd obstructed the fire brigade, but the outbreak was quelled.
>
> Quantities of literature and Red Flags were seized and burned when the building was evacuated by the occupants who had defended it for two hours.

During the scenes revolver shots were fired from the house.

The occupants escaped, some over the roof-tops where they encountered opposition, and hand-to-hand struggles took place in perilous positions in full view of the crowds. Baton charges were made in the adjoining streets until long after mid-night and, at least, twelve persons arrested.

An insight into establishment attitudes of the times are comments made in an *Irish Press* editorial on 29 March 1933. After expressing concern that a crowd singing *God Bless our Pope* while smashing windows of buildings might be mistaken by the demonstrators for Catholic Action, the editorial continued:

> If they [those attacked] hold public meetings and offend the feelings of their audiences so deeply as to stir up spontaneous anger against them, then they cannot expect to be listened to, and are in grave danger of suffering at the hands of the irate crowds. But it is an entirely different matter when organised groups go through the city attacking buildings and places which house those they dislike. It merely ends in the spectacle of one group of Catholic Irishmen (the police) being forced to disperse other groups of Catholic Irishmen (the demonstrators) . . . In this case although our views are the very antithesis of Communism, we think these organised attacks on property are wrong and inexcusable, and we hope the Government will take the appropriate action to prevent them . . .

Property, it seems, was more sacred than human life! Apart from its blatant sectarianism, the editorial's prejudice against those who dared challenge the contemporary orthodoxy is quite revealing.

Within months of the attack on Connolly House, the Communist Party of Ireland was re-formed.[14] Its rebirth was greeted by the *Irish Catholic* headline 'The Musk Rats of Russia—Squelch Them or Else'.[15] Apparently, in order to secure accommodation for its inaugural meeting, the CPI supplied the false information that it was a temperance gathering. The *Irish Catholic* commented adversely on this deception, evidently missing the irony that it was carried out to elude the attentions of the Catholic zealots. True to form, the paper concluded venomously: 'It is necessary that we should arm ourselves in the manner directed by the Church and take our share in the fight against these satanic forces. Those who neglect to range themselves on the right side should surely bear in mind the words of Our Lord, "I will vomit thee out of my mouth."' [16]

Following encouragement, or pressure, from the hierarchy, the Labour Party as well as Fianna Fáil, Cumann na nGaedheal/ Fine Gael harmonised their policies with the encyclicals. Fine Gael came into existence in 1933 following the merger of Cumann na nGaedheal, the National Centre Party and the Blueshirts. Cumann na nGaedheal's compliance with Catholic social teaching was evident in 1931 when the hierarchy issued a joint pastoral letter condemning communist influence in the IRA and Saor Éire. The latter organisation had been founded earlier the same year by Peadar O'Donnell,[17] George Gilmore[18] and other radical republicans. Its objects included the overthrow of Irish capitalism and the provision of an independent revolutionary leadership for the working class and working farmers. The Cosgrave Government responded by proscribing the IRA and Saor Éire.[19]

Corporatism had some influential Irish adherents, among whom were members and supporters of Fine Gael. This new political party immediately adopted a policy of vocationalism, a term deemed more acceptable than the discredited corporatism and fascism. None the less, General Eoin O'Duffy, Fine Gael's first President, and former leader of the fascist Blueshirts, was a committed corporatist and encyclical enthusiast. His presidential address to Fine Gael's first Ard Fheis in February 1934 makes this abundantly clear: '. . . The present Pope has proclaimed it as the primary duty of the State and of all good citizens to abolish conflict between classes with divergent interests . . . He, the Pope, has declared that the aim of social legislation must be the re-establishment of vocational groups . . .' The General continued: 'It is a practical proposition for Ireland and is now a complete everyday reality in the life of the Italian people . . . I expect that because I mention the word Italy—not to mention Mussolini— we shall have shrieks of fascism, dictatorship, sedition . . .'[20] O'Duffy's plans for the trade union movement had their origin in the encyclicals and in the practice of several fascist states. The unions in each industry were to be compelled to federate with employers' associations and strikes were to be outlawed.[21]

Corporatism had more sophisticated advocates than O'Duffy. Prominent among these were two academics, Professors James Hogan of University College, Cork and Michael Tierney of University College, Dublin. They were contributors to Fine Gael's weekly journal, *United Ireland*, which campaigned for the dissemination of power to vocational groups in accordance with Pope Pius XI's encyclical.[22] Notwithstanding O'Duffy's references to Mussolini and Italy, it was the Portuguese version of corporatism that found most favour in Ireland. Unlike Mussolini, Salazar, as a devout Catholic, could be relied upon to uphold the tenets of the papal encyclicals.

Fianna Fáil, founded in 1926, commenced its first of two continuous sixteen-year periods in government in 1932. It soon became evident that in relation to social policy de Valera and his republican colleagues were quite content to toe the Vatican line. True, the government did resist hierarchical pressure to suppress communism and abandon its neutral position on the Spanish Civil War. Yet, de Valera was responsible for the vitally important 1937 Irish Constitution which is still with us. Containing several sectarian provisions it appears to disregard non-Christian citizens. Take, for example, the preamble: 'In the name of the Most Holy Trinity from whom is all authority and to Whom, as our final end, all actions both of men and States must be referred, We, the people of Éire, Humbly acknowledging all our obligations to our Divine Lord, Jesus Christ, Who sustained our fathers through centuries of trial . . .' Probably the best-known sectarian provision was that in Article 44: 'The state recognises the special position of the Holy Catholic Apostolic and Roman Church as the Guardian of the Faith professed by the great majority of the citizens.' That clause remained in force until 1972 when it was deleted, following a referendum. Leaving aside the effects of such a provision on non-Catholics in the South, it is difficult to understand how it was to be reconciled with Fianna Fáil's cardinal policy of Irish unification.

Another sectarian provision is the prohibition, in Article 41, of the enactment of laws providing for divorce. An attempt to remove this ban through a referendum in 1986 ended in failure. Contributing significantly to that outcome was the combined opposition of the Catholic Church and Fianna Fáil. The emphasis in the Constitution on the family and on private property echoes the doctrines of the encyclicals.

Cardinal MacRory was pleased with the new Constitution. On 1 January 1938, in his new year message to the Irish people, he pronounced: 'The Constitution is a great Christian document, full of faith in God as the Creator, supreme Lawgiver and Ruler, and also of wise and carefully thought out provisions for the upbuilding and guidance of a Christian State.'[23]

Some of de Valera's papers released for public examination in July 1987 confirm earlier suspicions that Dr John Charles McQuaid, later to become Catholic Archbishop of Dublin, was involved in drafting the Constitution. The papers also reveal that the Dáil had access to the draft document only after it had been submitted for papal approval. That the Pope was dissatisfied with the text merely illustrates that nothing less than a wholly Catholic constitution would have been acceptable to Rome.[24]

Equally compatible with *Quadragesimo Anno* was the Commission on Vocational Organisation set up in 1939 on de Valera's initiative. The commission's terms of reference were, among other things, to report on the practicality of developing functional or vocational organisation, the rights and powers which should be conferred, and the duties which should be imposed on vocational bodies, and generally, the relations of such bodies to the Oireachtas and the Government.

The twenty-five person commission, under the chairmanship of the Bishop of Galway, Dr Michael Browne, included five clergymen and several leading corporatists. Among the latter were Professor Alfred O'Rahilly of UCC, who was later ordained a priest, Professor Michael Tierney, Fr Edward Coyne, the Jesuit sociologist, later prominently associated with the founding of the Catholic Workers' College (now the National College of Industrial Relations) and Fr Michael Hayes, founder of Muintír na Tíre. The four labour representatives on the commission included the unlikely figure of James Larkin, Sen. Larkin's labour colleagues were the trade union officials, Louie Bennett, General Secretary of the Irish Women Workers' Union; Senator Sean Campbell, Treasurer, Dublin Typographical Provident Society; and Senator Thomas Foran, the ITGWU's General President. Foran retired from union office in 1939 and was replaced on the commission by the Labour Party's General Secretary, Luke Duffy. Dissociating themselves from any suspicion of fascist tendencies that might be read into the recommendations, Louie Bennett and Seán Campbell signed the commission's report. Luke Duffy alone of the labour representatives dissociated himself from the report and published his own report criticising and ridiculing the commission's recommendations. Larkin, too, declined to sign the report, apparently holding the commission and its work in silent contempt.[25] Larkin's muteness elicited this caustic observation from Swift: 'What a pity the contempt was silent!'[26]

The *Irish Catholic* was in no doubt that the commission was a move towards the introduction of corporatism in Ireland. In an editorial on 2 February 1939, it welcomed the commission as:

> . . . a definite step towards bringing the principles of papal encyclicals to bear in Irish life . . . Among the many questions which the Commission will have to investigate will be the type of corporatism best suited for Ireland . . . The members of the Commission in investigating and deliberating on this fundamental point, will have the experience of Italy and Portugal to guide them.

Completed in 1943, the commission's report contained many quotations from the encyclicals which were its main inspiration. Among other things, the report recommended the development of vocational organisation to provide for joint employers' and workers' bodies in all areas of the economic life of the country. The recommendations made provision for the transfer of functions hitherto performed by the civil service and the government. Clearly, the report was recommending corporatism. Yet, when the document was published, the commission went to great lengths to emphasise it was not recommending a corporate state. Swift found the disavowal implausible and, instead, offered his own interpretation:

> To the members of the Vocational Commission . . . in the early years of the 1939–45 War, with the victories of the fascist powers, it must have seemed that fascism was invincible. Then, in 1943, came what is accepted as the decisive turn of the War, in the Battle of Stalingrad. The subsequent collapse of the fascist forces was not without its message for those who championed the corporate state, including its advocates on the Vocational Commission.[27]

As for the commission's recommendations, these were largely ignored by an unreceptive government and, as with so many findings of this kind, were otherwise left on shelves to gather dust.

The accommodation of Catholic social teaching by Fine Gael and Fianna Fáil did not greatly surprise Swift. Indeed, during his time in the Irish Volunteers, he had, to some extent, anticipated developments of this kind. What concerned him a great deal more was the Labour Party's abandonment of socialist objectives following pressure by the hierarchy. At the Party's annual conference in 1936, a new constitution was adopted calling for public ownership of all essential sources of wealth and the establishment of a Workers' Republic. These aspirations conflicted with the encyclicals which defended private property and condemned class war.

An affiliated union to the Party, the Irish National Teachers' Organisation (INTO), subsequently opposed these socialist provisions. Influenced, evidently, by their Treasurer, Michael Linehan, a prominent lecturer in Catholic social teaching, the union sought advice from the hierarchy who referred the matter to a *Committee of Experts*. The union was later informed that sections of the Party's constitution conflicted with Catholic social teaching. Attempts by the INTO to amend the constitution were pre-empted by the Party's administrative council which sought and secured authority from the 1939 conference to redraft the document. The council undertook to remove clauses which were objectionable to the hierarchy.[28] Commenting on this development, the *Standard* declared: 'The decision of the Irish Labour Party taken at a private session of its annual conference in Dublin this week to bring its constitution into line with Catholic teaching, marks the triumph of a movement started within the party over two years ago.' Nowhere was Labour's action more aptly described than in the *Standard*'s heading: 'Labour stands for Catholic View'.[29]

At the following year's conference the object of a 'Workers' Republic' was replaced by a 'Republican form of government' while the public ownership clause was qualified as follows: 'The Labour Party believes in a system of government which, while recognising the rights of private property shall ensure that where common good requires, essential industries and services shall be brought under public ownership with democratic control.' The INTO claimed credit for 'these desirable changes' and were rewarded by 'the express commendation of the body of the Bishops'.[30] During the period of this controversy, William Norton, the Leader of the Labour Party, sent a cablegram to the Pope assuring him that the Party 'never had and never would have any contact with communism'.[31]

As is clear from these policy changes by the Labour Party, workers were not immune from the religious fervour of those times. On the contrary, in temporal as well as spiritual affairs, they were quite prepared to be led by their priests. Such was the case, for example, in 1935, in Swift's native Dundalk, when the Republican Congress held a meeting in the Labourers' Hall. Present on that occasion were one hundred unemployed men and a Catholic priest, Fr Stokes. To the priest's query, if the Republican Congress stood for the abolition of private property, the chairman of the meeting replied in the affirmative. Fr Stokes then told the men that they had been brought to the meeting to be recruited to a movement condemned by the Church. When he thereupon asked the men to leave the meeting as a protest against an attempt being made to spread communism in the town, the men immediately vacated the hall.[32]

Also indicative of Catholic ardour among workers in that period was the granting of gifts to the Church. There were, for instance, the donations of pews to the Franciscan Church of the Immaculate Conception (Adam and Eve's) on Dublin's Merchants' Quay. Inscriptions on the pews show that these gifts were presented by the workmen in the sewer department of Dublin Corporation, the tramwaymen in Kingsbridge and Inchicore, and the Irish Municipal Employees' Trade Union. That the bakers were not found wanting in this regard is evident from an inscribed plaque in the same chapel. The inscription reads:

> The Electric Light Fittings of this Church were presented by The Members of The Dublin Branch Irish Bakers, Confectioners & A. W. Amalg. Union, for the Greater Honour and Glory of God and as a tribute to the memory of F. Moran (DECEASED) late Treasurer.
>   The presentation is due to the zealous efforts of the Executive and General Committee:

D. Cullen, *President*; C. Noonan, *Secretary*; J. Doyle, *Treasurer*; P. Dignan, Jn. Lea, *Trustees*.

At the 1933 AGM of the Bakers' Union Dublin No. 1 Branch there was discussion on the funding of this substantial gift to the Church. Having heard an appeal by the Branch President for voluntary contributions, the meeting empowered the executive committee to make up any deficiency from branch funds.[33]

Swift was utterly opposed to the union's involvement in this project which he regarded as sectarian. As we shall see, that stance was to be merely the beginning of his lonely crusade against sectarianism in the Bakers' Union.

Confronting Obscurantism

In 1933, following an approach by Peadar O'Donnell, Swift attended some meetings that led to the founding of the Republican Congress.[1] He and O'Donnell were already acquainted, having been introduced during the Civil War by Swift's cousin, Paddy White. Earlier in that war, O'Donnell and White had been on hunger-strike together in Mountjoy Gaol. The Congress was an anti-imperialist and anti-fascist body whose objects embraced the establishment of a workers' republic. Composed of radical republicans, tenants and unemployed associations, anti-fascists and others, its principal leaders included O'Donnell, George Gilmore, Michael Price and Nora Connolly-O'Brien, daughter of James Connolly. Attempts by the leadership to organise a united anti-fascist campaign with the Labour Party and trade unions were unproductive. There were other factors, however, that were to split the organisation and cause its dissolution after only a short existence.

While sympathetic to its aims, Swift did not become a member. He believed that in confronting the fascist threat, the Republican Congress would confine its criticism of corporatism to politicians and academics promoting that policy, leaving unchallenged the Church corporatists whose ideology emanated from the anti-socialist encyclicals. Swift elaborated:

> There were a number of us at that time who were quite critical of the activities of some churchmen here. We saw the Catholic Church as linked to some extent with the development of fascism in Europe. Mussolini had seized power in Italy in 1922, Salazar in Portugal in 1932, Hitler in Germany in 1933 and Horthy in Hungary. We did not feel that Republicanism, even as expressed by the Republican Congress, was strong enough to counter this trend.

Traditional Republicanism in this respect seems to be that, while they will condemn the Hierarchy for being pro-British and reactionary, they do not criticise and condemn the Church as a church. Some of us who had turned towards rationalism, did not consider this [the Republican Congress] worthy of our support.[2]

Believing that the Church's extensive control and influence in social matters demanded some response, Swift discussed the issue with some friends in the Contemporary Club. This resulted, in 1933, in the founding of the Secular Society of Ireland. As its contents and style suggest, the society's constitution was drafted by Swift:

Convinced that clerical domination in the community is harmful to advance, the Secular Society of Ireland seeks to establish in this country complete freedom of thought, speech and publication, liberty for the mind, in the widest toleration compatible with orderly progress and rational conduct. With this end in view, the Society takes for its aims the following programme:

To oppose unremittingly, with a view to terminating –
(1) the system of clerical management, and consequent sectarian teaching, in schools; (2) the immunity from payment of rates and taxes enjoyed by various churches; (3) the clerically dictated ban on divorce; (4) the Censorship of Publications Act; and (5) all other impediments by way of religious tests or regulations dictated in the interests of those who make a profession of religion.

The Society demands that men and women will be free to develop, conditioned only by what is reasonable in ethics.

The Society will be political in the sense only of seeking to establish for all citizens equality of citizenship as regards obligations to the State and the opportunity to develop freely therein.

Freedom cannot exist until the sectarian clergy of various denominations have been curbed of their power of interference and the people stand free of the worst of all despotism—hierarchy.

Where the clergy are powerful, liberty always suffers, no pursuit in thought or art, no act of the individual, even in one's own home can be free or sacred while the shadow of prelatism hovers to intimidate and bully.[3]

Some comments of Swift's throw further light on the nature of the society. Speaking as an officer of the organisation at one of its meetings, he declared that:

> The Society was not anti-religious but that it believed that religion unleavened by knowledge was nothing more than superstition. It did not advocate either divorce or birth control but would press for facilities in both matters for people who desired them, and would endeavour to have the law here amended accordingly. It would also press for full sex education for all classes.[4]

Church control of education was regarded by Swift as the most crucial issue facing the society. He challenged the churches' right to control schools which are funded almost exclusively by the state. As an alternative, he advocated the establishment of non-denominational state schools under the democratic control of parents, teachers and community representatives. He was opposed to the teaching of one particular religion in state schools, but had no objections to pupils being educated objectively in the many religions of the world.

Swift's long-held contention that the Catholic Church had enjoyed comprehensive control of education has been endorsed by John H. Whyte in his book, *Church and State in Modern Ireland.* Whyte states:

> Over most of the period since independence, the remarkable feature of educational policy in Ireland has been the reluctance of the State to touch on the entrenched positions of the Church. This is not because the Church's claims have been moderate: on the contrary, it has carved out for itself a more extensive control over education in Ireland than in any other country in the world. It is because the Church has insisted on its claims with such force that the State has been extremely cautious in entering its domain.[5]

Among members of the Secular Society were Denis Johnston, the playwright, and the critic, Mary Manning. Captain Jack White, trainer of Connolly's Citizen Army, was a founder member. Officers of the Secular Society were John Swift, chairman; Owen Sheehy Skeffington, vice-chairman; and Niall O'Leary-Curtis, secretary. Swift was already acquainted with his colleague officers through the Contemporary Club. A civil servant by profession, O'Leary-Curtis was a son of the Sinn Féin founder of that name. Sheehy Skeffington was a lecturer in French literature and language in TCD. Although usually described nowadays as a democrat or liberal, and he was certainly both of these, Sheehy Skeffington was also a convinced socialist who was prepared to campaign for socialism in a broad front with the Communist Party.[6] While Swift and Sheehy Skeffington became close friends, Swift admiring Sheehy Skeffington's integrity, many were the issues on which they disagreed. Sheehy Skeffington, for example, was a pacifist, a doctrine Swift found irrational if only because it ultimately precludes self-defence.[7] There were political differences, too, Sheehy Skeffington, unlike Swift, disapproving of the USSR's non-aggression pact with Nazi Germany and its intervention in Hungary in 1956. Sheehy Skeffington was also critical of what he regarded as the rigid line of the Communist Party of the Soviet Union.[8]

The Secular Society met fortnightly in the Contemporary Club's premises in Lincoln Place. To avoid disruption of its meetings by Catholic Action devotees, attendance was strictly by invitation. Its gatherings usually took the form of a lecture by an invited guest followed by a discussion. Among subjects addressed were: 'The influence of the Church against the Progress of Medical Science', and 'Sources of Christianity in Historical Perspectives'. The lecturer on the latter topic described the Gospels as 'mere conjecture being written at least a hundred years after Christ's death'.[9] At one of its meetings, the society passed a resolution calling on the government to cease trading with Germany on account of Hitler's treatment of the Jews in that country.[10] Copies of the *Freethinker*, obtained by Swift from the British Secular Society, were distributed free at lectures. Swift had been a constant reader of that paper for some time, having managed to secure copies from Lily O'Neill, known as Lily Geraghty after she married, and later from her brother, Jack O'Neill. They ran a newspaper stand at the Ballast Office where, concealed under national newspapers, socialist and secular periodicals were stocked. Lily Geraghty is the mother of a well-known family of trade unionists.[11]

Notwithstanding its controversial nature, the Society was never short of funds. Income from the annual membership fee of four shillings was augmented by substantial donations from middle-class people. These benefactors would not identify publicly with the organisation, but supported at least some of its aims.

Precautions by the society to restrict its gatherings to members and their friends failed to prevent the penetration of a meeting by an *Irish Press* journalist on 16 January 1934. The following day's *Press* published the constitution of the society and reported discussions that had taken place. Later that week, the Catholic press took up the story, leaving little ambiguity about its views on the new body. Under the heading, 'The Enemy in Our Midst', the *Standard* declared: 'The Society is really only another phase of the subversive campaign. Every reasonable measure should be taken to expose its iniquity and to repress it activities.'[12] This was mild compared with the virulence of the *Irish Catholic*. An editorial in that paper described the Society as 'a nefarious organisation' whose programme 'runs the full gamut of the Soviet No-Gods . . . and all the modern hateful inhuman and unnatural practices are enthusiastically endorsed . . . for that we surmise is where the screw is loose with them . . . the "liberty" of the debauchee is to them the most sacred of all liberties'.[13]

The *Irish Catholic* then resorted to the normal intimidation of the time. After disclosing the venue of the society's meetings, the editorial asked ominously: 'Did the landlord of the premises know the kind of foul birds to which he was giving a roosting place?'[14] Even the liberal Contemporary Club, the Secular Society's host, could not withstand this kind of pressure without risking attacks on persons and property. The Secular Society was informed that its further tenure of the Contemporary Club's premises was no longer desirable. Many members left the organisation following the press publicity. Swift was among a few who continued to meet in each other's homes and, occasionally, outdoors in the Dublin mountains, until 1936, when the society disbanded. Its remaining funds were sent to the Spanish Government.

By this stage the Spanish Civil War was under way, Franco having mounted his revolt against the legitimately elected Republican Government. Some months earlier an extremely hostile attitude had developed here against that government. It was based on allegations that, under that administration, vile acts were being perpetrated like the raping and murdering of nuns and the destruction of orphanages. Though little, if any, evidence was produced to substantiate such lurid and one-sided stories, they were widely believed.

A hysterical national campaign, based on the alleged atrocities, was whipped up by the Irish Christian Front, a pro-Franco organisation whose chief spokesman was the Fine Gael TD, Paddy Belton. Under the auspices of this new society, huge rallies were held throughout the country. In September 1936, for example, 40,000 attended a demonstration in Cork. Addressed by Church leaders and academics, it concluded with the singing of *Faith of Our Fathers*.[15] A month later, a crowd of 12,000 was present at a similar event in Waterford, at which the local Labour Party was strongly represented.[16] Later the same month, 100,000 participated in the first national demonstration in Dublin. The platform party on that occasion included the corporatist, Fr Edward Coyne, SJ. Among several resolutions endorsed by the crowd was one 'congratulating General Franco and his troops on their magnificent fight for religious liberty and European civilisation!'[17]

An indication of the emotive atmosphere that then prevailed may be gleaned from the public's response to two national collections. The Irish Christian Front alone raised £30,000[18] (approximately £970,000 in 1991 values) to supply medical aid for Franco's nationalists, while the hierarchy's efforts 'for the suffering Catholics of Spain' realised the even greater sum of £43,000[19] (approximately £1,400,000 in 1991 values). The atmosphere was further charged by the fact that the Irish hierarchy, like their Spanish counterpart, supported Franco and exhorted the Irish Government to do likewise.

Against this overwhelming pro-Franco campaign, few were prepared to support the Spanish Government. Most of the leading Labour and trade union leaders remained mute, with a small number actually speaking on Irish Christian Front platforms.[20] In the Dáil, Labour deputies remained silent after Cosgrave proposed recognition of Franco as the head of a legal government.[21] Apparently, even the Larkin-led WUI felt intimidated. Following the participation of its prominent official, Jack Carney, in the anti-Franco campaign, the executive prohibited its spokesmen from appearing on public platforms except on strictly union business.[22]

Among the handful of individuals who consistently and publicly championed the Spanish Republic were Peadar O'Donnell, Fr Michael O'Flanagan, the republican priest, and the CPI's General Secretary, Seán Murray. A further manifestation of support for republican Spain was the CPI's decision to form a unit of the International Brigade. That occurred after General Eoin O'Duffy had led an Irish Brigade to Spain to support Franco. Of the 140 Irishmen or so who fought on the Spanish republican side, a significant proportion came from the ranks of the CPI. Many had formerly been members of the IRA. The Irish republican contingent distinguished itself in that war, sustaining losses of some sixty volunteers who were killed in action.[23]

Not so illustrious were the experiences of O'Duffy's Brigade, which, as described by Michael O'Riordan in his book, *Connolly Column*, were of a comic-opera kind:

> The truth was that the 'Crusaders' had taken part in only one action when they clashed with a Moorish unit of Franco's army! The Moors killed four, and three others were to die later during a short period of trench duty. On the one occasion when they were ordered into attack O'Duffy refused to obey because it would possibly cause 'a huge loss of life'. Demoralised, they demanded to be sent home. In the course of their short service their only vigorous activities consisted of numerous mass parades and a mutiny against O'Duffy himself.[24]

Support for the Spanish Republic was the object, too, of the Spanish Aid Committee which came into existence at the height of the Irish Christian Front's campaign.[25] Hanna Sheehy Skeffington was chairwoman but, because of her numerous other activities, rarely did she attend the committee's functions. Consequently, Swift, who was vice-chairman, usually presided at its gatherings. The treasurer was Bobbie Walshe, later Bobbie Edwards [26] after she married Frank Edwards.[27] A native of Waterford, she had previously been involved in Cumann na mBan, the women's section of the IRA, and in the Republican Congress. Bobbie Edwards later worked as a caterer in the Irish Hospitals Sweepstake in Ballsbridge. Frank Edwards, a member of the

CPI, fought with the International Brigade and was wounded in action on the Cordoba front. He had earlier been sacked from his teaching post in the Christian Brothers School in Mount Sion in Waterford. The dismissal resulted from his refusal to accept an ultimatum from the Bishop of Waterford, Dr Kinnane, to sign an undertaking dissociating himself from the Republican Congress and not to join any similar movement in the future.[28] Blacklisted, subsequently, by the Catholic authorities and precluded from teaching in any Catholic school, Edwards was obliged to work as a labourer before eventually securing a teaching position in the Jewish national school in Dublin.[29] Swift was to be associated with Frank and Bobbie Edwards and others in the mid-1960s in founding the Ireland–USSR Friendship Society.

A room in the Court Laundry in Harcourt Street was the venue for meetings of the Spanish Aid Committee. This had been arranged through Robin (Robert) Tweedy,[30] a CPI member, whose family had some connection with that business. The committee raised funds for the Spanish Government and organised lectures and discussions on the situation in that country. Hospitality was also provided to International Brigade members home on leave. These social gatherings were frequently held in conjunction with a talk on the political and military position in Spain. Sometimes the speakers were volunteers home on leave from the war zone.[31] Swift recalled meeting two, the CPI member, Jack Nalty, who was killed in Spain in 1938, and Terry Flanagan,[32] who was wounded but survived the war. Terry Flanagan was a brother of Swift's Bakers' Union friend, Peter Flanagan, who died in 1987, and father of the well-known actress, Fionnula Flanagan.

In addition to his presidential responsibilities in the society, Swift organised the collection of funds in Dublin bakeries for the Spanish Government. He was assisted in this by two committee men or shop stewards, Michael Conroy and Jimmy Sweetman.

Swift's contribution to the Spanish republican cause has been placed in perspective by the International Brigade veteran and present CPI Chairman, Michael O'Riordan:

> Although the Labour Party and Trade Union Movement leaders kept a quiet silence, with here and there some of its prominent members actually speaking on pro-Franco platforms, many individual trade union leaders made generous

but anonymous subscriptions to the Irish Aid Committee for the Spanish Republic. One leading personality who refused to be anonymous but instead forthright in raising financial aid from his fellow trade unionists was John Swift.[33]

Secular Pilgrimages

The Swift family left their Clanbrassil Terrace home in 1936. This occurred after John's brother, Paddy, married Ann (Phoebe) Dowling on 31 August of that year and went to live elsewhere in Dublin. John's sister, May, stayed with friends for a while before moving in with Paddy and Phoebe. John, himself, lodged briefly at two Donnybrook addresses, at Auburn Avenue and then at Mount Eden Road, before moving to 40 Belton Park Gardens, Donnycarney, home of his Bakers' Union friend, Michael Conroy, and his wife, Grace.

Two years after assuming the full-time office of National Organiser of the Bakers' Union, Swift embarked on an extensive tour of Central and Eastern Europe. Work pressures had prevented him taking his holidays during the intervening period but, to compensate for this, the union's national executive committee granted him six weeks' leave in 1938. The main purpose of his trip, which was of an educational and cultural nature, and not merely confined to sightseeing, was to learn something about the trade unions in the USSR. Visits by Irish citizens to that country in the 1930s were extremely rare and foreign travel generally was much less common than now.

At the end of August or the beginning of September 1938, when he was 42, Swift left Dublin on a journey that was to take him to, among other destinations, the cities of London, Brussels, Cologne, Berlin, Köningsberg, Leningrad, Moscow, Warsaw, Prague, Budapest, Vienna, Munich, Zurich and Paris. A major reason for visiting these places was to acquire some knowledge of the bakery trade and the trade unions catering for that industry's workers. Accordingly, in most of these cities Swift visited bakeries to examine their products and production techniques. He also met representatives of bakers' and foodworkers' unions and acquainted himself with the policies and achievements of these organisations.

Swift's journey was relatively uneventful until he reached the German frontier where his occupation and Soviet visa provoked a hostile reception from the Nazi officials. Only after the most rigorous scrutiny of his modest luggage was he permitted to proceed. On his way to Berlin he passed through Cologne where he admired the magnificent cathedral, reputedly the largest Gothic building in Europe. It has another claim to fame as one of the longest building jobs in history. Though commenced during the thirteenth century, it was not completed until the nineteenth. Clearly, the productivity experts were not around then!

Swift had an unlikely contact in Berlin in Martin Plass, the Nazi whom he had first met in Dublin the previous year. Despite his familiarity with his fascist acquaintance, 'an amiable fellow, informed and broadminded in most matters, but aflame with the new patriotism of Nazi Germany', he was somewhat surprised on meeting Plass to find him sporting the brown shirt, jackboots and other insignia of a stormtroop leader. Having offered Swift hospitality should he ever visit Berlin, Plass suggested an inspection of stormtroop bases! The offer was declined politely in favour of visits to local bakeries.

With much apprehension, Swift expressed a desire to visit the city's Jewish quarter. He wished, if possible, to assess some of the anti-Semitic boycott and persecution. To his surprise, Plass immediately acceded to his request, bringing him to the principal fashionable shopping area, the Kurfürstendamm, where many shops were owned by Jews. To distinguish these from non-Jewish ones, the proprietors' names were printed in large white letters on the shop windows. A more explicit manifestation of anti-Semitism was the 'Jews not wanted here' notice displayed prominently in most hotels. More ominous than that was the message in a special issue of the hysterical anti-Semitic Nazi weekly, *Der Stürmer*, which declared in bold type on its front page, 'Der Juden sind unser ungluck' (the Jews are our misfortune). Plass's assurance that *Der Stürmer* was not regarded seriously by either the people or the authorities did nothing to reassure Swift. That Berlin meeting was to be their last. Some years later Swift learnt that his Nazi acquaintance had been killed on the Eastern Front fighting for the Führer.

There were special reasons why Köningsberg, then the Prussian capital and now Kaliningrad in the USSR, was on Swift's itinerary. He wished to pay homage to two of its famous sons, Eugene Sandow and Immanuel Kant. Sandow, reputedly the finest specimen of physical development of his day, had been a hero of Swift's youth. Lodging in the same hotel was a party of the Hitler Youth's 'Strength Through Joy' organisation which arranged cultural events such as workers' holidays. This particular group had come to Köningsberg to make a propaganda film about Sandow. That project was suddenly abandoned, however, when it emerged that he was of Russian and not 'Master Race' origin. Greater perseverance was shown by the Nazis when it was revealed that the nominally Catholic Viennese composer, Johann Strauss II, was of Jewish as well as Catholic ancestry. Still anxious to promote the music of the Strauss family for their own purposes, the authorities first attempted to suppress this information. Failing in that, they then confiscated the evidence, a marriage register in St Stephen's Cathedral, Vienna, replacing it with a forgery in which were excluded entries concerning the family's Jewish connection.[1]

Swift's tribute to Immanuel Kant, whom he regarded as one of the greatest philosophers of all time, led him to the Lutheran Church in Köningsberg. It is there that Kant is entombed in an outer wall, a position Swift found apt for one who was ambiguous about his religious beliefs, being neither in nor out of the Church. This did not detract from his admiration for the great philosopher, particularly for his proposition that all knowledge derives through experience, and not from experience as contended by the English philosopher, Locke.

From Köningsberg, Swift travelled through Lithuania and Latvia to Leningrad and from there to Moscow, where he stayed in the Metropole Hotel. By then he had become acquainted with an American male tourist, whom he had first met at the Soviet border with Latvia. It was at that frontier that the Soviet authorities had become suspicious of this visitor after discovering some women's underwear in his luggage. Whether this apparel represented the merchandise of a black marketeer or the clothing of a transvestite, Swift never discovered! It was certainly the cause of a delay and some argument between the parties, made worse by the American's impertinence to the Soviet officials.

Perhaps it was Swift's smattering of Russian that attracted the American to him. Whatever the reason, the two men travelled together on the train journey from Leningrad to Moscow. Both were later involved in an incident in a Moscow street when Swift's companion photographed a squad of Red Army soldiers approaching from the direction of a bridge. As this was forbidden, the American was arrested while Swift was questioned by an English-speaking, plain-clothes detective who accompanied him back to his hotel. There was more questioning at the hotel before the detective eventually left, satisfied that Swift was uninvolved with the American and his activities. As for the American, on meeting his Irish acquaintance later in Prague, he castigated the Soviet Union over the Moscow incident.

It was in the Czech capital that Swift was heartened to observe many anti-Nazi street demonstrations. He found the people defiant and confident that they would be saved from the Nazi invasion by their British and French allies. Swift cherished no such illusions and, unfortunately for the Czechs, his assessment turned out to be correct.

Budapest was Swift's next destination where he enjoyed a brief visit before taking the short rail trip to Vienna. Apart from his interest in matters pertaining to the bakery trade, he had come to the musical capital of the world to pay homage to Beethoven, whom he regarded as the greatest of all composers. At the State Opera House on the Ringstrasse (Ring Street), in the company of Inge Schine, a young German woman whom he had met on his journey to Austria, he attended a performance of Verdi's opera, *Don Carlos*. Inge was again his companion when he took the tram to the Zentralfriedhof (Central Cemetery), final resting place of Beethoven and many other celebrated composers. On the outward journey, Swift gave his seat to another young woman who was standing. She wore the badge that identified Jews from others. Earlier that year, Austria had been forcibly annexed to the German Reich. Swift's action drew disapproving glances from some German soldiers travelling in the same vehicle and, on arrival at his destination, he was informed by an officer of this group that he had acted indiscreetly.

Swift and Inge made their way to the composers' plot in the cemetery to find Beethoven's grave marked by a fine monument bearing simply his surname. Alongside lies Schubert, a fulfilment of his wish to be buried beside Beethoven. Mozart, buried elsewhere in an unknown communal grave, is honoured in the Vienna plot by a monument close to the tombs of Beethoven and Schubert. A little further away may be found the last resting place of other such famous composers as Brahms, Suppé and members of the Strauss family. The last mentioned includes Johann Strauss, the father, composer of *The Radetsky March* and his more famous son, also Johann, whose numerous popular melodies include *The Blue Danube Waltz.*

Swift's European trip was drawing to an end. After leaving Inge and Vienna, he visited Munich, Zurich and Paris before travelling back to Dublin.[2]

The following year, 1939, Swift returned to the Continent on an entirely different mission. A few years earlier he had participated in a labour seminar in Brussels run jointly by the British Labour Party and the Belgian Socialist Party. There he had met and become friendly with several underground anti-fascist Germans, one of whom was a socialist and a baker, while others were railway workers. Anxious to develop these contacts and, if possible, to help the anti-Nazi cause, Swift decided to go to Berlin. His arrival in London during the first week of September 1939 coincided with Britain's declaration of war on Germany. There was an immediate cessation of travel to that country. To circumvent this, Swift applied for a permit to visit Holland, aware that, once there, he would have no difficulty entering Germany. When his application was granted by the Foreign Office, he flew to Amsterdam. To avoid bombardment, planes then travelled at high altitudes and, consequently, Swift suffered a severe nose bleed during the flight. On arrival in Amsterdam he was taken to a surgery where a vessel of his nose was cauterised by an elderly doctor with shaky hands. Swift's painful ordeal was somewhat eased by the strains of Beethoven's Third Piano Concerto which was being rehearsed in the famous concert hall, the Concertgebouw (concert building), adjacent to the surgery.

A few days later, Swift travelled on to Berlin. Though aware that the Soviet Union and Germany had signed a non-aggression pact, he was surprised to find that the Germans had reasonably friendly attitudes to the USSR. In a bit of banter in a Berlin bank, Swift and a bank clerk were involved in a good-humoured exchange of the communist and Nazi salutes! The Soviet Union's negotiation of the pact with the Third Reich was fully justified, in Swift's opinion. The USSR, he contended, was neither prepared nor anxious to become involved in a war. He maintained that the West had since deliberately misrepresented the agreement as having been designed to facilitate Hitler's attack on 'The Democracies' when, in fact, it was purely for the Soviet Union's internal purposes. Swift's quest for anti-Nazi acquaintances ended in disappointment. The socialist baker whom he had met in Brussels no longer worked in the same bakery and had possibly been interned, while a clerical railway worker who had also attended the Brussels seminar had since become a Nazi supporter.

Swift returned to London by boat and train. Before reaching the Dutch frontier at Bentheim, where passengers changed trains to proceed into Holland, he was joined by two plain-clothes Nazi officials who had had him under observation for some time. He was questioned by one of them who spoke good English and it was evident that they were well informed about him and his attempts to contact anti-Nazis. On arrival in Bentheim, Swift was told he would have to come with them. They brought him to a hotel on the station platform, where the three of them had a meal. A wireless was playing Flotow's opera, *Martha*, incorporating Thomas Moore's melody, *The Last Rose of Summer*. The officers were rather sceptical when Swift explained the origin of this music. They proceeded to examine his papers and to search his pockets and suitcase. After some hours they permitted him to continue on his journey.

More problems awaited Swift in London where the authorities saw from his passport that he had visited Germany. He was placed under a kind of house arrest in a hotel near Euston station. Two secret service agents keeping him under observation allowed him to telephone William Banfield, Labour MP for a London constituency, and General Secretary of the English Bakers' Union. Swift and Banfield were already acquainted through their trade union contacts. Banfield came to the hotel and gave the authorities a good account of his Irish colleague, after which Swift was at liberty to return home to Dublin.[3]

A Dangerous Agitator

During the 1940s, the dissension that had plagued the labour movement for two decades was to culminate in splits in the Labour Party, the Irish Trade Union Congress (ITUC) and the Dublin Trades Union Council (DTUC). That dissension was based partly on rivalry between some Irish-based unions, notably the ITGWU, which were mainly nationalist and anti-communist in character, and their British-based counterparts whose outlook was generally mildly socialist and international. An equally important cause of discord was the bitter personal feud between the two most dominant figures in the movement, William O'Brien and James Larkin, Sen., General Secretaries respectively of the ITGWU and the WUI. They had been adversaries since their dispute over the leadership of the ITGWU, following Larkin's return from America in 1923. Their enmity had intensified the following year after Larkin and others had joined the new and rival WUI.

Swift's feelings on the contention between Irish and British-based unions were mixed. While favouring the notion of a united Irish-based trade union movement, he recognised that for historical and other reasons this was not a practical proposition and that the imposition of such a structure would split the ITUC. He was attracted by the concept of One Big Union (OBU), which was the ITGWU's objective, but found that union and its Irish-based allies rather parochial. With regard to the differences between the ITGWU and the WUI, more particularly between O'Brien and Larkin, Swift, though critical of what he considered Larkin's gradual depoliticisation over the previous decade, remained a firm Larkinite. He preferred the politics and trade unionism of Larkin and the WUI to that emanating from O'Brien and his ITGWU associates.

The ITGWU had responded to the formation of the WUI by isolating Larkin and obstructing his union's affiliation to the ITUC and the DTUC. Twelve years later, however, in 1936, the WUI finally succeeded in affiliating to the DTUC.[1] The following year, Larkin was elected to the DTUC's executive committee, a position he retained until his death ten years later.[2] He was also a DTUC delegate to conferences of the ITUC from 1937 to 1942.[3] However, in a move against Larkin, the 1942 conference decided that trades councils' delegates to future ITUC conferences would have to be members of unions affiliated to the ITUC.[4] Consequently, Larkin was ineligible to attend conferences of the ITUC until after that organisation had split.

Thus, disunited, the trade union movement was ill prepared to oppose effectively the Trade Union Bill, and Emergency Order No. 83, popularly known as the Wages Standstill Order, introduced by de Valera's Fianna Fáil Government in the spring of 1941.[5] Five years before that, the ITUC had established a commission to examine the restructuring of the movement. O'Brien dominated the commission, and his report, which was never implemented, proposed the reorganisation of the movement into ten industrial unions, each with exclusive organising and negotiating rights. This was to replace a structure of forty-nine unions representing a total affiliated membership of 134,000.[6] Supporting the plan was the Bakers' Union which stood to gain members from other unions operating in that trade. O'Brien's recommendations envisaged all bakery workers being members of the Bakers' Union.[7] The plan was opposed, however, by many other unions which perceived it as an attempt by O'Brien to strengthen the ITGWU at the expense of the British-based unions.[8]

The Trade Union Bill had much the same purpose as O'Brien's recommendations and was regarded by the British-based unions and the WUI as a threat to their existence. More than that, it was widely seen as embracing the ITGWU's OBU objective. Lending weight to suspicions of that kind was the failure of the ITUC and the ITGWU, both under O'Brien's influence, to mount a convincing campaign against the Bill and the Order. The Order was effectively a statutory wage freeze which, among other things, removed from workers striking for higher wages the legal protection of the Trades Disputes Act, 1906.

Notwithstanding the inertia of the ITUC and the ITGWU, a vigorous campaign of opposition to the new legislation was swiftly undertaken by the DTUC in conjunction with the Labour Party. As early as May 1941, on a proposal by Larkin, Sen., the DTUC established a Council of Action to deal with the matter. It was composed of the DTUC's executive committee and others like James Larkin, Jun. and Swift who were co-opted.[9] Swift had been a Bakers' Union delegate to the DTUC since 1933.[10] Under the Council of Action's auspices, many public meetings opposing the legislation were held in Dublin's working-class districts. Swift was much involved in this activity, organising some of the meetings and speaking on at least two occasions, in Marino and Larkhill.[11] His main contribution, however, was to launch and jointly edit a militant journal, *Workers' Action,* which dealt with every aspect of the campaign. His co-editors, Owen Sheehy Skeffington and Paddy Staunton, both socialists and Labour Party members, were co-opted to the council at his instigation. In selecting them for this task he was mindful that Staunton's experience as a professional journalist with the *Irish Press* would be a useful asset, while Sheehy Skeffington was not only capable of a valuable contribution himself, but could encourage some of his literary acquaintances to write articles for the paper. Other contributors included Roddy Connolly, James Connolly's son, and the playwrights Seán O'Casey and Paul Vincent Carroll. Swift wrote a considerable amount for *Workers' Action,* either anonymously or under the pseudonym *Bol,* short for *Bolivar.*

On 22 June 1941, in a mass demonstration against the Bill and the Order, the unions marched from Parnell Square to College Green, where a large public meeting was held. It was on that occasion that Larkin, Sen., the main speaker, staged one of his most celebrated gestures when, having told the crowd that 'he was given a Bill by Mr Lemass and he would do with it what he did with one in 1911', he produced from his pocket a copy of the Bill, and, to continuous cheers from the crowd, set it alight with a match, declaring defiantly: 'We will deal with this measure which is the same type as the rotten fascist government that has introduced it. There is a Bill on green paper for green people. This is the way the Bill and Order should be put out.'[12]

According to a police report, 7,000 people were present at that meeting. To those who remember the hundreds of thousands who participated in the Dublin Council of Trades Unions' tax marches in the early 1980s, the 1941 meeting may seem relatively small. Yet, that demonstration was one of the largest held in Dublin since the 1913 Lock-Out and the vast attendance worried many at the time, some of them in the labour movement. That same police report, a copy of which was presented to Swift on his ninetieth birthday by Ruairí Quinn, the Labour Party Minister for Labour and the Public Service, lists the ten members who constituted the Council of Action. It states that five of them were also members of the Fourth International. In the case of at least two, Swift and Owen Sheehy Skeffington, this information is false as neither was ever a member of that organisation. Interestingly, while the report lists the names, addresses and positions in the labour movement of all ten council members, Swift alone is the subject of special comment, being described as 'a dangerous agitator'.

During the march to College Green, Swift had been joined at O'Connell Bridge by Staunton who brought news from the *Irish Press* that Germany had invaded the USSR. Swift was elated by this development, interpreting it as a guarantee that the Nazis and their allies would lose the war. Up to then, it had appeared that the war would be won by Hitler.

At a meeting of the Council of Action's Standing Committee, some weeks after the demonstration, there was a report of a discussion between a council deputation and the General Secretary of the Irish Bookbinders' Trade Union, Michael Colgan. Colgan was also Vice-President of the ITUC at the time. It was mentioned that, in explaining his own and his union's inactivity and absence from the demonstration, Colgan had stated that his executive committee had refused to allow him to speak where persons of communistic or anti-clerical views were present and, elaborating, had added that he had in mind James Larkin, Jun., who was communistic, and John Swift who was anti-Catholic and anti-clerical.[13] Neither Larkin nor Swift had spoken at the demonstration.[14] There is no record of the basis of Colgan's allegations that Swift was anti-Catholic and anti-clerical. Swift's response to those assertions was recorded, however, in the minutes of a meeting of the Council of Action's Standing Committee held on 30 June 1941:

John Swift said he must combat charges made by Mr Colgan accusing him of being anti-Catholic and anti-clerical. He was definitely not anti-Catholic. As for being anti-clerical, if by that it meant being against sectarianism then that might be so, because in his union they had very many members in Northern Ireland who resented any attempt to use the union as a means of disseminating the views of one religion only, and that a religion to which they did not belong . . . Such sectarianism would destroy the national character of the union in twenty four hours if indulged in by any responsible official or member and he was proud that he was never a party to that, but always opposed such attempts to divide workers on religious grounds.

The Council of Action's Standing Committee, many of whose members held Catholic beliefs, refused unanimously to accept Colgan's explanation of his union's inactivity, and strongly objected to 'any attempts to introduce such mischievous and anti working class views into the Council of Action's campaign'.[15]

Following the demonstration and under the leadership of Larkin, Jun., its secretary, the Council of Action extended its campaign to include issues like unemployment, housing, food and fuel supplies and prices. These matters were also taken up by some Labour Party branches and among those active in this were Owen Sheehy Skeffington and his wife, Andrée.[16] One reason for extending the campaign was to provide Larkin, Sen. with a political and trade union platform.[17]

Opposition to the Bill and the Order was impeded, however, by the lack of unity in the movement and the failure of the ITUC to provide national leadership. Swift was exasperated with the situation and at a meeting of the Council of Action's Standing Committee held on 26 June 1941, he said he was opposed to asking the ITUC to lead the national demonstration. 'They had', he said, 'by their inactivity and lack of leadership forfeited any right to leadership of the national campaign. We should do it ourselves', he declared, 'and at the same time work to bring about a new leadership in the ITUC.' Before concluding, Swift reported that the national executive committee of the Bakers' Union had withdrawn their previous policy of support for the Congress in favour of the Council of Action.[18]

When the ITUC finally held a special conference on the matter on 23 October 1941, the Bill had become an Act. The Labour Party leader, William Norton, TD, Post Office Workers' Union, proposed the following motion: 'That this Congress instructs the national executive immediately to inaugurate a national campaign to compel the Government to withdraw the Trade Union Act 1941.' Swift's suggestion, effectively an addendum, that the campaign be launched in conjunction with the Labour Party, was carried. He saw the Party's involvement as an opportunity to attract new adherents: 'Until Labour ruled the country', he stated, 'they would be faced with the menace of such acts, bills and emergency orders.'[19] The subsequent campaign had little impact mainly because it lacked the support of the ITUC leaders. Swift was critical of them when the matter was considered at a second ITUC special conference held on 26 March 1942. 'The National Executive have not measured up to their duty and responsibility in lying down on this question', he said. 'We [the Council of Action] feel that they are not serving the best interests of the labour movement in remaining so inactive in the campaign that has been waged.' Later in the debate, in expressing what many were thinking, Swift described the state of the campaign thus: '. . . Our movement has failed to rally unity in opposition to the Act. The campaign is buried; this is the funeral service . . .'[20]

While the Council of Action's campaign ended in failure, it resulted in some favourable reverberations for the labour movement. Following consultations between the Labour Party and the DTUC, a number of DTUC activists who had led the campaign were selected as Labour Party candidates to contest the 1942 elections to Dublin Corporation. Among this group were Larkin, Sen., Archie Jackson,[21] Walter Carpenter[22] and Swift.[23] While Swift secured only a few hundred votes and was not elected, the Party had a notable success in that election, dramatically increasing its representation from two to twelve seats, thereby becoming the largest single Party on the corporation.[24] That victory was consolidated in the following year's general election when Labour's representation in the Dáil almost doubled from nine to seventeen seats.[25] Among those returned were the two Larkins.[26] The Labour successes, especially in Dublin, owed much to the Council of Action's campaign.

Both Larkin and his son had been admitted to the Labour Party in December 1941.[27] The younger Larkin had previously been a leading figure in the Communist Party of Ireland (CPI).[28] According to the CPI, he left that organisation without indicating any political disagreement: 'He never expressed disagreement with the Party, but ceased to play his part as a member at any level; he became involved in the affairs of the Workers' Union of Ireland and played the principal part in the next few years in transforming the organisational structure and democratic functioning of the union.'[29] As the CPI observed: 'The loss of Larkin Junior to the Communist Party was a grievous blow, as was the departure of Larkin, Senior ten years earlier.'[30]

Subsequent to the Council of Action's campaign, Swift and Larkin, Sen. were to exchange compliments. That occurred at the 1943 national delegate meeting of the Bakers' Union, which Larkin attended as a representative of the DTUC. Introducing Larkin to the assembly, Swift said that as Vice-President of the DTUC he was learning much from its President, Jim Larkin. Responding to this tribute, Larkin stated that his comrade, Swift, was far from being an apprentice. Continuing, Larkin declared: 'The fact that they now had a Labour Lord Mayor of Dublin [Martin O'Sullivan, the first Labour Party Lord Mayor of the city] and a few new Labour Deputies in the Dáil was due to men like Swift and others who worked so hard on the Council of Action against the Trade Union Act and the Low Wages Orders. But for that fight things would have been much worse for the movement.' Larkin went on to regale his audience with a colourful and wide-ranging speech in which fascist Portugal was described as 'one of the seven depths of Hell', and de Valera as 'the omnipotent Taoiseach who ought to be away in an eleventh-century monastery'. He said that some of the people now in power had given out handbills at his meetings years ago. This, Swift believed, was a reference to the Fianna Fáil minister, Seán MacEntee. It appears that in his younger days in Belfast, MacEntee had been a follower of Larkin's meetings. In a rousing conclusion to his address to the Bakers' Union delegates, Larkin declared:

> The workers of the earth must unite to control it. The workers of the earth are on the march; Joe is in Toganrog [*sic*] today, tomorrow he may be in Dublin. Why have

these borders? No government, neither the cursed crew in the North, nor the nitwits here, could keep us back if we only willed. The inarticulate dream of the workers is stirring. We will not submit much longer.[31]

Perhaps it was Swift's contribution to the Council of Action's campaign that led to his election to the vice-presidency of the DTUC in 1942, a position he held for three years before being elected president in 1945.[32] He retained vivid memories of the executive meetings of that period, particularly the two-year term of office of his immediate presidential predecessor, Larkin, Sen. At that time, the executive met at eight o'clock every Thursday evening in their council room at 44 Lower Gardiner Street. The top end of the oval table around which they sat was dominated by the huge frame of Larkin, who occupied the chair, and P. T. Daly, the council's reserved secretary who had difficulty retaining sufficient space for the minute book and papers. Larkin's usual sign to start the proceedings was the raising of his hooked stemmed pipe in the style of a conductor's baton. The meticulous Daly, whom Swift admired for his cultural interests as much as his trade unionism, passed his carefully prepared agenda towards Larkin who, more often than not, swept it aside and started talking about himself. A typical Larkin discourse consisted of an exposition of his views on world affairs, coupled with reminiscences of some of his more dramatic experiences. The latter were drawn from such diverse places or events as Liverpool docks, the 1913 Dublin Lock-Out or his incarceration in Sing Sing Prison in America. Though less flamboyant at these meetings than when addressing the multitudes on Dublin's streets, Larkin had no difficulty captivating the smaller audience with his lively and rebellious talk. As Swift was later to remark: '. . . Listening to Larkin in this mood at this time one might define the art of good talk as knowing how to muster your irrelevancies. The golden rule in selecting your subject would be: keep always to the line of least persistence!'[33]

Swift was among a group of five or six executive members, all Larkinites, who sat opposite Larkin at the end of the table near the door. This facilitated their exit from the meeting before the pubs closed, closing time then being 10 p.m. Their custom of leaving the meeting early for a drink did not meet with the approval of the strict teetotaller, Larkin, who, in his earlier days, had condemned Dublin stevedores for paying dockers their wages in pubs. At about 9.30 p.m. one of Swift's coterie would stand up saying 'Excuse me, Chairman', before leading the others from the meeting. Their venue was Doran's bar in Marlboro Street, which was close to the Pro-Cathedral and, like it, almost opposite Larkin's WUI headquarters. The pub lounge was only beginning to appear in Dublin at that time and Doran's was one of the first to introduce this facility. Their lounge had acquired a reputation as the haunt of 'adventurous women'. On one occasion as Swift and his friends were leaving the meeting for Doran's bar, Larkin was heard to shout after them: 'There they go to the pros' cathedral!'[34]

The Men whose Goal is Man

In the early 1940s Swift was fairly active in the Labour Party, serving for a time as an administrative council member.[1] With a number of friends, including Michael Conroy and Jimmy Sweetman, he formed a new Party branch in Donnycarney. He was motivated in that by a desire to assist Larkin, Sen.'s election as a city councillor. The DTUC's campaign against the Trade Union Bill and Wages Standstill Order had given Larkin new life and a base from which to contest a seat on Dublin Corporation. In the 1942 local elections, Larkin and Swift were the Labour Party candidates in the Dublin North East constituency,[2] where Swift was also director of elections.[3] As we have seen, while Swift received a small vote and was not elected, Larkin won a seat.

It was also with a view to assisting Larkin that Swift and others joined the Labour Party's Central Branch in the early 1940s. Specifically, the objective was to secure Larkin's nomination as a candidate in the 1943 general election. The admission of both Larkins to the Party in 1941, and their adoption as candidates in the 1943 general election were opposed by William O'Brien. When both secured seats in the Dáil,[4] the ITGWU sought unsuccessfully the expulsion of Larkin, Jun., chairman of the Party's Dublin committee, on the grounds that Larkin, Sen.'s candidature had been in breach of the Party's constitution.[5] Earlier than that, on instructions from their union, ITGWU members on the Party's administrative council had successfully opposed Larkin, Sen.'s candidacy. However, with its sights set on an extra Dáil seat, the Party's Dublin executive committee subsequently disregarded this decision and supported Larkin's candidature.[6]

Later, in January 1944, the ITGWU disaffiliated from the Party, with five of the eight ITGWU deputies seceding to form a rival organisation, the National Labour Party. In a joint statement the five declared that they were taking this action because of communist influence in the Party.[7] On 15 January 1944, O'Brien issued a circular to ITGWU branches charging the Labour Party's administrative council with having 'allowed and encouraged admission into the Party of people who had been active members and well-known propagandists of the Communist Party'.[8] A pamphlet issued by O'Brien on behalf of the ITGWU charged that communists had taken possession of the Labour Party in Dublin, and that the Party had allowed Communism to permeate it to such an extent that there was no hope of its recovering its independence.[9] O'Brien availed of the Catholic weekly, the *Standard*, to pursue his campaign. Information on communists and socialists was supplied to the *Standard* by O'Brien, who, through an intermediary, was in contact with Alfred O'Rahilly, President of University College, Cork, and author of the *Standard*'s anti-communist tirades.[10] Swift judged this action of O'Brien's as extremely cynical. In his younger days O'Brien had welcomed the Bolshevik Revolution enthusiastically.[11] Nobody realised more than O'Brien that this communist scare was a red herring, devised by himself to consign Larkin, Sen. to the political wilderness.

Although grossly exaggerated, some allegations of O'Brien's and the *Standard*'s were not entirely without foundation. The two Larkins, for instance, had been actively and openly involved in the communist movement. In addition to that, the Dublin Branch of the CPI had decided in July 1941, 'to suspend independent activity and to apply the force of the branch to working in the labour and trade union organisation'.[12] These CPI members had joined various branches of the Labour Party, a few enrolling in the Central Branch which sometimes met in New Books, the CPI's bookshop, then located at 16A Pearse Street, Dublin.[13] New Books had opened in January 1942 with the twin purpose of making available left-wing, communist and progressive literature and being a centre for left-wing supporters.[14]

Presumably because of its support for Larkin, Sen., the Central Branch was selected for a special attack by O'Brien. The *Standard* commented: 'Mr O'Brien's charge that the Central Branch of the Labour Party was under Communist control was well founded as was demonstrated very effectively when the 1943 Branch Committee was elected. Comrade Ireland was elected hon. treasurer;

Comrade Ryan hon. secretary; and Comrades Musgrove, Herbert, Nolan and Kenny, members. The only non-CPI men elected were Messrs Tucker, Chairman and J. Swift.'

Inclusion of Swift's initial while omitting the initials of the others was neither a gesture nor a mistake. Rather, it was to reveal that the J. S., author of the following verse, published in bold type in the middle of the anti-communist article, was none other than Swift.[15]

The Men Whose Goal Is Man

Have we forgotten the real men,
The good men, the lone men,
The saints whose visions plan;
The men whose faith is writ in deeds
Above the narrow sects and creeds,
The cursed men, the best men,
The men whose goal is man.

These last lines were reproduced from the September 1940 issue of the *Torch*, organ of the Dublin Constituencies Council of the Labour Party.

Whatever success the CPI members achieved in the Labour Party, and they were certainly influential in Larkin, Sen.'s nomination as a candidate in the 1943 general election, their weakness was exposed when the 1944 Labour Party conference endorsed overwhelmingly the administrative council's decision to expel several of their number, including Johnny Nolan and Robert Tweedy.[16] Another victim of that purge was the distinguished teacher, historian, author and maritime expert, Dr John de Courcy Ireland.[17] Between 1942 and 1944, he had been Secretary of the Dublin executive of the Labour Party to James Larkin, Jun.'s chairmanship. Against strong opposition from William O'Brien and the ITGWU, he had played a leading role with Larkin, Jun. in Larkin, Sen.'s nomination and election to the Dáil in 1943.[18] Although never a member of the CPI, de Courcy Ireland's transgression, apparently, had been to attend a conference of that Party in Belfast.[19] Collectively, these expulsions from the Labour Party, particularly by such a decisive majority (203 in favour, with ten dissenting)[20] illustrate how preposterous was O'Brien's contention 'that the party had . . . no hope of recovering its independence'. Actually, the Labour Party was then a deeply conservative organisation whose independence had recently been surrendered, not to the CPI, but to the Catholic hierarchy. As has already been observed, sections of the Party's constitution dealing with private property and the establishment of a workers' republic had been diluted to conform to Catholic social teaching. That had not elicited a murmur from O'Brien.

Swift was a delegate to several annual conferences of the Labour Party in the early to mid-1940s.[21] Opposing the expulsions of Nolan, Tweedy and others at the 1944 conference, Swift declared that he had done worse than those fellows; he had visited the Soviet Union. Rejecting this plea, the conference chairman, William Davin, TD quipped: 'So, too, Mr Swift, has the Minister for Justice!'[22]

Further evidence of the Labour Party's conservatism in the early to mid-1940s was the expulsion in 1943 of Swift's socialist and liberal friend, Owen Sheehy Skeffington, who was never a member of the CPI.[23] The reason given for his removal from the Party was that he had been publicly critical of its leaders, Norton and O'Brien. Sheehy Skeffington was convinced that he had been simply too radical for the Party.[24] Swift believed that he himself narrowly escaped a similar fate, being saved only by the leadership's fears of disaffiliation by the Bakers' Union.

The campaign by O'Brien and the *Standard* had a devastating effect on the Party and in the May 1944 general election, the total Labour vote decreased by a third, or 74,000 votes. There was a reduction from twelve to eight in the number of seats secured by the Irish Labour Party while the National Labour Party suffered a loss of one of its five seats.[25]

The Labour Party split was characterised by the two bodies vying with each other to enunciate their loyalty to Catholicism. An example of the National Labour Party's position on this matter was the statement of its secretary, Frank Purcell, when addressing the Party's Limerick branch in October 1944.

> The lessons of the fate of the Irish Labour Party is that if we mean to build up a really effective Labour Movement there must be the utmost clarity as to where the movement stands in relation to the teaching of the Church, and with regard to the popular rights and directive principles of social policy, embodied in the Constitution of the State.

The people of this country would always recoil from anything or anyone that could be suspected of being subversive
of Catholic teaching. National Labour would present no
difficulty of conscience to those who embraced its membership.[26]

Norton, the Leader of the Labour Party, and member of the
conservative, Catholic organisation, the Knights of St Columbanus,[27] declared that the Labour Party proudly acknowledged
the authority of the Catholic Church in all matters which related
to public policy and public welfare.[28]

The Labour Party split ended effectively with the election of
the 1948 Inter-Party Government, which included members of
both Labour Parties.[29] During the period leading up to reunification, the *Standard* devoted an editorial to the subject, much
of it an attack on Swift:

> We look forward to the implementation of the new United
> Labour policy. Those who take the task in hands will have
> plenty to do, particularly if they extend their activity into
> the trade union movement. For instance, they will have to
> make up their minds as to the desirability of allowing pro-
> minent members of the Labour Party, and even members
> of the Dáil, as well as executive heads of Irish trade unions,
> to co-operate with the Communist organisation in Britain
> which calls itself the Connolly Association, or of writing in
> the organ of that Association, the so-called 'Irish Democrat'.
> For instance, the bakers who are in their vast majority Cath-
> olic, should ask Mr John Swift, their leader and President
> of the Irish Trade Union Congress, whether he is speaking
> for them when he writes in the 'Irish Democrat' that
> Ireland should have diplomatic relations with Communist-
> dominated Poland or the Communist State of Yugoslavia.
> That is, should the Irish bakers by implication range them-
> selves up against Archbishop Stepinac and for Tito or in
> favour of the Lublin Committee murderers of the trade
> union leaders of Poland?
>
> Those who compare Mr Swift's affection for Yugoslavia
> with the account given in our last issue of the persecution
> of the Church there, as described by the Vatican City
> newspaper *Osservatore Romano* will readily see how far
> Mr Swift is from being a person who does not participate
> in Communist activity.[30]

No mention here of Catholic Church collaboration with fascism! No recognition either of the rights of individuals to hold and express unorthodox opinions. Never did Swift purport to represent anyone but himself when advocating the establishment of diplomatic relations between socialist states and Ireland.

The ITUC split, which was to be mirrored in the DTUC, occurred in April 1945. A consequence of that was the resignation of five members of the ITUC's national executive and their replacement, initially through co-option, by five others including Swift and Larkin, Jun., the WUI having affiliated to the ITUC on 10 May 1945.[31]

Swift had first been a delegate to the ITUC annual conference in 1937, a memorable occasion for him if only because it was held in his native Dundalk. From 1937 to 1967, the year of his retirement, he was present at a total of twenty-two ITUC or ICTU annual conferences, missing those from 1939 to 1941 and 1960 to 1966. At all the conferences he attended, excluding 1942 when representing the DTUC, he was a delegate of the Bakers' Union. Swift was an officer of the ITUC for eleven of his thirteen years on the national executive, serving as Vice-President in 1945/6, President in 1946/7 and Treasurer from 1949/50 to 1957/8. The 1946 annual conference had special significance for the Bakers' Union and Swift, for it was at that conference, held in Four Provinces House, the union's new national headquarters in Harcourt Street, Dublin, that Swift was elected President of Congress.[32]

Swift's period on the ITUC's national executive virtually coincided with the fourteen-year division in the movement, a division that occurred when ten Irish-based unions led by the ITGWU disaffiliated from congress and formed a rival body, the Congress of Irish Unions (CIU). A decision by the ITUC to participate in a world conference of trade unions was the immediate cause of the split. Among items on the conference agenda was the reconstruction of the trade union movement in the post-war era.[33] The secessionists contended that the ITUC's representation at the conference would infringe the Free State's neutrality as many participants would be representing trade union national centres in the allied nations.[34] Those seceding also alleged that for several years leading up to the rift, the ITUC had been dominated by the votes of delegates belonging to unions having their headquarters in Britain.[35]

Regarding the Bakers' Union's reaction to the split, it has to be said that, in unions generally, the average rank and file, and even NEC member, had little interest in such matters. Consequently, policy of this kind was often determined by the leading full-time official, and this was the case when the Bakers' Union formulated policy on the Congress crisis. Account, of course, had to be taken of the union's Northern Ireland members, many of whom would have baulked at the prospect of being affiliated to the CIU. At the 1944 ITUC Annual Conference, Swift influenced the union to support the Congress's representation at the world trade union conference.[36] Moreover, after the rift had occurred, he convinced the NEC that the union's best interest lay in remaining affiliated to the ITUC.

Although general secretary of an Irish-based union, albeit with a significant unionist membership in Northern Ireland, Swift firmly supported the ITUC's position on the split. He believed that the main objective of the secessionists was to rid the movement of British-based unions and that the issues raised by the world trade union conference were merely a pretext. O'Brien and the ITGWU, in Swift's view, also perceived the schism as a means to advance their OBU aspirations. It was widely believed that the ITGWU had influenced Fianna Fáil's Trade Union Act, 1941, granting sole negotiating rights to the majority union in an employment. That stipulation proved to be unconstitutional. Had it complied with the constitution, the main beneficiary undoubtedly would have been the ITGWU, primarily at the expense of the Amalgamated Transport and General Workers' Union (ATGWU), the largest British-based union in the Free State, and the WUI.

Conscious of the political dimension to the rift, Swift declared in May 1945: ' . . . The lion rampant at the moment is not the protagonists of the OBU or indeed anyone with status in our common movement. The Fianna Fáil Government, with its post-war plans for greater production and greater regimentation for the Unions, is the real lion in the slaughter contemplated . . .'[37] In an address to the ITUC's annual conference two months later, Swift again referred to the government's role in the matter:

> . . . Some of the leaders of the breakaway, at least, have the hope that they will be the sole body to be consulted

with regard to Trade Union affairs, and Mr Lemass (Minister for Industry & Commerce), as you read in the press recently, has expressed regret that there is not one single body to represent the Trade Unions. In my opinion, that does not represent the true feelings of the Government. My opinion is that the reaction of the Government will be that they would prefer to have two bodies at each other's throats and that Mr Lemass and the Government spokesmen will give sufficient encouragement to the breakaway body to entertain the hope of becoming the sole body at some future date. My reading of the situation is that they will take very good care that that does not materialise . . .'[38]

A year later again, in July 1946, Swift referred to the passing of the initiative in labour matters from the trade unions to the de Valera Government. Citing the 1946 Industrial Relations Act, whose main provision was the introduction of the Labour Court, he expressed the concern of many trade unionists then that the legislation might impose penalties on trade unions and curtailment or even forfeiture of the right to strike. He alluded, too, to the collaboration between the government and the employers in resisting union demands for a fortnight's holiday with pay, an issue of considerable concern to the movement at the time.[39] That battle was spearheaded by the Dublin laundresses, members of the Irish Women Workers' Union (now part of SIPTU), whose three-month strike in 1945 ended in victory.[40]

Efforts to reunite the movement commenced almost immediately following the split. As early as 1945, discussions began between the ITUC and the CIU 'to explore the possibility of reuniting the movement'. Representing the ITUC at those talks, which were unfruitful, were Tom Johnson (Acting Secretary, ITUC, and former Labour Party Leader); John T. O'Farrell (Railway Clerks' Association); Philip Cairns (Post Office Workers' Union); and John Swift (IBCAWAU); the CIU's delegation comprising William O'Brien (ITGWU); Cathal O'Shannon (ITGWU); Leo Crawford (Operative Plasterers' and Allied Trades Society of Ireland); and Michael Drumgoole (Irish Union of Distributive Workers and Clerks).[41] In another attempt in early 1947, Swift and James Larkin, Jun. were appointed by the ITUC to meet CIU representatives with a view to finding a basis for ultimate unification of the two congresses.[42] Neither this nor the many other reconciliation efforts of the late 1940s and early 1950s were successful.

By then, of course, some of the leading personalities had left the movement. O'Brien's retirement in 1946[43] had been followed in 1947 by the death of Larkin, Sen.[44] Also by then, with the ending of World War II in 1945, followed in the late 1940s by the start of the Cold War, the issue, spurious or otherwise, of the ITUC's involvement in world trade union conferences had become almost irrelevant.

The ITUC had sent two representatives to the world conference in London in February 1945.[45] Later that year, Tom Johnson and Swift had represented the ITUC at a second London conference called to ratify the founding of the World Federation of Trade Unions (WFTU).[46] Later still, in October 1945, Gilbert Lynch, President of the ITUC, had attended the inaugural meeting in Paris of the WFTU.[47] With the rise of the Cold War in the late 1940s, the WFTU itself split, the American affiliated unions and some Western European union centres led by the British TUC seceding to form the International Confederation of Free Trade Unions.[48] For that reason, the ITUC's connection with the WFTU had lapsed, the ITUC, and indeed, its successor, the ICTU, subsequently remaining unaffiliated to any world trade union body. Since 1974, however, the ICTU has been a constituent of the European Trade Union Confederation, an organisation representative of trade union centres in the European Community and in other non-socialist states such as Finland, Sweden and Austria.

Prospects for unity of the Irish trade union movement were boosted in 1956 by the establishment of the Provisional United Trade Union Organisation (PUTUO). Representative of the two congresses, the committee of PUTUO had as its principal task the drafting of a constitution for a new united trade union centre. The committee's endeavours over several years culminated in 1959 in the disbandment of the ITUC and the CIU and their replacement by the present Irish Congress of Trade Unions.[49] Though Treasurer of the ITUC and a member of PUTUO's Committee,[50] Swift acknowledged that John Conroy and James Larkin, Jun., General President and General Secretary, respectively, of the ITGWU and the WUI, were the chief architects of unity.

Patrick Swift and his wife Alice in Dundalk about 1893.

John Swift in Germany immediately after the Armistice for World War I.

The Bakery Trade's Social Club Committee 1927–34. John Swift, as Honorary President is seated in the centre.

The Dublin Trades' Union Council in 1942. James Larkin is second from left in the back row with John Swift to his left.

At the official opening of the Irish Bakers' Union Library in Four Provinces House, Harcourt Street, Dublin. From left, James Brown, President of the Bakers' Union, John McCann, Lord Mayor of Dublin and John Swift.

The Committee of the Provisional United Trade Union Organisation about 1957 under the chairmanship of Professor John Busteed. James Larkin, Jun. is beside John Swift, left-hand side.

Seán Lemass and John Swift at the International Bakery Exhibition on 25 August 1953

The National Executive Committee of the Irish Bakers', Confectioners' and Allied Workers' Amalgamated Union in February 1958.

John Swift, speaking as President, at the Conference of the International Union of Food and Allied Workers' Associations, Dublin 1967. In the back row are Michael Mullen (DCTU), John Conroy (ITGWU), Eugene Timmons, TD (Lord Mayor of Dublin), An Taoiseach, Jack Lynch, Michael O'Leary, TD (Labour Party), Dr Patrick Hillery (Minister for Labour) and A. Dawson (ILO).

John Swift, Roddy Connolly, the Chief Justice Cearbhall Ó Dálaigh and Austin Clarke at an Irish-USSR Society reception in Dublin on 18 July 1970.

With the Soviet Ambassador, Mr Gennadi Uranov, at a reception to celebrate the 72nd anniversary of the Great October Socialist Revolution in 1989.

John and Harriet Swift in Washington DC, August 1964 and with their children and grandchildren twenty-three years later in November 1987.

Father and son at the DCTU May Day March in Dublin 1984.

Later efforts by Conroy and Larkin, Jun. to unite the ITGWU and the WUI were foiled, however, by their deaths within a week of each other in 1969.[51] A further twenty years were to elapse before these unions would amalgamate to form a new organisation, the Services, Industrial, Professional and Technical Union (SIPTU).[52] Leading figures in that merger were John Carroll and William (Bill) Attley, General President and General Secretary, respectively, of the ITGWU and the FWUI. On the institution of SIPTU on 1 January 1990, Attley and Carroll became Joint Founding General Presidents.[53] The reunification of the Republic's two largest unions, following some sixty-odd years of divsion, was welcomed very much by Swift. Considering this development to be of some significance, he believed it would provide much needed impetus to the rationalisation of the Irish trade union movement.

In contrast to his peripheral role in the unity of Congress, Swift had been among the founders of the People's College which came into existence in 1948.[54] For several years beforehand, the establishment of an organisation for workers' education had been discussed on the ITUC's executive. There existed within the executive a divergence of views on the kind of education that might be deemed suitable for such a venture. Some, including Sam Kyle, James Larkin, Jun. and Swift, felt that courses should not be restricted to cultural subjects such as art appreciation, but should embrace economics, politics and sociological subjects generally. That view was probably not shared by Louie Bennett, Swift's immediate successor as ITUC President, as she, apparently, was an admirer of Salazar and his Portuguese version of corporatism.[55] It was cultural subjects, however, that were to dominate the college's curriculum.[56]

While the People's College, through its courses, avoided ideology, others were less hesitant in entering that domain. These included such well-known opponents of the People's College as the *Standard*; Alfred O'Rahilly, Professor of Theology and President of UCC, who was closely associated with that paper; and Fr Edward Coyne, SJ. The principal declared concern of these forces was that the People's College should provide education of a non-denominational character. Apparently, Professor O'Rahilly also regarded the college as an affront to his workers' education endeavours in UCC.[57] Catholic social teaching, as expounded in the anti-socialist papal encyclicals, was the basis of O'Rahilly's courses. Launched around the same time as the People's College, this UCC undertaking was followed in 1949 by the commencement of similar courses in UCD, under the guidance of Fr Edward Coyne, SJ. That led, in 1951, to the founding by the Jesuits of the Catholic Workers' College,[58] an institution that was to cater for managers as well as workers.[59] In relation to ideology, there was no ambiguity about the position of the Catholic Workers' College: 'The original aims and objectives of the college had their inspiration in the Catholic social principles expressed mainly in the social encyclicals of Popes Leo XIII, Pius XI and Pius XII.'[60] Moreover, when, in 1966, the Catholic Workers' College was renamed the College of Industrial Relations (now the National College of Industrial Relations or NCIR), one of its founders, Fr Edward Kent, SJ declared: 'It is unnecessary to say that the teaching and influence of the College is and will always be the teaching of the Church.'[61]

Within the trade union movement there was considerable support for the courses based on Catholic sociology. This found expression, for example, in 1954 when the ITUC, at its annual conference, reviewed the work of the People's College. In the course of that debate, Senator R. S Anthony, representing the Typographical Association, Cork, recommended that the People's College should emulate Professor O'Rahilly's workers' education classes. Supporting that view, another delegate, Mr M. Hill of the Plumbing Trades Union declared:

> I think that first and foremost education should be Christian education and that is why I support what has been done by Professor O'Rahilly because the courses have been Christian, Catholic education . . . These lectures gave me some education and one of the things it taught me was that I was Irish and Christian. It is necessary to be a Christian both at work and at meetings of this kind. I am afraid that the Irish worker is frightened of the trade union movement's educational schemes unless they are assured beforehand that the education has Christian as well as trade union principles.[62]

It was disconcerting to Swift that the NCIR, an institution he considered to be inherently sectarian and anti-socialist, managed to attract considerable numbers of trade union students. Equally distressing to him was the support given to that body by many ICTU affiliates.[63] He found it particularly disturbing that practically as many unions were affiliated to the NCIR as to the People's College.[64] This, Swift believed, said something about the Irish trade union movement.

Despite being a founder and, for a period, a central council member of the People's College,[65] Swift was disappointed with what he regarded as its non-political nature. When advocating the establishment of the college he had had in mind an institution where workers would learn something about socialism. Enlarging on that theme at a Labour Party Connolly Commemoration meeting in Dublin in 1970, he said:

> Why does not the Congress and the Labour Party start their own school of socialism and socialist industrial relations? Why should they be content to leave it to outside bodies like the College of Industrial Relations to teach this subject so important in any study or appreciation of socialism? This college is run by the Jesuits whose aim and motto is 'Ad Majorem Dei Gloriam'—To the greater Glory of God— meaning, of course, to the greater glory of the Church, not to the greater glory of socialism. And what is the message of institutions like the Irish Management Institute and the College of Industrial Relations? The message is simple— that the worker—lamb or sheep should lie down with the capitalist tiger, that the tiger is not as fierce or hungry as he used to be, and if you snuggle up to him he'll pat you with his paw and lick you with his tongue and if you're really nice to him, instead of tearing you to pieces and eating you at once, he'll eat you by instalments![66]

In the spring of 1988, Swift was offered a Foundation Honorary Fellowship of the NCIR by the college's Executive Director, Fr Tom Morrissey, SJ. While not doubting the good intentions of Fr Morrissey and others associated with this gesture, Swift politely but firmly rejected the offer.[67]

Swift's year as ITUC President was marked by two notable events for the trade union movement. The first was the institution of the Labour Court in 1946. Prior to that, negotiations between employers and unions were generally rather informal and confined to the employment or industry concerned. Rarely had either party recourse to significant statistical or other research data. That changed considerably with the establishment of the Labour Court. Its two-stage process, which remained substantially unaltered until 1990, when new legislation was enacted, consisted of a conciliation conference and a formal hearing. The first step, involving a verbal presentation of the case before a conciliation officer, was a relatively informal affair. Issues unresolved at that level were referred to a formal hearing of the court. To meet the court's requirements, unions pursuing claims for improved wages and working conditions likely to increase living costs had to furnish accurate particulars of wage rates and working conditions in comparable employments. This information was presented in a written submission detailing changes in members' living standards and indicators in the national economy justifying the improvements sought. The case presented was then considered by the court, comprising three members, an independent chairperson, and two colleagues nominated by trade union and employer organisations.[68] The court later issued a written recommendation on the issue in dispute.

With most unions unprepared for this challenge, the ITUC decided to appoint its own research officer.[69] Swift was a member of an ITUC subcommittee which, in 1948, interviewed candidates for the position. Many of the applicants were university graduates who had neither knowledge of the purpose of Congress nor interest in the labour movement. One interviewee, the local correspondent of a French newspaper, defined the purpose of Congress as being the establishment of the corporate state! The only candidate to impress the interviewing subcommittee was Donal Nevin. Familiar with the role of Congress, Nevin expressed his desire to serve the labour movement. At that time he was employed by the Department of Industry and Commerce as a statistician, the very skill required by Congress. Short of funds following the CIU defections, the ITUC explained that the position advertised might not have much future or be pensionable. Despite that, Nevin left his existing permanent and pensionable post to work as a research officer for Congress. Later, for a period, he served as Assistant General Secretary of the ICTU, before being appointed General Secretary of that body in 1982. He retired in January 1989.[70]

The second notable event during Swift's ITUC presidency was the death on 30 January 1947 of James Larkin, Sen.[71] Swift had last met Larkin six months earlier at the 1946 ITUC annual conference in Four Provinces House. Larkin's declaration, on that occasion, that he was 'going down to the grave rapidly'[72] was interpreted by some as a typical Larkin recourse to the dramatic. Shortly after the conference, however, James Larkin, Jun. informed Swift that his father, who had been married in a civil ceremony,[73] was arranging to go to Liverpool to escape the solicitations of local concern, not so much for his physical, but his spiritual welfare. But, as Swift was to observe later, Larkin 'did not go to Liverpool, being apparently content to remain in the care, physical and spiritual, of the concerned at home'.[74] Indeed, as the following account shows, Larkin, Sen. was given an elaborate send-off by those concerned about his spiritual welfare:

> He [James Larkin, Sen.] was attended in his last days by Rev. Father Aloysius O.F.M. Cap., who attended James Connolly before his execution by a British firing squad in 1916.
>
> His Grace, the Archbishop of Dublin was present while the dying veteran of many a bitter industrial struggle received the Sacrament of Extreme Unction from Rev. W. Kealy, M.A., C.C., St Kevin's, Harrington Street, Dublin, Chaplain to the hospital.
>
> His body, clothed in the brown habit and scapular of St. Francis, lay in state in the Thomas Ashe Hall, headquarters of the Workers Union of Ireland, until Sunday, when it was removed to his parish, St. Mary's, Haddington Road, where the Bishop of Thasos, Most. Rev. Dr. Wall, received it.
>
> His Grace the Archbishop presided at the Requiem Mass, which preceded the funeral to Glasnevin on Monday. The Bishop of Thasos was the celebrant.[75]

Swift was asked by James Larkin, Jun. if, as President of Congress, he would care to make the graveside oration. Having worked together in the Dublin Trades Union Council and on the national executive of Congress, Swift and Larkin, Jun. had long been good friends. It was thus embarrassing for Swift to decline the honour offered. He explained his reasons for not accepting:

> I was never one disposed to or gifted in formal public oratory of the kind that would have been thought appropriate to the occasion. Besides, the Larkin they were now

about to inter with the pomp of bell, book and candle, and the genuflections of sycophants who had maligned and despised him, was not the Larkin that for me had once rung bells of challenge, cited books of revolt and lit candles of socialist vision.[76]

Larkin, Jun. and Swift agreed that an orator more accomplished, more appropriate to the occasion, would be William Norton, the Labour Party leader.[77] Nevertheless, six months later, in his presidential address to the 1947 ITUC annual conference, Swift paid his own tribute to Larkin:

> . . . Since our last Annual Congress our movement has lost one of its greatest men, one of its pioneers. Jim Larkin has passed from us, leaving our movement the poorer. For none can fill the place he occupied; none can do the things he did. Perhaps some of the things he did do not need to be done again. Let us hope that the foundations laid by him and his fellow-pioneers are of permanent duration and that the organised workers of Ireland shall never have imposed on them the task, as our fellows in many countries in Europe have had, of laboriously rebuilding a movement shattered by anti-labour elements. It is true that before Larkin's coming we had trade unions in this country. For many years before there was trade union organisation, principally among the crafts, and to a slight extent with the general workers, such, for example, as the Dublin quay labourers. Still, the unions were more in the nature of friendly societies, timid of militant trade union action and in some cases secret conspiracies allying themselves to the current political agitations in the hope that political changes might bring amelioration of the workers' conditions. Thus, instead of direct trade union action, hope was placed in the dominant political leader—one time O'Connell, then the Young Irelanders, Davitt, the Fenians, the Parliamentary Parties. Then came Larkin and his co-workers. Soon thousands of despised rabble became ennobled with the dignity of trade union organisation. Larkin taught them the duty of struggle, the imperative of rebelliousness. He breathed fire into the dead eyes and the cringing breasts of slaves. They heard him and their supplications to their

masters became defiance, their despair became a challenge.
He taught them self-reliance. They followed Larkin because
he had convinced them in his person and in his teaching
that there was no more noble duty or destiny for men and
women than that of raising themselves from bondage.
Some of us are old enough to remember how Dublin
throbbed to Larkin's fiery slogans. A Titan of a man, he
needed no banners on which to scroll his burning poetry.
He made banners of the air: his voice wrought magic
patterns compelling attention and exultation. In the city's
gutter, in the fetid slums, in the stinking holds of ships, on
the quay-side, where men fawned and flunkeyed for
wretched bread, in the poor-house, even, and the prison,
there was exultation when Larkin spoke. Men and women,
made dumb and abject by injustice and destitution, listened.
What new hurricane from the heavens was this that said
'The great appear great because we are on our knees. Let
us arise.' or, 'Who is it spoke of defeat? I tell you a cause
like ours is greater than defeat can know—it is the power
of powers!'

   This man of power was loved by little children and was
himself, throughout his life, in many ways a child. He was
a great artist, working towards the ideal that consumed
him. His music was livid thunder, hurtled at injustice and
hypocrisy. At times his harmonies were strange, as of
forces eruptive and elemental. But who could doubt the
main chords of the symphony he sought to fashion, with
its tones and overtones that told of chains breaking and
dungeons tottering, and the wild elation of serfs made
free! Let us stand to honour Larkin—Larkin who taught the
despised rabble to stand erect, unafraid and hopeful . . .[78]

The Catholic rites associated with the death and burial of
Larkin are not irreconcilable with his declared religious position
during his life. At one of his first meetings in New York, for
instance, in the course of a speech to a socialist and largely non-
Irish and atheistic audience, Larkin unbuttoned his shirt and
produced a golden cross. Holding the cross before him, he
professed:

> There is no antagonism between the cross and socialism. A man can pray to Jesus and be a better militant socialist for it. There is no conflict between the religion of the Catholic Church and Marxism. I stand by the Cross and Marx. I belong to the Catholic Church. In Ireland that is not held against a socialist and a revolutionist![79]

Furthermore, during a visit to Moscow in 1928 to attend an executive committee meeting of the Comintern, Larkin declared that he had faith, there was a God and he would hold to such a faith until he was proved wrong. He was replying to Bukharin who had asked him if he believed there was a God, Bukharin being under the impression that Larkin postured as a Catholic for opportunistic reasons.[80]

From his own observation of Larkin, Swift was inclined to the view that Bukharin's assessment was correct, Larkin's posing as a Catholic being part of his general depoliticisation during the last couple of decades of his life. At the root of that depoliticisation, Swift believed, was the dissension in the movement, particularly between O'Brien and Larkin, and, of course, involving the ITGWU and the WUI. The feud between these adversaries was conducted in a conservative Catholic society not noted for its tolerance of the unorthodox.

It is Swift's belief that in pursuing his vendetta with O'Brien, especially in the climate of the time, Larkin practically abandoned socialism and became politically *respectable*. According to Swift, this involved Larkin in ingratiating himself with the Church, particularly after his communist past had been publicly exposed in the Catholic press. Dr McQuaid's ministering to the dying Larkin had not been their only contact, Larkin having visited Archbishop's House with other Dublin City Councillors in 1941 to present the then newly appointed Dr McQuaid with an address on behalf of Dublin's citizens.[81] Moreover, at a public meeting in Dublin's Mansion House the following year, Larkin declared that 'they were particularly blessed that they had an Archbishop who was in such intimately close touch with the people's needs'.[82]

According to Swift, Larkin's depoliticisation involved the virtual abandonment of radical politics, an early indication of that being his departure from the communist movement in 1931.[83] Despite this, the CPI has always been reluctant to criticise him. Yet, that

Party was to castigate Larkin for his attacks on British-based unions, interpreting them as a mask for his abandonment of militant politics. They condemned, too, his action during the prolonged builders' strike in the early 1930s in storming off the platform of a public meeting in Dublin because other listed speakers included strikers who were communists.[84]

The failure of most Irish socialists to assess objectively revolutionary figures like Connolly and Larkin was something that concerned Swift. Too often he found the Left accepting uncritically the words and deeds of such leaders. Intolerant of almost any criticism of Connolly and Larkin particularly, many socialists, it seemed to Swift, appeared to regard these figures as almost infallible. Rejecting that approach, he could admire and respect greatly the likes of Connolly and Larkin without, as he often put it, making 'plaster saints' of them. The Left, he believed, could learn much from examining the failures as well as the achievements of such leaders.

What then is Swift's evaluation of Larkin? In his youth, the period before and during the 1913 Lock-Out, he had been captivated by Larkin. Subsequently, he and Larkin had been colleagues on a joint bakery union committee, and later, on the executive of the DTUC. He found Larkin egotistical, always seeking to dominate proceedings, and difficult to work with on a committee. He had to report correspondence with the constituent unions and any consequent action taken. Rarely did Larkin reply to his letters and when on more than one occasion this occurred and Swift reported it to the meeting, Larkin was emphatic he had never received any letters. Challenging Swift's assertion, Larkin would extract from the large inside pocket of his long seaman's-like jacket a fistful of much-handled papers. After sorting them out on the table, he would snarl: 'I got no letter from you, Swift!' Swift learnt not to argue with Larkin about such matters.[85]

However, these were the least of Swift's worries about Larkin. Of much greater concern were what he regarded as Larkin's political shortcomings, not least his silence on the threat posed by fascism from the early 1930s to the mid-1940s. It was this issue more than any other that provoked him to voice his most trenchant criticism of Larkin. Accusing Larkin, amongst others, of 'having failed the [labour] movement' in this matter, he declared:

Much has been written about the harm done the Labour movement here by the break-away from the IT&GWU and the ensuing faction fighting, made the more bitter by the vicious enmity between William O'Brien, chief spokesman for the IT&GWU, and Larkin, leader of the WUI.

But, to my mind, the worst injury done the movement was its political enfeeblement by the apparent political emasculation of the two antagonists, with each making public postures of mild or no politics, in order to discredit the other.[86]

Is there then a contradiction in Swift's judgment that, in efforts to effect political and socio-economic change in the country, Larkin was the greatest Irishman of his time?[87] It appears not, for here Swift is referring to a younger Larkin, Larkin the socialist visionary and internationalist who campaigned relentlessly, not only for the material rights of his class, but their dignity as human beings. This is the Larkin of the first three decades of the century, the Larkin of the 1913 Dublin Lock-Out, who has deservedly secured an honoured place in labour history. This was the Larkin who inspired Swift.

Mixed Blessings

John Swift became General Secretary of the Irish Bakers' Confectioners' & Allied Workers' Amalgamated Union in 1943.[1] The circumstances leading to his election were less than ideal for, in May that year, his predecessor, Denis Cullen, had resigned from that office[2] having been suspended a month earlier from the part-time position of President of the Dublin No. 1 Branch.[3] Cullen's suspension arose from his failure to attend an important conference on night work with the bakery employers.[4] Despite opposition from Cullen and others, strike notice had been served on the employers on this issue following pressure from the younger members, including Swift. The members were incensed with Cullen's attitude, particularly his failure to attend the conference, and he was subsequently charged by the branch executive, of which Swift was a member, with a breach of discipline.[5] His explanation for being absent, that he 'went to do a good turn for strangers not connected with the trade',[6] was not accepted by the executive, which suspended him for six months.[7] At a well-attended branch meeting held immediately afterwards in the Rotunda, Swift was elected unopposed to the presidency for the period of the suspension.[8]

Cullen's resignation as General Secretary of the union followed the revelation of a 'very big deficit'[9] (£1,300,[10] or approximately £26,000 in 1991 values) in the union's accounts. Excessive alcohol was the cause of Cullen's downfall. For many years he had been practically a teetotaller but had acquired a taste for liquor following his election to the Dáil in 1927. Cullen's drinking gradually led to the neglect of his union duties and responsibilities, and to the misappropriation of union funds.[11]

Swift had had a high regard for his predecessor before these transgressions became apparent. Although full-time colleagues for almost seven years, Cullen and Swift never exchanged a harsh word. In private discussion, perhaps while travelling together on union business in Cullen's car, Swift found the self-educated Cullen interesting and well informed. Though a socialist and free-thinker by conviction, believing in modern science, Cullen was timorous about expressing his views publicly. Of friendly and courteous disposition, he was well liked by many in the trade union movement.[12] President of the ITUC on two occasions, in 1925/6 and 1930/1, Cullen was also, for a short period, a Labour Party TD and chief whip of the Parliamentary Labour Party.

At its meeting on 3 June 1943, the NEC elected Swift as Acting General Secretary pending the national delegate meeting due three months later.[13] On the second day of that three-day delegate meeting, 2 September 1943, when he was forty-seven, Swift was elected General Secretary of the union by thirty-four votes to five.[14]

That 1943 national delegate meeting had another significance for Swift. It authorised the NEC to procure new union premises,[15] an objective he had initiated many years earlier in the Dublin Branch's Bakery Trade's Social Club. Aware of the successful campaign of the Labour Party and trade unions to replace the Dublin slums with new suburban, working-class dwellings, it seemed somewhat incongruous that the union's headquarters should remain in the slum area of Lower Gardiner Street. More important, almost from its inception, the club had advocated the acquisition of new union premises to cater, not only for the administrative requirements of the union, but the social, cultural and educational interests of the members.

Swift was delegated by the NEC to look for a suitable premises or site. When the Baptist Church in Harcourt Street was purchased in October 1944,[16] it was said more than once that he had closed his first church! Michael Scott, the eminent architect, was employed to plan the transformation of the building to suit the union's needs. Much of the architectural work, however, was executed by Scott's colleague, Uinseann MacEoin, who later produced and edited the book, *Survivors*, a chapter of which is devoted to Swift. Alderman Martin O'Sullivan, Labour Party TD for Dublin North West and first Labour Lord Mayor of Dublin, laid the foundation stone of the new building in May 1945.[17]

The pseudo-Gothic façade extending some seventy feet along Harcourt Street was replaced by a five-story, brick building. Behind that, and extending almost to the back entrance of the site in Charlotte Street, was the high-roofed part of the church used for services. It was retained as the union's main auditorium.

Frances Kelly, the well-known contemporary mural painter, was commissioned to paint murals on the auditorium's north and east walls. She took as subjects features from Swift's book, *History of the Dublin Bakers and Others*. These included depictions of early domestic baking in Ireland and the rise of urban or trade baking which developed under the Dublin trades' guilds. Frances Kelly's husband was Frederick Boland who later became President of the United Nations and, later still, Chancellor of Trinity College, Dublin. Eavan Boland, the poet, is their daughter. The murals of vivid colours adorning the south wall were the work of Nano Reid. One mural devoted to Irish labour writers depicted Seán O'Casey while others featured the Ralahine Co-operative, James Connolly at a meeting in Belfast docks and Larkin addressing a meeting in College Green, Dublin. At the entrance of the new building fronting Harcourt Street were engraved plaques executed by the sculptor, Laurence Campbell. These featured aspects of bread production and distribution, and trade union struggles in the last century when the combination laws were being enforced. One panel depicted felon-workers being whipped through the streets of the Coombe, while another showed them embarking on convict ships for transportation to British colonies.

On the fourth and top storey of the building were situated the union's administrative offices and NEC room. Also for a time on that floor was the Irish office of the International Labour Organisation whose representative, Ronald Mortished, a former Assistant Secretary of the Labour Party, was appointed first Chairman of the Labour Court in 1946. Mianraí Teoranta, the State agency responsible for mineral resources, occupied the third floor. Below that again was the Guild Room which was used for a variety of purposes such as lectures, film shows and gramophone recitals. Ballet classes run by the union for members' children were also held there, as were rehearsals by the Dublin Orchestral Players under Brian Boydell. A library for union members occupied the first floor of the building. In appropriate places throughout the library were wooden carvings depicting the heads of James Connolly and writers like Goldsmith, Shaw and Yeats. These were the work of the sculptress, Hilary Heron. She was related to the Labour Party TD, Archie Heron, husband of Connolly's daughter, Ina. Situated in the library was a café, later developed into a restaurant that extended to a balcony overlooking the adjoining auditorium. As the headquarters of one of the few Irish-based unions with branches in Northern Ireland as well as throughout the Free State, Four Provinces House was deemed an appropriate name for the new premises. To emphasise this aspect of the union, four paintings illustrating typical scenery of each province were commissioned from the painter, Frank McKelvey, for display in the NEC's room.[18]

Four Provinces House was opened in February 1946. Two months later, on 10 April, the day of the official opening, Swift expressed his views on the significance of the project:

> A building such as Four Provinces symbolised the aspirations of a working class organisation to be something more than an instrument for improving the economic conditions of their members. It indicated that the union felt a responsibility in regard to the cultural, educational and social activities of the members. The day should be gone when trade unions regard the securing of a sufficiency of the elemental needs such as food, shelter, clothing to be the final objective of working people. Trade unions should aspire to the highest standards of living for their members. They should encourage the members to insist on a higher cultural life and not a life tied to mere food, shelter and clothing.[19]

The formal opening was marked by a dinner, to which were invited representatives of the Royal Irish Academy, the universities, the Labour Party, the ITUC and DTUC. Seán Lemass, Minister for Industry and Commerce, represented the Government. Earlier, the NEC had proposed that Dr McQuaid, Catholic Archbishop of Dublin, be invited to the function. Swift had opposed this on the grounds that the union was a non-sectarian organisation and that it might be resented by some members, particularly in the North. To meet this objection, it was decided to invite also the Church of Ireland Archbishop, Dr Barton. While Dr Barton accepted and attended, Dr McQuaid failed to turn up. An explanation heard later was that he declined the invitation because the function was being held during Lent.[20]

Acquiring the site, building, reconstructing and furnishing the union's premises cost £64,000 (approximately £1,280,000 in 1991 values). Funding was provided by the sale of some of the union's investments, bank borrowing, loans from certain branches of the union and profits from dances.[21] The national union invested £14,000[22] (approximately £280,000 in 1991 values) while branch loans included £6,000 (approximately £120,000 in 1991 values) by Dublin No. 1[23] and £2,000 (approximately £40,000 in 1991 values) by Belfast.[24] To raise finance, dances were held in the auditorium, better known to Dubliners as the Four Provinces Ballroom. On Saturdays, Sundays and suitable public holidays, these were run by the union while on week nights the ballroom was rented by private clubs who ran their own dances. The union employed its own vocalist and band of ten members composed partly of union members formerly working at the trade, and formerly members of the union's orchestra.[25] Among more accomplished players were the pianist, Paddy Malone, and the tenor saxophonist, Johnny Devlin. Malone resigned from the band on becoming General Secretary of the Irish Federation of Musicians. Devlin later joined the Radio Éireann Light Orchestra (now the RTE Concert Orchestra). Later still, he worked as an arranger and a producer with RTE.[26] For the first few years of its operation Four Provinces House was a financial success. In its first year the National Treasurer could report that every department in Four Provinces House was showing a credit balance and that the profit for the three months up to mid-November 1946 was more than £3,000.[27] During the first three and a half years of operation, the average annual profit from the ballroom was £9,000.[28]

The success of the undertaking was threatened, however, in 1947, when rumours began to circulate that the Four Provinces was a centre for disseminating communism. Two years or so before that, in March 1945, Swift had sought and received sanction to purchase second-hand books for the library.[29] Approximately 8,000 volumes were acquired[30] mainly from Eason's of O'Connell Street which then had an excellent second-hand bookshop located in the basement. It was managed by John Quinn, a great authority on books. The Four Provinces library had a cultural section comprising the arts, classical fiction and poetry, while a special Irish section had works by Goldsmith, Shaw, Yeats, O'Casey and others. There were also books of special interest to women, youth and children. The main section was devoted to sociological subjects such as philosophy, social theory, labour history, politics and economics. Though the library contained works by socialist writers like Marx and Connolly, prominent capitalist and other writers were also represented in volumes by such authors as Adam Smith, Ricardo, Marshall, John Stuart-Mill, Henry George and Tolstoy.[31] At their meeting on the day of the official opening of the library, the NEC complimented Swift whom, they said, 'was chiefly responsible for the project'.[32] To the official opening on 4 June 1947 were invited representatives of the National University, Trinity College, the Labour Party, the DTUC and the Labour Court.[33] Not invited, but nevertheless present, was a reporter from the Catholic weekly, the *Standard*. A week or so later, the *Standard* brought to its readers notice that in the library's section on citizenship, readers could borrow or refer to such books as *The Philosophy of Communism*, by John MacMurray; *The Socialist Movement in England*, by Broughan Villiers; *The Socialist Sixth of the World*, by the Dean of Canterbury, (Hewlett Johnson); *Socialism over Sixty Years*, by Fenner Brockway; *Soviet Communism, a New Civilization*, by Sydney and Beatrice Webb. While the *Standard* acknowledged as an afterthought that the library also had a volume entitled *Christianity Confronts Communism*, it neglected to refer to the library's many books by capitalist writers on the social sciences.[34]

The issue of the communist books was first raised in the national union in August 1947 when a deputation comprising the executive of the two Dublin branches met the NEC in connection with complaints that had been received by those branches concerning the character of certain books in the library. There was reference to the reports in the *Standard* stating that the library contained communistic books. The delegation was assured by the chairman that on a recommendation of the resident management committee (RMC), comprising the union's president,

Treasurer and two Trustees, it had been decided 'to seek the advice of the clergy who could be regarded as authorities on the matter of what books would be suitable for a library such as that being operated by the union'.[35]

On 1 August 1947, almost three weeks before the NEC's meeting, the *Standard* had published an anonymous letter highly critical of Swift.

> Sir, in your issue of the 11th. inst. you stated that there is Marxist literature to be found in the library of the Four Provinces Houses (headquarters of the Irish Bakers Union). Again in your issue of the 18th you stated that Mr John Swift, General Secretary of the same Union (IBC & AWAU) has collaborated with the Communists in the 'Irish Democrat'. This should not be strange news for the Dublin bakers if they remember some years ago he (Mr Swift) said that 'Maynooth College was a bar to progress and culture in this country.' The Dublin Executive and the National Executive should know their Mr Swift, and, if they lack the courage to take a definite stand against him and all for which he stands, then it is high time the bakers cleared them out along with him. It was not on Mr Swift's ideals that the Bakers' Union was reorganised and built up to what it is today. As good Irishmen, democrats and, in their great majority, Catholics, it is about time they put a stop to this kind of treachery.[36]

This was but one of several anonymous letters critical of Swift which were published around that time in the Catholic and provincial press. Responding to a particular letter of this kind published in the *Standard* the NEC unanimously passed a resolution 'deprecating the cowardly attacks made on the General Secretary and placed on record their trust and absolute confidence in the General Secretary'. However, the suggestion of the National Treasurer, that Swift should raise the matter with the editor of the *Standard* was hardly likely to have been productive.[37]

The library was discussed again by the RMC at its meeting in October 1947 when Christopher Noonan, National Treasurer, referred to complaints he had received from clergymen that the library contained irreligious books and was being hired to communistic bodies. As a response to this, the RMC decided to invite Fr Edward Coyne, SJ to advise them on the matter.[38] Faced with the NEC's decision that the books be vetted by a cleric [39] and in a bid to save the library, Swift had suggested that a Jesuit undertake this task. His proposal had been made in the knowledge that a priest from that Order would have some education and would therefore be unlikely to find fault with any of the books. When Fr Coyne attended, Swift explained that in selecting the books, great care had been taken to exclude any that might be regarded as indecent, offensive or hostile to religion. He added that only books that were obtainable from public libraries in the city had been included in the library. That criterion had been suggested by Swift in the knowledge that his socialist friend, Paddy Stephenson, soon to become Dublin's chief librarian, could supply almost any work he required. The list of books complained of, which was identical to the titles published earlier by the *Standard*, was submitted to Fr Coyne. After examining this, Father Coyne said that he had read some of the books and that, in his opinion, none of them could be regarded as objectionable.

If Swift's strategy for protecting the library appeared to have been successful, there was a price to be paid. Taking advantage of the situation, Fr Coyne advised that the best way to meet such complaints or criticism might be for the union to organise lectures in Four Provinces House on Catholic social teaching by clergy approved by the Archbishop, Dr McQuaid.[40] Subsequently, at least one such lecture was held under the auspices of the Dublin No. 1 Branch, when Johnny Byrne, President of that branch, presided at an anti-communist talk by the Rev. Father Paul, OFM. A vote of thanks to the speaker was proposed by another priest, Rev. W. Deasy, CC, and seconded by T. J. M. Sheehy of the *Irish Catholic*.[41] Swift was not present at that meeting.

The complaint regarding the hiring of the library to communistic bodies probably had reference to a series of lectures held there in the autumn of 1946. These were run by *Review*, a political, literary and cultural journal of democratic opinion run by communists. Speakers at those gatherings, none of whom was a communist, were Owen Sheehy Skeffington; R. M. Fox, the author; Desmond Ryan, the historian; and Thomas Johnson.[42] The complaint may also have related to a meeting in the library of the Promethean Society at which Sheehy Skeffington presided at a lecture by a Professor Thompson on 'Marxism and Poetry'. Apparently a large group from Trinity College was present, which included some communists. After the lecture, a speaker from the floor declared that the time had come, in fact it was long overdue, when workers should band together and smash for ever their greatest obstruction to progress, i.e. the Catholic Church.[43] Whatever the reason for the complaint, the RMC decided that future lectures on political and allied subjects in the Four Provinces would only be permitted by bodies affiliated to the ITUC or the Labour Party, or approved by them.[44]

However, even these measures failed to satisfy the Catholic press or the more zealous Catholic members of the union. At the union's national delegate meeting in September 1948 it was suggested that lectures on matters of importance to Christian workers be held in Four Provinces House and that literature of a communistic nature be removed from the library. Contributing to the debate, Swift said that if books advocating communism were to be excluded it would be difficult to decide where to begin. 'Should James Connolly's books be excluded or Karl Marx's book on "Capital"?', Swift enquired. He suggested that in order to discover the 'errors of communism' it was first necessary to study the subject. A proposal by an NEC member, James Bradbury, that some form of repudiation of communist philo-sophy as a way of life be sent to the press and that the library should be left as it was, was agreed.[45]

In a discussion on the Four Provinces House controversy at the union's 1948 national delegate meeting, Swift was obliquely criticised by James Bradbury and Johnny Byrne, prominent members of the NEC. Responding to this, Swift defended the Four Provinces project and stated that rumours circulating about it were designed to undermine his position as General Secretary. He told the delegates that if they considered him an unfit person to hold office they knew the answer to that (they could remove him from office) and he would return to the bakery trade.[46] Support for Swift in the ensuing debate was led by the Tralee delegate, Michael O'Regan, followed by others such as Christy Fitzgerald, Cork Bakers' Branch, and David Condon of Dungar-van.[47] O'Regan informed the meeting that he had received several anonymous letters stating that as Swift was a communist he should be removed from the position of General Secretary. The authors of the correspondence had indicated that they would be present at the delegate meeting. Aware of this fact, O'Regan demanded that they identify themselves. Not surprisingly, that failed to elicit a response. Having expressed his contempt for those who had written the offending letters, O'Regan rejected the criticism of the Four Provinces and complimented Swift on his work as General Secretary.[48] In paying this tribute, O'Regan possibly had in mind the improved pay and working conditions which had recently been secured by the union under Swift's leadership. Indeed, the meeting had already noted that the Dublin journeyman's wage of £6. 19s. for a 44½ hour week without night work was greater than any comparable rates in Britain.[49] Moreover, the union had recently secured for its members in the Free State a second week's holidays with pay.[50] Another factor working in Swift's favour was the tension that existed between the Dublin branches and those in the provinces. Attempts by the former to dominate the national union were resented by the provincial branches. The provincial delegates were appreciative, therefore, that on becoming General Secretary in 1943, Swift had confronted this issue.

A Labour Party member of Tralee Urban District Council, Michael O'Regan was later several times mayor of that town. Although now totally blind, O'Regan is still a member of the union's NEC, a position that requires him to travel regularly to Dublin for meetings. O'Regan is also currently President of the Tralee Council of Trade Unions.

Following the 1948 delegate meeting, the controversy concerning Four Provinces House continued and, at the following month's NEC meeting, Noonan recommended that books on communism be removed from the library.[51] Referring to an earlier instruction by the RMC to report on books in respect of which complaints might be entertained.[52] Swift stated that he had prepared a list of books which might be a cause of controversy. He undertook to remove these from the library if directed to do so by the NEC. He was so directed.[53]

A general boycott of Four Provinces House was well under way at this stage. It followed the rumours and whispering campaign that there was a communist library on the premises. Many societies and clubs, for example, the nurses who made regular bookings for dances and other functions withdrew their patronage. The restaurant which had prospered from wedding breakfasts and other functions was also adversely affected.[54] Allegations that the dances were attracting prostitutes and that drugs were available in the ballroom exacerbated the situation. Without a shred of evidence, it was alleged that the drugs had been introduced by 'coloured' medical students.[55] The national executive of the Catholic Boy Scouts issued a circular to branches advising them not to hold functions at Four Provinces House. That particular boycott was raised by the Dublin No. 1 Branch with a priest who consulted the Archbishop. Surprisingly, Dr McQuaid expressed approval of the Four Provinces, following which the Catholic Boy Scouts withdrew statements made in their circular.[56]

It was around late 1948, that an unofficial union delegation, composed of officers of the Dublin No. 1 and No. 2 Branches,[57] visited Dr McQuaid to seek his advice on removing Swift from his position as General Secretary. The four officers concerned, all of them members of the union's NEC, were Christopher Noonan, National Treasurer, Johnny Byrne and Cecil Bradbury, National Trustees, and Bradbury's brother, James, an ordinary NEC member. This action was taken without the knowledge or authority of the NEC. The principal concern of the delegation was the library and allegations that it was communist. A lesser worry was the reputation that the premises had acquired for prostitutes and drugs. Having established that Swift was married with three young children, and that his work was satisfactory, Dr McQuaid told the delegation to leave Swift alone and to go home and pray for him![58]

However, with the boycott continuing, the NEC became alarmed about the risk to the union's substantial financial investment in the premises. In Swift's absence abroad on union business, some members of the NEC sold the entire library to Greene's Bookshop in Clare Street, for £600[59] (approximately £11,000 in 1991 values). This occurred sometime between November 1948 and March 1949 without the NEC's approval.

On 20 December 1948, seemingly without the NEC's authority, Four Provinces House was blessed and dedicated to Mary Immaculate by the Rev. P. Crean, CC, Spiritual Director of the Bakery Trade Branch of St Joseph's Young Priests' Society, assisted by the Rev. W. Deasy, CC. Executive members of the two Dublin branches, most of whom were also NEC members, organised and attended these ceremonies.[60] Swift did not attend. During the solemnities, he was in his office in a different part of the building awaiting an important telephone call. This was resented by his colleagues who could understand his absence from the ceremonies but not his presence in the building. The suggestion that the premises be blessed had first been mooted almost three years earlier at an RMC meeting. James Bradbury and Christopher Noonan had proposed that Catholic clergy, preferably the Archbishop of Dublin, should bless the new building. Swift's reaction to that is recorded in the union records:

> The General Secretary [Swift] said that it would be a demonstration of sectarianism to have any religious ceremonies in connection with the opening of the new premises. We have to bear in mind that the union was a non-sectarian body and that it had members of various denominations. We had to consider particularly our non Catholic members in Northern Ireland who formed a big section of the union.[61]

Support for this view had come from Swift's full-time colleague, James Coleman, the Organising Secretary, who had said that if the RMC proceeded with the proposal it would undoubtedly cause trouble in the Belfast Branch.[62] Coleman had previously been president of that branch.

Controversy concerning Four Provinces House continued within the union, or more precisely within the Dublin No. 1 Branch, and at a branch meeting held on 6 November 1949, a special committee was elected to 'investigate the running of Four Provinces House since the premises was embarked on'.[63] Under union rules this ad-hoc committee had no authority to carry out such an investigation. Matters of that nature were the prerogative of the NEC and ultimately a national delegate meeting. Two such meetings in 1946 and 1948 had already approved the accounts in respect of Four Provinces House. For these reasons the NEC was not in favour of the proposed enquiry. Nevertheless, with nothing to hide in relation to the matter, they decided to permit the investigation to proceed. The special committee set its own terms of reference which were: 'To find the reason for the high losses incurred in the running of Four Provinces House, to enquire into the losses on the sale of certain assets and to determine why an outsider could run Four Provinces at a profit whilst we could not.'[64]

That last item referred to the letting of the ballroom and library to a tenant. Published on 7 March 1950, the committee's report stated that Four Provinces House 'had always shown a very large profit'.[65] Thus, the committee had found no grounds for the assertions in its first and third terms of reference. The remaining question, the contention that, in relation to the sale of chairs, 'sufficient efforts were not made to secure the highest possible price and that these assets should have been sold by public auction'[66] was a moot point which could neither be proved nor disproved. Needless to say, the committee made no comment on the fact that the library had been sold for a song!

Generally, the report was characterised by prejudice, misrepresentation and inaccuracy. For instance, presumably due to an inability to interpret the accounts, the committee miscalculated losses and expenditure totalling almost £13,000 (approximately £231,000 in 1991 values). A detailed and critical reply to the report by the NEC, written by Swift, was issued to Dublin No. 1 Branch members who perversely adopted the report. Swift believed that for at least some of the special committee's members, the real purpose of the investigation was to discredit him. Observations by the committee on projects closely identified with Swift lend weight to this view. For instance, they described as 'a further example of wasteful expenditure' the persistence shown in publishing the union's publication the *Bakery Trade's Journal*.[67] As might be expected, they were even more dismissive of the library which, in their opinion 'should never have been started at all'.[68] Swift would also have been aware that Denis Cullen, his immediate predecessor as General Secretary, was a member of the special committee.[69] Moreover, though not obvious then, the committee's secretary, James Young, was to become General Secretary when Swift retired.

As for Four Provinces House, the ballroom and first floor of the building were let for an annual rent of £6,250 (approximately £111,000 in 1991 values) to Lorcan Bourke,[70] a member of the well-known family associated with theatre entertainment. Later, when his son-in-law, Eamonn Andrews, became involved in the tenancy in the 1960s, the premises was known to the industry as the Television Club. That tenancy lapsed in the early 1980s. In 1987, the union sold the premises to a property developer and moved to new headquarters at 12 Merrion Square. Four Provinces House was demolished by the new owner in March 1988.[71] Lost in the rubble were the murals of Frances Kelly and Nano Reid. Earlier efforts by Swift and others to save these works of art had been unfruitful.[72]

Carnival of Reaction

The opposition Swift encountered from sections of the Bakers'
Union reached its nadir during the late 1940s and early 1950s.
A contributory factor was that related to the relocation of the
union's headquarters. Hitherto, with the union and its Dublin
branches sharing premises, and the General Secretary also serving
as the Dublin No. 1 Branch president, the Dublin branches had
considered themselves to be the national union. That changed
in 1946, not only with the union's relocation, but also Swift's
resignation from the branch presidency to concentrate on his
national union duties. Resenting these changes, many Dublin
members had difficulty accepting that their branches, representing approximately one third of the total union membership,[1] did
not constitute the national union.[2]

There was also among Dublin members a widespread belief
that Denis Cullen, Swift's predecessor as branch president, had
been treated harshly by the branch executive and that Swift had
been primarily responsible for his removal from office. That,
too, was a cause of some antagonism towards Swift. However, it
was his religious and political outlook that engendered most of
the antipathy he encountered in the union. It was almost inevitable, therefore, that the resulting disharmony between sections
of the Dublin members and Swift would surface at NEC level.

The NEC tended to be a rather conservative body concerned
primarily with the material well-being of the union's members.
Apart from James Brown, its long-serving Belfast-based Pres-
ident, a Unitarian, and one or two other Catholic and Protestant
Northerners, the NEC was composed of Southern Catholics.
Some of the last mentioned held moderate socialist opinions, a
few being members of the Labour Party. Leaving aside its
Northern Ireland dimension, the Bakers' Union was otherwise

fairly typical of unions in the South and this was reflected in its policies and general outlook.

To most of the Bakers' Union's Dublin members, including those on the NEC, Swift's strong socialist and secular convictions were anathema. While difficult to believe now, a large number of the Dublin members, particularly in Boland's bakery, were convinced that Swift was the leading communist in Ireland, that he had been approved by Moscow and that in the event of a communist take-over in the South, he would be its leader! Swift's pro-Soviet views, his visit to the USSR in 1938 and the false information that he had received medical treatment in that state were the basis of these beliefs.[3]

From the 1930s, there existed in the bakery trade, effectively in the union's Dublin branches, a Catholic lay organisation, St Joseph's Young Priests' Society. Although the society originally had some connection with a religious body in France, it was actually founded in Ireland in 1895 by a Galway woman, Olivia Mary Taaffe. The principal stated aims of this institution, which still has members in the bakery trade and elsewhere, were to foster vocations to the priesthood and religious life, and help financially in the training of students for the priesthood.[4]

That the society had a wider brief than that is manifest from a statement of the Very Rev. M. Kirwan, SJ, Superior, St Francis Xavier's, Gardiner Street, Dublin. Addressing the 1939 annual general meeting of the society's Dublin United Tramway Company Branch, Fr Kirwan said that he was constantly being informed that in the depots of the Tramway Company there was a considerable amount of communistic literature such as the *Moscow News* being distributed weekly. He went on to state that he 'did not see a Catholic body such as the tramwaymen allowing communism to creep in. Things of that kind should be contradicted', he declared, 'but if they were true', he considered that 'St Joseph's Young Priests' Society was missing some of its work.'[5]

Fr Cyril Crean, spiritual director of the society's bakery trade branch, was, for all practical purposes, also spiritual director of the Bakers' Union's Dublin branches. Collections of members' contributions to the society, which in 1949 were six pence per month,[6] were the most overt activity of that body. Periodically, to boost these collections, Fr Crean would visit the larger city bakeries. The society sponsored the education of bakers' sons as priests. Among those to avail of this facility was a son of the union's NEC member, Johnny Byrne. Byrne's son, Father Damien Byrne, OP, served as President of the Conference of Major Religious Superiors of Ireland in 1980.

Apparently the bakers were diligent members of the priests' society for, at the 1935 annual general meeting of the organisation's commercial branch, it was said that: '. . . The bakery and allied trades had always been the branch's mainstay . . .'[7] Thirteen years later, in 1948, at the height of the crisis over Four Provinces House, more than a thousand members[8] of the union's Dublin No. 1 Branch, virtually the entire membership,[9] were enrolled in the priests' society.

In addition to its presence in the bakery trade, the society's other branches included tram and bus workers, railway workers, bank and insurance workers, ESB workers, civic guards, teachers and civil servants.[10] In 1944 the society claimed a membership of 40,000.[11]

St Joseph's Young Priests' Society was not the only Catholic body in the bakery trade. In Boland's bakery in Grand Canal Street, Dublin, there was the Parish Council, a group of stalwart Catholic members of the Bakers' Union whose leader, Michael (Mick) McGuinness, was known as the *Pope*. It was Swift's conviction that this body was a front, perhaps of St Joseph's Young Priests' Society, whose members promoted Catholic Action. That view, however, is not shared by Luke MacKeogh or Michael O'Halloran, two members of the Bakers' Union who worked in Boland's. While acknowledging that the Parish Council comprised long-standing Catholic members of the union, MacKeogh and O'Halloran maintained that it was not involved in any form of Catholic action. Moreover, O'Halloran, currently Education and Training Officer of the ICTU, and a recent Labour Party Lord Mayor of Dublin, contended that McGuinness's title, the *Pope*, related more to his portly appearance than to any religious fervour. What is not at issue, however, is that Swift was subjected to more hostility from Boland's bakers than from others. Nor is it disputed that McGuinness was the mentor of Johnny Byrne, who, with others, sought Dr McQuaid's advice about removing Swift from the general secretaryship of the union.[12]

That the Bakers' Union was not alone in practising what Swift regarded as sectarianism is evident from the actions of other unions at the time. For instance, at its 1952 annual meeting, the Irish Women Workers' Union, whose first General Secretary was Delia Larkin,[13] sister of James Larkin, Sen., decided to promote officially the celebration of the feast of St Brigid. The meeting unanimously passed a resolution invoking the 'powerful intercession of our Patron St Brigid to get Divine help for our collective efforts to establish the principle of justice, charity and peace in our everyday lives'.[14]

The objects of the Marine, Port and General Workers' Union (MPGWU) provide another example of what Swift found sectarian:

> The objects of the Union shall be to organise on a national basis the Port and General Workers of Ireland and to take such steps as may be necessary for the purpose of making full provision for the relations between employer and employee, and between worker and worker, from time to time, having special regard to the Christian principles as laid down in 'The Workers' Charter' and other Christian Encyclicals and teachings . . .

Retention of the last lines of these objects, following numerous revisions of the rules in recent years, could not, Swift believed, be dismissed as an oversight.[15]

A more common manifestation of what Swift considered to be sectarianism in unions was the blessing of their headquarters. In that regard Four Provinces House was not unique. When, for example, in 1954, the WUI transferred to new headquarters in Parnell Square, Dublin, the premises, formerly Vaughan's Hotel, was blessed and dedicated to the Immaculate Heart of Mary.[16] Eleven years later, in 1965, the ITGWU's new Liberty Hall in Dublin was blessed by Dr McQuaid. That particular ceremony was held on May Day, a day described by the ITGWU as the Feast of Saint Joseph the Worker![17]

Sectarianism, as defined by Swift, increased in the Holy Year, 1950, with several union delegations, including the Bakers' Union, making pilgrimages to Rome. With extraordinary insensitivity to non-Catholic members, the Bakers' Union appealed to its branches throughout the thirty-two counties for 'some contribution towards the making of a suitable presentation to Pope Pius XII'. The delegation was composed of three NEC members, James Bradbury, Christopher Noonan and Johnny Byrne, the last two representing the Dublin No. 1 Branch. At an NEC meeting, following their return to Dublin, Bradbury expressed the belief that their visit to the Pope 'would have material results for the union'![18] A more significant mission to the Vatican that year was that of the Congress of Irish Unions (CIU). Led by Frank Purcell, General Secretary of the 32-county ITGWU, the delegation was presented to the Pope by Dr McQuaid, whose gift to the Pontiff was a special bouquet of 500,000 Masses, 300,000 Holy Communions and 700,000 Rosaries of our Lady from the faithful of Dublin. No doubt His Holiness was equally pleased to receive the CIU's address of loyalty on behalf of approximately 200,000 Irish workers. Purcell's colleagues in the eternal city included William (Billy) Whelan, General Secretary, Dublin Typographical Provident Society, a forerunner of the present Irish Print Union, and Joseph Murphy of the Irish Local Government Officials' Union,[19] now the Irish Municipal, Public and Civil Trade Union or Impact. Not to be outflanked by the CIU, a nine-member WUI delegation that included its President, John Smithers, and Denis Larkin, a son of Larkin, Sen., travelled to Rome to join in the Holy Year ceremonies.[20] The trade union movement, it seemed to Swift, had indeed travelled far from the ideals of Connolly and Larkin!

These actions by the trade unions did not, of course, occur in isolation. While the fascist threat had receded by the end of World War II, the Irish Free State, or Irish Republic as it became known in 1949, remained a deeply conservative society, with the Catholic Church continuing to exercise enormous influence. Testimony of that was the Inter-Party Government's decision in 1951 to withdraw Noel Browne's Mother and Child Scheme following the hierarchy's statement that 'they must regard the scheme proposed by the Minister for Health as opposed to Catholic social teaching'.[21]

The Labour Party participated in this capitulation and in a subsequent Dáil debate, the Party leader, William Norton, who was also Tánaiste, declared:

> If this question is raised as one in which the Bishops are to be on one side and the Government on the other side, I

say, on behalf of the Government, that issue is not going to arise in this country. This Government will not travel that road . . . There will be no flouting of the authority of the Bishops in the matter of Catholic social or Catholic moral teaching.[22]

In his resignation speech following the government's withdrawal of the Mother and Child Scheme, Noel Browne, himself, who had been a member of the republican Party, Clann na Poblachta, stated: 'I as a Catholic accept unequivocally and unreservedly the view of the Hierarchy on this matter.'[23]

Swift had some difficulty with this statement. To say the least, he found it a profoundly disappointing conclusion to Browne's courageous attempt to introduce an important health provision. He had difficulty, too, accepting the inference in Browne's argument that, while the scheme conflicted with Catholic social teaching, it was not opposed to Catholic moral teaching.[24] Was there an implication here, Swift wondered, that Browne would have abandoned the scheme had it conflicted with Catholic moral teaching? If so, Swift would have found that incompatible with republicanism as well as socialism. None of this, however, lessened his admiration for Browne's outstanding contribution to Irish political life. Paradoxically, for Swift, the most important element of that contribution had been Browne's persistent campaign for a socialist and pluralist society.

Another example of Catholic Church influence was manifest in 1950, when, with complete disregard for non-Catholic citizens and seemingly without a murmur from the politicians, the state-owned Radio Éireann commenced daily broadcasts of the *Angelus*.[25] This sectarianism, later extended to the state's television service, continues to the present day.

Presumably the intense Catholic ethos of the country explains the bizarre statement made by Alderman Robert Briscoe, TD at a meeting of Dublin Corporation in January 1950. After a resolution had been passed tendering the corporation's and the citizens' filial homage and devotion to His Holiness on the occasion of the opening of Holy Year, Briscoe, a member of the Jewish community, declared that the Republic was a Catholic country and the more Catholic the people became the more he would like it![26]

These events illustrate the difficulties that confronted those aspiring to a socialist and secular state. Socialists had also to contend with the consequences of the Cold War that had developed between East and West. They were not helped by the pro-Western and anti-socialist reporting of that war in the national media. May Day 1949 was an example of the challenge faced by socialists and secularists. In Dublin that day, 150,000 participated in a demonstration, not a socialist celebration of international working-class solidarity, but 'to protest against the imprisonment of Cardinal Mindszenty and Archbishop Stepinac and the persecution of the Church in Eastern Europe'. According to contemporary reports, the immense throng included large contingents of trade unionists and representatives of many organisations. This resolution, proposed by the Ceann Comhairle of the Dáil and seconded by the Lord Mayor, was carried by acclamation:

> We the citizens of Dublin, assembled in a vast meeting of protest in our capital city, humbly desire to express our profound sympathy with your Holiness and to record, without equivocation, our detestation of the cruel tyranny of atheistic communism which has so inhumanly persecuted the Catholics of Eastern Europe. In particular, we abhor the barbarous injustice done to Archbishop Stepinac, and to his Eminence Cardinal Mindszenty. We wish to avail of this opportunity to assure your Holiness of our steadfast loyalty to the teachings of our holy faith in face of the present menace of atheistic communism throughout the world.[27]

How selective these protesters were! How silent they had been when millions of Jews, socialists, communists and others had been exterminated by the fascists! They were silent again when members of the Irish Workers' League (IWL), a forerunner of the present Communist Party of Ireland, were being persecuted in Dublin during the early 1950s.

Joe Deasy[28] was among a small group of IWL members who, from the late 1940s to the early 1950s, were active in the Inchicore/Ballyfermot Co-operative Society, a non-political, non-sectarian body, whose members and committee held various political and religious beliefs. By 1951, with a membership of approximately 700, the society was running its own shops in Inchicore and Ballyfermot. So successful was the Ballyfermot co-op during its first year of operation that it provoked a campaign by local reactionaries, led by local Catholic clergy, to wreck the society.

An open-air public meeting propagating the co-operative concept was disrupted by these forces simply because some of the members of the co-op's management committee were associated with the IWL. The committee was then led to believe that the local clergy were prepared to withdraw their objections to the society if the IWL members resigned their official positions. Despite this injustice and the years of work they had contributed to the organisation, the IWL members offered to resign. Even that was insufficient for the clergy and their allies; the society was denounced from the pulpits of churches in Inchicore and Ballyfermot.

After three members of the society's management committee had been prevailed upon to resign, a general meeting of the remaining members was held. In an attempt to placate the clergy and protect the society, IWL members declined nominations to the committee. Despite this, the attacks continued and the new committee was also denounced from the pulpits. Eventually, the hostility inspired by the local clergy and shopkeepers, some of the latter being in competition with the society's grocery store, forced the closure of the co-op's shops. Supporting that vicious campaign unscrupulously were sections of the national and Catholic press. Worst of all was the *Standard*. Apart from the half truths, the smears and the innuendoes, blatant lies were told against the society, the principal one being its portrayal as a 'communist plot', a 'cover' for other activities.[29]

The *Standard* also ran a relentless campaign of persecution against the IWL members in 1953. Influenced, no doubt, by McCarthyism in America, and presumably to encourage victimisation of IWL members by their employers, this Catholic weekly published the names and, in some instances, the photographs, of a number of league members. In this sinister campaign questions addressed to individual IWL members appeared in the *Standard*. Frank Edwards, a schoolteacher, was asked, for example: 'In your spare time do you teach the fundamentals of communist ideology to your recruits in Dublin? Did you organise Irish Communistic Relief for the Spanish Reds?' Similarly, Geoffrey Palmer, then a salesman in Walpole's in Suffolk Street, was questioned: 'Do you, during your leisure hours, put your undoubted qualities of salesmanship into good use in New Books?' (the IWL's Dublin Bookshop) As Robin Tweedy discovered, even actions in the privacy of one's home were not immune from this kind of intimidation: 'When the visiting country delegates of the Irish Workers' League came to Dublin last week did some of them, in fact, hold a meeting in your private home?', the *Standard* enquired.[30]

The following year, 1954, a new campaign against the IWL and its General Secretary, Michael O'Riordan, was launched by the *Standard*. O'Riordan was a candidate of the league in the general election that year, a development not welcomed by the *Standard*'s special representative:

> . . . Mr O'Riordan belongs to what is in fact the Irish Communist Party. Therefore, he must believe in the mass extermination of our clergy, in forced labour camps, in the complete absorption of the individual, not alone by the state but by the Party. He is endeavouring to use freedom, dearly bought, to end freedom of conscience, freedom of speech, freedom of the press . . .[31]

Throughout the Dublin South West constituency, the *Standard*'s posters proclaiming 'You Can't Vote for the Red O'Riordan' were rendered counter-productive by O'Riordan's supporters who altered them to read, 'You Can Vote for the Red O'Riordan'. A statement by the Catholic Archbishop of Dublin read in the churches in the constituency warned that Catholics might not vote for any candidate supported by the IWL. Turning the tables on the *Standard* and the Church, the IWL placed an advertisement in a Dublin evening paper quoting the Most Rev. B. G. Sheil, D.D., Catholic Bishop of Chicago, on anti-communism: 'In this day and age anti-communism is sometimes a scoundrel's first defence.' O'Riordan's vote of 375 alarmed the *Standard* and led to this warning for its readers: ' . . . The number of first preference votes cast for Mr O'Riordan gives us an accurate indication of the number of Communists or Communist sympathisers who live in just one constituency. We must, all of us, remain alert to the danger . . .'[32]

Although not a member of the IWL, Swift, of course, as a socialist, was sympathetic to that organisation. On friendly terms with many IWL members including Deasy, Edwards, Palmer, Tweedy and O'Riordan, Swift followed the campaigns against that body with much interest. He was not very active in the Labour Party then on account of his trade union responsibilities, which extended beyond the Bakers' Union to the ITUC, of which he was Treasurer, and the International Union of Food and Allied Workers' Associations. Nevertheless he had his own political battles to fight in the trade union movement. It was in the Bakers' Union that the communist question arose once again in 1954. At the union's national delegate meeting that year, the following addendum to rule XII(b) was carried: 'Any member who is a member of the Communist Party shall be ineligible to be a delegate to Delegate Meetings, or to be a candidate for any position in Head Office . . .'[33] This motion was designed specifically for Swift. A further addendum to the same rule was carried at the union's next national delegate meeting in 1956: 'Any fraternal delegate who is a member of the Communist Party shall not be eligible to attend the Delegate Meeting . . .'[34]

Significantly, both motions were proposed and seconded by Swift's main adversaries, the Dublin NEC members, Johnny Byrne and James Bradbury.[35] Although the second motion, like the first, was carried, it provoked opposition from several delegates including John Cullinane, Cork Confectionery Branch; Jimmy Bennett, Mullingar Branch; and Michael O'Regan, Tralee Branch. Swift expressed the view that the motion was ill advised. Referring to the union's affiliation to the ITUC, he said that the union sent delegates to the annual conferences of that organisation and to the conferences of the English/Welsh and Scottish Bakers' Unions. Mentioning that the Irish Bakers' Union was well aware that communists were present at those conferences, Swift explained that they were not there as communists, but as representatives of their unions. Continuing, he asked how the union was going to implement the motion and how would the union be assured that delegates coming to the conference from different bodies were not communists. 'The motion was dictatorial', he said.[36]

The adoption of the second motion led the union into a farcical position. Three months after the delegate meeting, two delegates of the union, Johnny Byrne and John Power, attended the Scottish Bakers' Union's delegate conference in Prestwick. On arrival in Scotland they learnt that Russian delegates, guests of the Scottish TUC, would be present. Interpreting the second resolution rather liberally, the Irish delegates decided to boycott the conference session, at which the Russians would be present, and an official dinner for the Russians. Yet, following a special plea from the General Secretary of the Scottish Bakers' Union, Byrne and Power subsequently decided to attend a civic reception for all delegates given by the Provost and Council of Prestwick. Quite a fuss was created by the absence of the Irish from the conference session, particularly when the local Scottish press took up the story.

At a subsequent meeting of the Bakers' Union's NEC, Cullinane asked Byrne and Power if their objection had been that the delegates in question were Russians or communists, to which Byrne replied, 'communists'. After establishing that at least three Scottish communists had been present, Cullinane said he could see no sense in objecting to a Russian and not a Scottish communist. There was no answer to that! As a solution to their dilemma, the NEC adopted Swift's suggestion that in the event of communists advocating communism at such conferences in the future, delegates of the Irish Bakers' Union should protest, the form of protest to be left to the delegates' discretion. In proposing this, Swift was well aware that there was little chance of communists advocating their ideology at assemblies of that kind.[37]

The anti-communist rules of the Bakers' Union were deleted entirely in 1980, thirteen years after Swift's retirement from office.[38] It was also after his retirement that the first Communist Party member was elected to the union's NEC.

17

Extending Horizons

Several factors influenced Swift's voluntary retirement from the ITUC's executive in July 1958.[1] Two months earlier, at the age of sixty-one, he had suffered from several severe nose haemorrhages, caused, according to his doctor, by tension from overwork. As a result he had been, for almost a fortnight, a patient in Dublin's Royal Victoria Eye and Ear Hospital. His indisposition had prevented him from attending that year's biennial national delegate meeting of the Bakers' Union. But, quite apart from his ailment, he had been finding it increasingly difficult to discharge his responsibilities to the union as well as attending to his ITUC duties. Membership of the Congress's executive entailed participating in, not only the deliberations of that forum, but several of its subcommittees.

A further consideration was his increasing involvement in the International Union of Food and Allied Workers' Associations (IUF). It will be recalled that, following the prompting by Swift and the Bakery Trade's Social Club, the 1936 national delegate conference of the Bakers' Union had instructed the NEC to take steps to affiliate to the international body, which was then known as the International Federation of Food and Drink Workers.[2] On his extended European trip two years later, Swift had visited the IUF's Zurich headquarters to enquire about affiliating procedures. Later, in 1939, the Bakers' Union's application was accepted by the international body,[3] and the union was represented at its first IUF conference that year when James Brown, President, and Swift attended an International Bakery Workers' Conference in Zurich.[4]

Overshadowing that meeting which heard reports from underground German and Spanish delegates was the impending World War II, which was to disrupt greatly the work of the IUF.

However, it was agreed that during the war delegates from neutral countries would maintain contacts. This fell principally to the organisation's Swiss President, Herman Leuenberger, and Swift, who corresponded with each other throughout the war. Through his clandestine visits to Nazi Germany, Leuenberger, a Labour member of the Swiss parliament and subsequently President of the Swiss TUC, was also in touch with underground German trade union leaders.[5] Towards the end of the war Leuenberger appointed Swift and two others to draft a new constitution for the IUF. Colleagues of Swift's on the drafting committee were Karl Mantler, an Austrian ex-internee of Auschwitz and Lo Vitte, a Dutchman.[6]

Before the war ended Leuenberger and Swift met in London to prepare for the IUF's revival. At that meeting, held in the English/Welsh Bakers' Union's headquarters, were trade union leaders in exile from the Nazis. Absent, alas, were colleagues of Swift's who had been tortured and exterminated in fascist concentration camps, and elsewhere, in defence of trade unionism. At the first post-war conference of the IUF held in Copenhagen in 1946,[7] Swift and Brown again represented the Bakers' Union,[8] and Swift, Karl Mantler and Lo Vitte were among those elected to the IUF's management committee.[9]

In 1955, Swift was elected to the IUF's executive committee,[10] comprising a president and a number of vice-presidents representing the principal language groups of the constituent bodies. Initially, these were English, French, German, Scandinavian and Spanish, the last mentioned serving refugees resident in France since the Spanish Civil War. Swift, of course, was a vice-president representing the English language group. A second English language group was introduced later to cater solely for the American unions.

Among the functions of the IUF was the interchange of information on working conditions in the food and allied industries of the various countries. Also occupying that organisation, particularly after World War II, were many new challenges emanating from the proliferation of trans-national companies. Aside from such central considerations, it was Swift's aim to combat anti-Sovietism in the IUF and encourage links between that body and the Soviet trade unions. These were ambitious objectives in the Cold War period, particularly after the imposition by the IUF of a ban on relations between its affiliates and unions in the socialist countries. Neither the Scottish nor the Irish Bakers' Unions were penalised, however, for defying the ban.[11]

In the case of the Irish, that occurred in 1963 when Swift led a three-person delegation to the USSR.[12] Arranged by Swift through the Soviet Food Workers' Union, hosts of the Bakers' Union, this was the first trade union mission from the Irish Republic to the USSR since that of the Dublin Trade Union Council in 1929.[13] Opposition to accepting the Soviet invitation was expressed on the Bakers' Union's executive. Two executive members, both prominently involved in the Labour Party, opposed the visit, one of them contending that there was nothing to be learned in Russia to warrant the sending of representatives to that state.[14] The executive's decision to send a delegation was condemned in anonymous press correspondence.[15] Taking cognisance of that, the Wexford No. 1 Branch of the union passed a resolution criticising the NEC's action.[16] There is no evidence of further opposition within the union to the Soviet trip.

The hospitality of the Soviet Food Workers' Union was reciprocated in April 1967 when, again on Swift's initiative, a delegation from that body visited Ireland as guests of the Irish Bakers' Union.[17] By the end of that year, exchange visits between Soviet trade unions and the ICTU, the ITGWU and the WUI had been initiated.[18] Nowadays, such contacts are commonplace and relations between the Irish and Soviet trade union movements have been formalised in an agreement, signed in 1988, between the ICTU and its Soviet counterpart, the All Union Central Committee of Trade Unions.[19]

Membership of the IUF's executive involved Swift in a great deal of foreign travel. Although associated more with the Soviet Union, having journeyed to that country on seven occasions, Swift was an equally frequent visitor to the US. On these visits he represented either the Bakers' Union or the IUF, usually the latter, at trade union conferences, or conventions as they are known in the US. Among the conventions he attended were those of the American Bakery Workers' Union, the American Brewery Workers' Union and the Amalgamated Meat Cutters and Butcher Workmen.[20]

Of the American union conventions he attended, Swift found the Amalgamated Meat Cutters and Butcher Workmen to be the most advanced politically. Its chief official, Patrick Emmet Gorman, supported the American Socialist Party and was President of the Eugene Debs Foundation. Radical, particularly by American standards, Gorman had a long history of open and energetic disagreement with the leadership of the American Federation of Labour—Congress of Industrial Organisations (AFL–CIO), the American congress of trade unions. Among the issues he opposed were the purging of communists from organised labour, the anti-communist witchhunt of Senator Joe McCarthy in the 1950s and American action in Vietnam. Gorman was also a tireless campaigner on behalf of the rights of women, minorities and the handicapped. It has been claimed that Gorman's attitude cost him a position on the executive council of the AFL–CIO. Like Swift, with whom he became a close friend, Pat Gorman was a vice-president of the IUF. The son of Irish immigrants, he was proud of his ancestry and visited Ireland several times. He died in Chicago in 1980 at the age of eighty-seven.[21]

Swift's friendship with Gorman contrasted with his encounter with another American union official. On a visit to Washington DC to attend a meeting of the IUF's executive, Swift and some colleagues were invited to visit the AFL–CIO's headquarters, situated close to the White House. Following a brief interview with George Meaney, then the AFL–CIO's President, Swift was directed to the office of an official he believed to be on the staff of the AFL–CIO. Of special interest to this official, known as Andy McClelland, was the extent to which left-wing influences were affecting the trade unions in Ireland. Suspicious of such an unsubtle line of enquiry, Swift left McClelland no better informed on the matter. Nor was he surprised to learn later that McClelland was a CIA agent, well known as such by leaders of the American unions. He had previously been an official of the Amalgamated Meat Cutters and Butcher Workmen's Union but, as Swift observed, 'That was no reflection on Pat Gorman.'[22]

During his American visit in 1956 to attend a bakery workers' union convention in San Francisco, Swift encountered some unorthodox theology. Each day of the week-long convention was opened with a non-denominational prayer or invocation, calling on God to bless the proceedings. Reciting these prayers were preachers of various persuasions, representing the main religions of the members. Thus, the first day's blessing by a Jesuit priest was followed on subsequent days by a Jewish rabbi, a Mormon elder and an Episcopalian minister. Short of preachers on the final day, a lay preacher from among the delegates was invited to officiate. Coming from a union branch in the southern, Bible-belt part of the country, his preaching style was reminiscent of other lay preachers heard earlier by Swift at Belfast's Custom House and in London's Hyde Park. Later that day, this lay preacher approached him to comment on some aspect of Swift's fraternal address to the convention. He enquired of Swift how he and his religion might fare in Ireland, declaring that from what he had heard, Ireland was a priest-ridden country. Swift was more interested in ascertaining the preacher's particular sect and while probing this matter his acquaintance suddenly pronounced 'You know the Holy Ghost—he's a phony'! Swift considered this a strange piece of theology and on querying the matter further his acquaintance declared: 'There are only two Divine persons: God the Father and God the Son. The Holy Ghost is an invention of the priests to justify themselves'![23]

An interest of Swift's in visiting the US was to acquaint himself with the attitude of the minority peoples, particularly the Black people, to white domination. Before his visits, he had conceived the Black people in America as being in all but open rebellion against their White masters and exploiters. But, he altered that view as he gradually became acquainted with how Blacks were faring and acting in the unions. At the conventions he attended, he met many Blacks on the unions' executive committees and amongst the rank and file. He was enlightened but disheartened by his discussions with them concerning the ideas and ideals which inspired their membership of the union: 'Pondering these experiences, I came to speculating that the Whites and Blacks in America had been staring one another so long they had come to sharing identical vision. That vision was formulating itself in convention resolutions, and, it was hoped, in the busier clatter of the supermarkets' checking-out machines.'[24]

This brings us to the question of Swift's impressions of Americans generally, impressions formed on his first visit to that country and confirmed in subsequent visits. He found the Americans to be an extremely hospitable people. While attending the 1956 Bakers' Union's convention in San Francisco, he was invited to the home of a local delegate. There he spent some hours with this man and his wife and their three sons, the eldest being about twelve. From the start, the children participated in the conversation, questioning Swift in a most adult fashion about the type of cars and television that were available in Ireland, subjects on which Swift had little interest and even less knowledge. Undaunted by his ignorance of such matters, the children continued questioning him in this vein, displaying knowledge as well as curiosity in these technological subjects. Reflecting on this experience later, Swift declared:

> Their [the children's] whole bearing was so assured and adult, I was given to speculate if the Americans hadn't abolished childhood, abolished it as a waste of valuable time. Their expertise had succeeded in creating instant adulthood, spontaneous knowledge and know-how. At the same time I thought there was something of naivety, something suggesting childishness in perhaps all Americans, whatever their age, something that could be charming or captivating. This made for easy and friendly social converse. But was naivety a virtue or asset in politics?[25]

With regard to American society generally, Swift found little that was admirable in this citadel of capitalism, where virtually everything had a price and nothing was valued more than the almighty dollar.

If aspects of American society were repugnant to Swift, he found much that was commendable in another capitalist country, the state of Israel. It was to preside at an IUF management committee meeting that brought him there in 1965. He was impressed greatly by the conversion of large desert areas into fertile land, yielding such crops as grapes, oranges, grapefruit and cotton. Equally impressive to him were the experiments in co-operative collectives and small holder co-operatives, kibbutzim and moshavim, respectively, run by subsidiaries of the Histadrut, the Federation of Labour in Israel, and counterpart of the Irish Congress of Trade Unions. At the time of Swift's visit, these co-operatives constituted a significant sector of Israel's economy, contributing two-thirds of the value of national agricultural output. As well as that, more than 550 kibbutzim and moshavim villages supported directly a population of 160,000.

Through its subsidiaries, the Histadrut was involved in many other important spheres of economic activity. Indeed, in 1965, a quarter of Israel's industrial output was being produced in enterprises owned by the Histadrut. Metal, cement, glass, plastics, chemicals, rubber, timber products and electrical equipment were among the produce of subsidiaries of this trade union centre. The Histadrut's building and public works enterprise was responsible for more that 40 per cent of all construction in Israel. Most of the buses and freight lorries were run by its co-operatives while another of its agencies had a controlling interest in the country's civil aviation and merchant shipping. The Histadrut had, among many other ventures, its banking and insurance enterprises as well as trading and consumer co-operatives.[26] Impressed though Swift undoubtedly was with these projects, he nevertheless concluded that the kibbutzim were too primitive a form of socialism to withstand the spread of American monopoly capitalism.[27]

On the Palestinian question, Swift had some sympathy with the Jews as well as the Arabs. Like many others, he empathised with the Jews on account of their horrendous treatment by the Nazis. His visit to Israel in 1965 inspired him to write sympathetically about that country.[28] However, following the 1967 Six-Day War, his attitude to Israel modified. Israel's subsequent occupation of vast areas of neighbouring Arab states, in which new Jewish settlements were established, was opposed by Swift, as was the ill-treatment of Arabs living under Israeli control. Against that, however, he had reservations about the Arab position, believing that Israel, too, had rights, and that the Arabs had been as intransigent as the Jews in failing to reconcile their differences. He was in no doubt that given the choice of residing in a fundamentalist Moslem state or a secular Israel, he would choose the latter.

Did Swift see any solution to this most intractable of Middle East disputes? One possibility, he believed, that could form the nucleus of a settlement, would involve Israel's withdrawal from territories occupied since 1967, recognition by the Arab states of Israel's right to exist, and the creation, outside Israel, of a new Palestinian state. Such an arrangement, Swift believed, would have to be guaranteed by the United Nations.

As an executive member of the IUF, Swift made it a practice to address international conferences in the languages of the host countries. Accordingly, his grasp of foreign languages, acquired through self-education, was an important asset. Fairly fluent in French and German, he could also converse in Italian, Spanish, Danish, Norwegian, Swedish and Russian. With assistance from Professor Jacob Weingreen, his old Jewish friend, he learnt sufficient Hebrew to address the IUF's management committee meeting in Israel, in 1965.

Many years earlier, in 1948, at the German Foodworkers' Union's conference in Hamburg, Swift's facility with foreign languages almost provoked an incident. With representatives present from nearly all the IUF's affiliates, the President of the host union, Hans Nätscher,[29] yet another Nazi concentration camp victim, explained that, due to time constraints, only German-speaking delegates would be permitted to address the conference. While enabling Swift to speak, this ruling precluded the British delegates, some of whom were demonstrably incensed.

A more substantial grievance of the British related to Swift's executive position in the IUF. Conscious that, with a membership of less than 6,000, the Irish Bakers' Union was by far the smallest of the seven Irish or British organisations linked to the international body, some of the British unions resented Swift's exalted position, being especially aggrieved that he held the vice-presidency of its English-language group. Aside from the American unions, this group represented affiliated bodies throughout the English-speaking world, chiefly in colonies or former colonies of the British.[30]

How then, against such a background, and for more than twenty years, did Swift retain an executive position in the IUF? While ability must certainly have been a consideration, his manifest interest in the organisation, together with his facility with foreign languages, a facility not shared by his British colleagues, were arguably more decisive factors.

Swift was elected president of the IUF at its fourteenth triennial congress in Stockholm in May 1964.[31] Three years later, in Dublin's Liberty Hall, he presided at the IUF's fifteenth congress. By then, the IUF represented more than 1,600,000 members in sixty countries.[32] The Dublin congress was officially opened by the Taoiseach, Jack Lynch, in the presence of Dr Patrick Hillery,

Minister for Labour, the city's Lord Mayor, Eugene Timmons, TD and representatives of the labour movement, including the Labour Party TDs, Michael Mullen and Michael O'Leary; and John Conroy, President of the ITGWU.[33] At the end of that fifteenth congress, Swift retired from the IUF.[34] He was then seventy.

18

A Man's A Man for A' That!

By the mid-1960s, Swift was married with three grown-up children. He had met his future wife in 1940, on April Fool's Day! Swift had gone to Howth to obtain granite rocks for the garden of his friends and landlord, the Conroys. After placing the granite in a sack he entered a café opposite the harbour. Not long afterwards, two women, one of whom he was attracted to, arrived and sat at a nearby table. There followed an incident in the café when the waitress carrying hot water to Swift's table stumbled on some steps. When it had been established that she was uninjured, the café resounded to relieved laughter. Taking advantage of the ensuing relaxed atmosphere, Swift offered his fresh supply of water to the women. They were Harriet Hendy, 'an attractive young woman', and her friend, 'a matronly type', whose surname was Hickey. Both were enjoying a day's outing from their nursing duties in Dublin. A conversation developed between Swift and the women, the three of them chatting about various matters, including his foreign travel experiences. Nurse Hickey enquired if he had ever visited Lourdes!

Surely only romance could explain their subsequent uncharacteristic behaviour? Nurse Hickey began to read the cups and Swift, normally one to scorn such nonsense, was inveigled into participating. When told he would meet a fair-haired woman, he retorted, 'I hope so!' In an equally untypical act, the fair-haired Harriet, a non-smoker, left the café to buy herself cigarettes and matches! On her return she and her friend bade him goodbye before leaving to stroll down the pier. In due course, Swift took the same route, waving to his new acquaintances when they came into sight. Later still, he sat down beside them. There was more chatting before Harriet and her friend accepted his invitation to partake of some refreshments. On their return to the same café, the women enjoyed ice-cream while John drank some wine. Before finally parting, John invited Harriet to the opera. Two days later they attended the Dublin Grand Opera Society's performance of Verdi's *Rigoletto* in the Gaiety Theatre. Backstage, during the interval, Harriet was introduced to Peter Flanagan,[1] Swift's friend and a member of the opera chorus. Six weeks after they first met John and Harriet became engaged, and sixteen months later, on 26 September 1941, they got married. John was forty-five[2] and Harriet thirty.

Swift's late marriage was not due to any lack of faith in that institution or interest in women. Rather, it derived from his determination not to marry in a religious ceremony or raise children in a particular religion. To the mainly Catholic women with whom he had had relationships, his position on these questions had been unacceptable. There had, however, been exceptions to that where Swift's friendship with women had ended for other reasons. For example, religion had not been an impediment in his relationship with Inge Schine, the German woman whom he had met in 1938 on his journey to Austria. Like Swift, Inge Schine was non-religious, but she was a Nazi sympathiser, and it was her politics that he had found objectionable. Such then had been his tribulations with the opposite sex when he first met Harriet.

Though a member of the Church of Ireland, Harriet consented to marry John in a non-religious ceremony. Their children, they decided, would be raised in a free-thought atmosphere, free of instruction in a particular religion and at liberty to determine their religious positions as adults. When making his will, a decade later, in 1951, Swift inserted a provision to that effect: 'I . . . request that my children shall not be taught or brought up in any sectarian religion until they shall attain the age of 15 years and at that age they shall then be free to choose their religion or none if they so desire.' To avoid the intolerance that prevailed in the South, John and Harriet's civil marriage ceremony was held in Lurgan, Co. Armagh, in the registrar's private residence. They were facilitated in this by distant family connections of John's called Magill, who lived in that town. Witnesses at the wedding ceremony, a quiet affair attended by less than ten, were John's aunt, Sarah Millar, and Dr Arthur Darley, medical officer of the Bakers' Union's Dublin No. 1 Branch. Swift had attended musical evenings in Darley's home after being introduced to him by Peadar O'Donnell. Darley and O'Donnell had become acquainted through their mothers, both Donegal women. Darley's father, also called Arthur, was a celebrated violinist and principal of Dublin's Municipal School of Music. Swift knew him, too, through the Bakers' Union's sponsorship of members' children attending the school.

Harriet was born on 14 August 1911 in her parents' home, 'Ladytown', situated about two miles beyond Naas, Co. Kildare, off the Newbridge road. She was the third of eight children, five girls and three boys, of John and Harriet Hendy who were farmers. When she was five, the family moved their home to 'Spring Lodge', a few miles outside Athy, where they had a 250-acre farm. In 1933, at the age of 22, Harriet left home to work as a nurse in the Royal Hospital for Incurables (now the Royal Hospital) in Donnybrook. She left there after four years to take up a similar post in a private nursing home in Maidstone, Kent. Homesick, she returned to Dublin after nine months, at the end of 1937, and worked in a succession of private nursing homes up to the time of her marriage. She was then residing with family friends called McNamara, at 66 Lower Leeson Street, Dublin.

Harriet, an affectionate and considerate person, loved children and had a natural way with them. For much of her married life she suffered badly from asthma and chronic rheumatoid arthritis. Yet, when rearing her children, she thought nothing of losing a night's sleep to care for family members who were ill. Typically, when in her early seventies, she was the constant companion of her friend and neighbour who was dying of cancer for more than a year. Harriet, like John, was gregarious and had a good sense of humour. She liked nothing better than a chat, being almost as much at ease with strangers as in the company of friends. Topics of conversation that interested her most were family related matters. Harriet was not a socialist, nor did she share John's other philosophical interests.

After their marriage, John and Harriet's first home was a terraced house at 131 Celtic Park Avenue, Donnycarney. They left there about the beginning of 1947 after Harriet had suffered severe asthma attacks which her doctor attributed partly to the relatively high altitude of the district. A different problem awaited them at their second residence, another terraced house at 213

Upper Rathmines Road, where a couple of family members narrowly escaped serious injury when some ceilings collapsed. Consequently, in March 1948, after about only a year in Rathmines, the family moved again, this time to a new bungalow situated across the end of a cul-de-sac, at 54 Westbrook Road, Dundrum.

John and Harriet had three children, Alice, John, the present writer, and Patrick (Grosvenor), born respectively in 1942, 1945 and 1947. Grosvenor is called after a friend of John's, Dr Grosvenor Lowry, an American of old English stock, more English than American in outlook, who was educated in the Sorbonne in Paris. Lowry was a medical officer during World War I, quartered at the American base in Derry. So impressed had he been with a visit to Dublin at the time that he decided to settle there on his discharge from the American Army. John was introduced to Lowry by his first cousin, John Swift, whose daughter, Gladys, first suggested that the new arrival be called after Lowry.

Alice, Grosvenor and I were sent to school at what was then probably the Republic's only non-denominational national school. Known as the Damer, it was run by, and adjacent to the Unitarian Church, 112 St Stephen's Green West. Before the Damer's closure in 1954, Alice won a scholarship from there to Wesley College, then located in St Stephen's Green South. Accompanied by Harriet and Alice, John went to see the Rev. Gerald Myles, headmaster of this Methodist secondary school, to secure an assurance that religious education would not be imposed on his daughter. Alice, however, expressed an interest in participating in this aspect of school life and it was agreed to try that for a month. In the event, during her five years in Wesley, Alice attended the daily morning service in the college chapel and a couple of weekly scripture classes.

Grosvenor and I completed our primary education in Church of Ireland national schools where the main feature of religious education was Old Testament biblical stories. For secondary education I was sent to St Andrew's College, a Presbyterian establishment, then situated on Clyde Road, Ballsbridge, while Grosvenor attended the non-denominational Dalton School at Leinster Road, Rathmines. As with Alice in Wesley, John visited the headmaster of St Andrew's, Mr P. J. Southgate, and got an undertaking that I would not participate in religious education classes. John and Harriet did agree, however, that I would attend a brief morning prayer at assembly. Exemption from religious education gave me an unexpected advantage over most of my schoolmates. For forty minutes weekly, the two forms comprising my school year were redivided into religious instruction classes run by the Church of Ireland and the Presbyterian Church. Much to the envy of my Protestant fellow pupils, this left three Jewish boys and me free to play football in the school yard, overlooked by at least one of the religious education classes.

Classical music, played on gramophone and on radio, or wireless as it was then known, was an important feature of life in our home. It was mostly played informally and without obligation to listen. On only one occasion can I remember John asking us to leave our toys and listen to some music, a Sunday afternoon BBC symphony concert. All three children were enrolled in piano classes and while Alice and Grosvenor discontinued after a short period, I struggled through the examinations of the eight grades of the Associated Board of the Royal Schools of Music, London. My teacher in the Municipal School of Music, was the gifted but self-effacing Gerard Shanahan, with whom I became friends, and from whom I learnt something about art generally. He had no interest in material things beyond the absolute necessities of life. There was no time limit on my piano classes which could be continued at his home. Nor were extra fees expected for this dedication. John was keenly interested in my musical education, cherishing hopes of my becoming a concert pianist, perhaps an unfulfilled ambition of his own. His disappointment with my failure to succeed in this field was magnified by the success of three of my contemporaries, the international celebrities, John O'Conor, Míceál O'Rourke and Philip Martin. While music was a passion of John's he also had a wide knowledge and appreciation of literature and the visual arts. Seldom would he read less than a book a week, usually on loan from Dundrum Public Library. Subjects, reflecting his wide interest, were diverse and included both fiction and non-fiction and poetry as well as prose. Among the authors he liked best in literature were Shakespeare, Gogol, Zola, Maupassant, Wilde and Shaw; Burns and Byron being his favourite poets. In painting he admired the work of the great masters of the Italian, Spanish, French, Flemish and English schools. Where sculpture was concerned, the work that most impressed him was that by Rodin.

Walking was another great pastime of his. Almost every Saturday before he was married he walked from the city to Dun Laoghaire, where he bathed in the public baths. His rambles during the 1950s and 1960s, usually accompanied by his children, were mostly in the foothills of the Three Rock and Kilmashogue mountains, beyond the villages of Dundrum and Rathfarnham. The route most often taken was a six-mile trek from our Dundrum home to the then virtually unbuilt Ballinteer area. On the outward journey, often on a Sunday afternoon, there would be a stop in Dundrum village for sweets or ice-cream. Turning right into Ballinteer Road, on leaving the village, we would glimpse the Pye factory, employing up to one thousand workers. In earlier years, Peadar O'Donnell and Frank Edwards had worked for that firm, Edwards being sacked for attempting to organise a trade union.[3] From roughly the half-way point on Ballinteer Road we would walk the loop formed by Ballinteer Avenue, Grange Road and Harold's Grange Road and the upper part of Ballinteer Road, before returning home via Dundrum. With the dearth of footpaths for much of our ramble, we would be obliged to walk on the roads. That was feasible then as cars, mostly black in colour, were few in number. On some occasions we would return from Ballinteer by bus. During the soccer season there could be a long wait for a bus, delayed by the throngs leaving Shamrock Rovers' ground in Milltown. At that time soccer was a very popular spectator sport in Dublin.

Soccer was not a sport that interested John, though he preferred it to rugby which he disliked as much for the snob element it attracted as for what he regarded as the tomfoolery of the game itself, especially the scrums. In his youth he had followed Gaelic football in Dundalk and had travelled to Croke Park several times to see Louth play. In the year he came to Dublin, 1912, Louth had won the All-Ireland final, having qualified for the finals in two of the preceding three years. Although Swift continued to follow the game for a while in Dublin he found intolerable the sectarianism of the GAA. At Croke Park, for instance, before the commencement of a match, the Artane Boys' Band would play *Faith of Our Fathers*. Furthermore, the game would usually be started by a priest throwing in the ball. Clerics were also to be found in leading committee positions at club and county level. Apart from all that, he was not keen on field games, preferring indoor sports like weight-lifting, wrestling and boxing, the last mentioned being his favourite. He had boxed in the British Army during World War I and, in the 1950s and early 1960s, was a fairly regular patron at amateur boxing tournaments held in the National Stadium, on Dublin's South Circular Road.

Alice, Grosvenor and I were brought on many special outings. During the summer, John and Harriet would bring us on train trips to Bray, Dundrum then being served by the former Harcourt Street line. For the first few years, the trains were driven by steam engines. Among other special treats were coffee and cakes in Bewley's cafés, and visits to a carnival, the zoo or a circus. John enjoyed the circus very much and was always fascinated by the bears. The fact that we had neither family holidays together nor a car did not bother any of us. Fearing for the safety of himself and others, John had declined the Bakers' Union's offer to place a car at his disposal.

During the late 1950s and early 1960s John brought me to some meetings of the Irish Workers' Party (IWP) and its antecedent, the Irish Workers' League (IWL), including at least one congress. The congress, to which John had been invited as an observer, was held in the long since demolished Moira Hotel in Trinity Street. I was also brought by John to several public meetings of the IWL and the IWP, held outside the former Irish Press offices at the corner of O'Connell Street and Middle Abbey Street. Perhaps John found sustenance there for his socialism, sustenance sadly absent from the Labour Party at that time. Principal speakers at those meetings were Joe Deasy, George Jeffares, Sam Nolan and Michael O'Riordan. Prior to his enrolment in the IWL, around 1950, Deasy had been a Labour Party Councillor on Dublin Corporation. Subsequently, in the mid-1970s, Deasy, Jeffares and Nolan became active members of the Labour Party. In addition to being Regional Organiser of UCATT, Nolan is currently Correspondence Secretary of the DCTU. Together with Peadar O'Donnell, George Jeffares was a co-founder of the Irish Voice on Vietnam. O'Donnell and Dan Breen, the Fianna Fáil TD, were the organisation's joint chairmen, while Jeffares served as its secretary.[4] In an impressive campaign from the late 1960s to the mid-1970s, this society organised and led Irish opposition to American intervention in South East Asia, particularly in Vietnam. John was a keen participant in the society's many demonstrations and meetings.

The annual trade union commemoration of James Connolly's death was another event that I attended regularly with John. Held on the Sunday nearest to 12 May, the anniversary of Connolly's execution, this demonstration was always regarded as sectarian by John. Some of the unions marched to Mass, celebrated at the Church of St Mary of the Angels in Church Street. After Mass the procession proceeded to Connolly's grave in Arbour Hill, where a decade of the Rosary was recited. To avoid these aspects of the commemoration, John would join the procession later at Parnell Square before it proceeded down O'Connell Street to a public meeting at the GPO.

In the early 1950s, immediately before television became popular here, John and Harriet entertained a lot at home. There were the occasional and sometimes informal visits of John's friends from earlier days, people like Owen Sheehy Skeffington, Jacob Weingreen, Robert Hannan and James Larkin, Jun. They were all very interesting and Hannan, John's philosophical friend from the 1930s, was also a most amusing character whose out-rageous tales, told in impeccable English, never failed to entertain.

Sometimes the visitors were John's trade union colleagues from abroad, some from as far away as America and the USSR; more often they were members of the Irish Bakers' Union. These included John Cullinane of Cork and Frank Prendergast from Limerick, who shared a musical interest with John. Cullinane and Prendergast served as president of the union during the 1960s, Prendergast later becoming a full-time official of the ITGWU. A member of the Labour Party, he was subsequently elected to the Dáil. Their most frequent guests, however, were Dublin bakers, Michael Conroy, Jimmy Sweetman, Peter Flanagan, and his brother, Paddy Swift. All were socialists, but of different hues, and none was more radical than their mentor, John. He was also between eight and fifteen years older than any of them. They usually visited as a group, sometimes enlarged by one or two others. The others could include two of the wives, Nellie Sweet-man, a close friend of Harriet's and Phoebe Swift; or Cormac Kenny, a full-time official of the Irish Garment Workers' Union and member of the IWL, whom John had met through the DTUC. Kenny's eccentricity on arrival at our house was to change into his slippers!

Of the four regulars who visited, the closest to John was Conroy. Conroy and Sweetman had been apprentices in Rourke's Bakery in Store Street when John had first met them. Under John's influence, Conroy had left the Catholic Church to become a free-thinker, as did Conroy's brothers, Frank and Dan. These two brothers later lost their lives in the fight against fascism. Frank, a member of the CPI and the International Brigade, was killed in the Spanish Civil War, while Dan, an RAF pilot, was shot down over Nazi Germany. Michael Conroy worked as a foreman in Johnston Mooney and O'Brien's Ballsbridge bakery. He had accepted the foreman's position on the strict understanding that he would retain his membership of the union. Sweetman was a soft spoken, reserved but friendly man, who worked in Rourke's until the 1960s, when he became Assistant Secretary and later Secretary of the Dublin No. 1 Branch of the union, succeeding Flanagan. Flanagan and Paddy Swift had commenced their apprenticeship on the same day in Wilson's bakery in Fleming's Place, off Mespil Road, Dublin. John's friendship with Flanagan, the only bachelor in this group, had as much to do with music as with trade unionism. A light-hearted and entertaining type, Flanagan had worked in Johnston Mooney and O'Brien's Ballsbridge bakery before being elected Secretary of the Dublin No. 1 Branch.

Paddy Swift, whilst he did not possess as fine a mind as John's, shared his general outlook on philosophical matters and his interest in music. Paddy and Phoebe lived at 10, Lansdowne Park, Ballsbridge. Unlike John, Paddy was very easy going, being quite content with his night job in the dough loft of Johnston Mooney and O'Brien's bakery. The lack of supervision at night suited Paddy who, during slack periods, would lie on sacks of flour and have a nap. He loved playing practical jokes on his workmates and, though he died in 1960, his exploits were still being recounted in the Ballsbridge bakery up to its closure in 1989. When John had had the human skeleton in the 1920s and 1930s, Paddy brought it on a bus ride, asking the conductor for two fares!

The visitors would arrive around tea-time on Saturdays. After a drink or two, they would have high tea. Afterwards they would return to the rectangular shaped sitting room which was known to the family as the middle room because of its central location at the front of the house. Over the fireplace there was a print depicting a west of Ireland scene by Paul Henry. Other walls of the room displayed photographs of John's mother and George Bernard Shaw. Flanking the fireplace to the right was a hot press, while to the left was a large alcove occupied by our piano. For a couple of hours after tea the conversation would include subjects such as literature, music, foreign places, trade unionism, politics and philosophy. Amid the informal chat, amusing stories would be told. While John's were usually based on personal experience, the one he related most often was heard from Jim McCauley, a conciliation officer of the Labour Court, who later became Deputy chairman of that institution. The story concerned the Belfast street preacher, Arthur Trew, who many years earlier had addressed public meetings on the steps of Belfast's Custom House, then a sort of Hyde Park, but exclusively religious. Damnation and hell were the themes most often chosen by Trew. He would warn the large assembled crowds that they would be down in the dungeons of hell, and they would look up at the Almighty to plead forgiveness, and they would say: 'We did na' know, we did na' know'; and the Almighty would look down at them and would say: 'Ye did na' know, ye did na' know; well, ye bloody well know now!'

Sometimes during the evening, the men would pay a visit to O'Neill's pub (now The Millrace) in Windy Arbour. It was owned by our next door neighbour. After an hour or so in O'Neill's, they would return with their replenishments, loose bottles of stout and ale packed in thick brown paper bags. The brash advertising and packaging revolution had not yet arrived in Ireland! In the increasingly relaxed and informal atmosphere, the evening would gradually progress from chat to music and verse.

Typically, the proceedings would commence with an operatic contribution from the extrovert Flanagan. If he could find a suitable partner, there might be a duet, perhaps *The Moon Has Raised Her Lamp Above* from Benedict's opera *The Lily of Killarney*. On one occasion, Flanagan and Dessie Moles, a baker from Bewley's, tackled the famous tenor/baritone duet from the opera *The Pearl Fishers* by Bizet. Not over-endowed vocally, Conroy might follow Flanagan with Percy French's amusing song *Abdul*

Abulbul Amir. Whatever the performance lacked musically, Conroy's spirited rendition always entertained. Standards would improve appreciably with Pady Swift's choice of the Prelude to Act III of Verdi's opera *La Traviata,* played on record on our hand-wound gramophone. Alternatively, prompted by John, he might settle for one of Moore's Irish melodies or a waltz by Johann Strauss, played by me on the piano. In the case of a melody by Moore, the entire company would sing the words.

Strangely enough, though a great lover of music, John's offering would usually be poetical, probably from the works of his favourite poet, Robert Burns. *A Man's a Man for A' That* was a frequent choice or the *Address To The Unco Guid, or the rigidly righteous.* His most zestful recitation was usually reserved for these opening lines of Burns's *Holy Willie's Prayer*:

> O Thou, who in the heavens does dwell,
> Who, as it pleases best Thysel',
> Sends ane to heaven, an' ten to hell,
> A' for thy glory,
> And no for ony gude or ill
> They've done afore Thee!

For an encore, John might be persuaded to sing *The Volga Boatman,* in Russian!

With the exception of Conroy, the guests would depart in time to catch the last bus home. At social functions of that kind, Conroy was oblivious of time and thought nothing of walking home to Donnycarney, a distance of more than seven miles. On one such occasion, shortly after leaving our home, he mounted a traveller's horse at St Columbanus Road and rode the whole way home to Donnycarney!

Zest for Life

A couple of weeks or so before his seventy-first birthday in August 1967, having held the position for twenty-four years, Swift retired as General Secretary of the Irish Bakers' Confectioners' and Allied Workers' Amalgamated Union.[1] Eleven months earlier, he had attended his last delegate meeting of the union in that capacity. His final year in office had been devoted mainly to familiarising his successor, James Young, with the work of that position, Young having been elected at the 1966 delegate meeting.[2]

At that same meeting, Swift's influence was much in evidence, not least in the musical programmes which opened the proceedings and entertained delegates and guests at social functions held each evening after conference sessions. In earlier times, this music had been performed principally by the union's orchestra and choir. But following the demise of these bodies, senior students of Dublin's Municipal School of Music had been engaged to play. This and the choice of music had been arranged by Swift through the principal of that school, Michael McNamara. In this way many of the country's more famous musicians possibly made their debut at delegate meetings of the Bakers' Union! Among artists Swift recalled performing at these events were Kathleen Watkins, the singer and harpist, and the pianists, Veronica McSwiney and John O'Conor.

Reflecting Swift's tastes, music played on those occasions would generally be selected from the classical repertoire with perhaps some of Moore's Irish melodies. However, he sprang something of a musical surprise at the 1966 meeting by engaging the celebrated Irish ballad group, The Dubliners. Their lively concert of Irish ballads and traditional music delighted the audience, particularly the continental visitors. Swift had enjoyed earlier concerts of The Dubliners, including one run by Sceim na gCeardchumann[3] in Liberty Hall on May Day 1966.

Although almost seventy-one years of age when relinquishing the general secretaryship of the Bakers' Union, Swift was under no obligation to retire. He was not suffering from ill health. Nor was there provision in the union's rules to prevent him remaining in office for life. Moreover, it was the unanimous wish of the union's NEC that he should continue to act on their behalf.[4]

What then induced Swift to make this important decision? For some considerable time beforehand, he had been finding aspects of his work unrewarding. His vision of the trade union movement was shared by few of the union's members, including those on the NEC. For Swift, trade unionism devoid of political objectives had little meaning or appeal. Confining the union's role merely to collective bargaining aimed at improving rates of pay and working conditions was a limitation that he found unacceptable. Yet, for the vast majority of members, that limited role, the repetitive and endless cycle of wage claims chasing cost of living increases, was the zenith of their ambitions. It was his exasperation with this situation, together with a desire to write, that determined his decision to retire.

Swift was particularly interested in writing his memoirs, not so much those of his trade union career as his childhood in Dundalk and his subsequent prison and war experiences. His first drafts of such early episodes in his life had been written on the Western Front during World War I. In an attempt to retain his sanity in that arena, he had resorted to recording these experiences. His many subsequent versions of these events were written as much from his imagination as from his memory, and always in a literary style. For weeks and even months at a time, he would write on these themes only to abandon the project in favour of pursuing other interests. This occurred several times during his retirement and was explained by him as a paradox whereby, when writing, he would become dissatisfied, feeling that he should be participating in life and influencing events, and conversely, when active in other spheres of his life, he would yearn to write.

Swift's *tour de force*, of course, is his book, *History of the Dublin Bakers and Others*. On publication, in 1948, it was reviewed favourably by the three Irish national daily newspapers.[5] It was also adopted by University College, Dublin as a standard reference on the old trade societies and guilds of Dublin.[6] In

Swift's view, the book's main value is its exposure of the corruption of Dublin's medieval guilds. Francis Devine, current president of the ILHS, has offered an alternative evaluation: 'Until the publication of T. J. O'Connell's centenary history of the Irish National Teachers' Organisation in 1968, Swift's book remained the only official trade union history for any Irish union. Even then it is a remarkable book in that it catalogues the history of the union and of the bakery industry from the earliest times to the then present times in a scholarly and unchallenged fashion and in that classic and highly readable prose style that was his own . . .'[7] *History of the Dublin Bakers and Others* has become a collector's item, a fact reflected in its current second-hand price of up to £20 per copy. When first published in the late 1940s, it sold for 18s. 6d.

Swift's other published writing consists of hundreds of articles he contributed to newspapers and other periodicals. From the 1920s to the 1940s, he wrote extensively in Labour Party journals such as the *Irishman* and the *Torch*. In the early 1940s, he wrote much for *Workers Action*, a publication of the DTUC's Council of Action, which he co-edited with Owen Sheehy Skeffington and Patrick Staunton. From the 1950s to the 1970s, Swift contributed more than thirty articles to the *Irish Times*, most of them dealing with political and trade union affairs. Exceptions to these were two articles on sources of Irish secularism and one commemorating the bicentenary of the birth of Hegel, who was regarded by Swift as the greatest of all the philosophers. From the early 1980s onwards, most of his published writings appeared in the *Irish Socialist*, an organ of the CPI. As with the earlier *Irish Times* articles, these contributions, some thirty in number, related almost exclusively to matters of political and trade union interest. Usually written from a historical perspective, this particular series was based largely on his experiences in the labour movement. Of greatest significance in the *Irish Socialist* series was his critical reassessment of Larkin, Sen.

Writing, however, was not the dominant occupation of Swift's retirement. Never content to be a mere spectator of life, he availed of this period to engage in numerous radical and cultural causes which sometimes anticipated change in Irish society. Before considering these activities, let us first examine some of the political, economic and social developments that emerged here in the 1960s.

A significant phenomenon that decade was the economic boom experienced by many Western economies, including Ireland. This was reflected here in reduced unemployment and emigration. Average unemployment of 51,000 in the 1960s was 10,000 fewer than the 1950s and less than a quarter of today's staggering figure of close to a quarter of a million.[8] With regard to emigration, it has been estimated that in the ten-year period ending in March 1971, net emigration fell from 409,000 to 135,000.[9]

Among other important factors influencing Irish Society that decade were rapid industrialisation and urbanisation, the introduction of the free post-primary education scheme, the growth in the number of Irish people travelling abroad, the mass availability of television and, of course, the Second Vatican Council. These are some of the developments that have led to the slow but inexorable liberalisation of Irish society since the 1950s.

To the secularist Swift, the effect of these influences on Irish Catholicism was never less than intriguing. He observed that, in that post-1950s era, many Catholics openly questioned their inherited beliefs, including their faith. This was manifest in the ever increasing number of lapsed Catholics and in the widespread challenge to papal authority on such issues as attendance at Mass, confession, contraception, divorce, priestly celibacy, the role of women in the Church and, to a lesser extent, even abortion. By their acceptance of certain papal rulings while rejecting others, increasing numbers of Irish Catholics were adopting what the media described as an à la carte approach to their religion. No longer could the Church sustain the monolithic image it had portrayed up to the 1950s. Furthermore, clerical influence on the thoughts and actions of members of that Church diminished greatly during that period, the laity having recourse to alternative sources of knowledge and morality. One alternative source was television. On national television programmes such as *Seven Days* or the *Late Late Show*, mass audiences could hear discussions on subjects which, up to the 1960s, had been taboo. This is to say nothing of the influence here of British television. For the Republic's few socialists and secularists the 1960s represented a glimmer of light, the emergence of a period of relative tolerance hitherto unknown in this state. It even became possible for communists to hold public meetings in Dublin without being physically attacked. A sign of those times was the demand for social justice by a small number of Catholic clerics. This was evident, for example, in the late 1960s when Fr Michael Sweetman, SJ, sharing a public platform with the CPI's General Secretary, Michael O'Riordan, condemned government inaction on Dublin's housing crisis. This unprecedented action by a priest drew the wrath of Kevin Boland, the Minister for Local Government, who attacked Fr Sweetman in the Dáil.[10]

Such was the atmosphere in Dublin, if not throughout the country, when Swift retired in 1967. Immediately following his retirement, he went on holiday to the Soviet Union. Unusual for Swift, who normally travelled by air, this seventeen-day trip was by sea and rail. It comprised a cruise by Soviet liner from London to Copenhagen, Helsinki and Leningrad and thence by rail to Moscow, returning after eight days in the USSR to London via the same route. On that vacation, he was accompanied by Grosvenor and myself and some colleagues and friends, including Peter Flanagan and the impresario, Lorcan Bourke.

Prior to this visit, Swift and several others including Frank and Bobbie Edwards, Nora Harkin, Brendan Scott and George Lawlor had inaugurated the Ireland–USSR Friendship Society (now the Ireland USSR Society).[11] Frank Edwards was the founding secretary,[12] a position he retained until his death in 1983. The founding chairperson was Swift.[13] He was later made honorary president for life. As its original title implies, the society's principal object is the promotion of understanding and friendship between Ireland and the USSR. Discussions and film shows on various aspects of Soviet life are organised by the society. These are usually preceded by a lecture delivered by a Soviet or Irish speaker who has special knowledge of a particular topic. In addition to arranging holidays to the USSR, the society receives many Soviet groups visiting Ireland. Swift was disappointed, however, that so few Irish trade unionists visited the Soviet Union. The establishment of diplomatic relations between Ireland and the USSR in 1973 fulfilled a central objective of the society. On that occasion, Dr Garret FitzGerald, Minister for Foreign Affairs, acknowledged that the society had helped to create the climate for such a development.[14]

Coinciding with Swift's retirement was an upsurge of interest in left-wing politics. Influencing that development were some of the many changes then taking place in Irish society. Also, following the jubilee of the Easter Rising, Connolly, long over-shadowed by Patrick Pearse, began to emerge as by far the most significant of the 1916 leaders. Moreover, the centenary of Connolly's birth in 1968 gave impetus to that development and to renewed interest in Connolly's socialist writings. As well as that, the struggle for socialism in Vietnam and elsewhere in South-East Asia, coming as it did in the aftermath of the Cuban Revolution, added momentum to the increasing interest in socialism. Benefiting from these developments were the parties of the Left. Numerically stagnant as a consequence of such factors as emigration and the Cold War, the Irish Workers' Party (IWP), immediate antecedent of the Communist Party of Ireland, recorded a modest growth in membership in the 1960s which continued into the 1970s.[15] Consolidating the IWP's position was its merger in 1970 with the Communist Party of Northern Ireland to form the present Communist Party of Ireland.[16] In 1965, the IWP launched the Connolly Youth Movement (CYM), a broadly based socialist organisation which later evolved into the youth section of the IWP.[17] In the many public demonstrations that took place in Dublin at that time, the CYM could muster several hundred members and supporters.

About the same time, a significant section of Sinn Féin adopted a more radical position, campaigning with organisations like the IWP and CYM on issues such as housing, unemployment, apart-heid in South Africa and the Vietnam War. When, in 1970, the traditional section of this Party seceded to become Provisional Sinn Féin, the radical wing adopted the title Official Sinn Féin, later Sinn Féin–the Workers' Party and, later still, the Workers' Party, its present name. Official Sinn Féin attracted large numbers of new recruits, many young, active trade unionists.[18]

The Labour Party, too, profited from this left-wing swing, hundreds of young people swelling its ranks.[19] More important from Swift's perspective were signs that the Party might be shift-ing to the Left. However, that was hardly evident at the Party's Connolly commemoration ceremony held in May 1967. This took the form of a Mass celebrated in the Church of St Mary of the Angels in Dublin's Church Street, followed by a visit to

Kilmainham Gaol, site of Connolly's execution. At Kilmainham, a decade of the rosary was recited after the Party leader, Brendan Corish, had delivered his oration. Those present at the Mass heard a lecture by Fr Leonard. In the course of his address Fr Leonard said:

> . . . You have come to assist at this Mass which is said for the repose of the soul of James Connolly. You have come to pay homage to his name, and the best tribute you can give to him is to try to achieve in your own lives the ideals that he has put before you.
>
> Some may object and say those ideals were communistic and socialistic. Yes, Connolly was a socialist, so was St Francis, so am I, but Connolly's socialism was not a Godless thing. It was a socialism that could well be reconciled with the teachings of the Catholic Church and the Papal Encyclicals.
>
> To portray Connolly as a man without faith would be to do him a great injustice, and the records of the Easter Rising which are kept in the archives of the Capuchin Order prove beyond all doubt that Connolly was a man of faith as well as a man of great character . . .[20]

Fr Leonard's opinions conflict with those of Connolly's biographers, C. Desmond Greaves and Samuel Levenson. From studying Connolly's writings, Greaves and Levenson concluded that Connolly was a marxist.[21] Let Connolly himself speak of his religious beliefs. This is what he said in 1908:

> . . . For myself, though I have usually posed as a Catholic I have not gone to my duty for fifteen years and have not the slightest tincture of faith left. I only assumed the Catholic pose in order to quiz the raw freethinkers whose ridiculous dogmatism did and does annoy me as much as the dogmatism of the Orthodox. In fact, I respect the good Catholic more than the average freethinker.[22]

Presumably, Fr Leonard's contention that Connolly was a 'man of faith' was based on Connolly's death-bed request to be attended by a priest. Yet, excluding a few Sunday visits to chapel, this was the first religious duty that Connolly had performed since his marriage twenty-six years earlier.[23]

How, then, are Connolly's conflicting religious positions to be reconciled or, at least, assessed? While Swift always found Connolly ambiguous on this question, he would not disagree with the conclusions set forth in Levenson's biography of Connolly. Levenson states:

> The causes of this step [Connolly's request to be attended by a priest] are open to argument. The pious will maintain that, like many others, he 'saw the light' on his death bed. The rationalist will argue that he was in a weakened mental condition. Others will say that he was moved by a desire to be closer to his comrades; that he was influenced (like Constance Markievicz, who decided during the rising to convert to Roman Catholicism) by the Catholic fervour exhibited by Padraic Pearse, Joseph Plunkett and The O'Rahilly.
>
> It is unlikely that Connolly underwent any kind of mystical experience; or that, at the age of forty-eight, he abandoned his life long belief in Marxist materialism and regained his faith in organised religion.[24]

In that very year that Fr Leonard attempted to sanctify Connolly, the Labour Party decided that henceforth the Party would be a socialist organisation with the object of establishing an Irish Socialist Workers' Republic.[25] That object, it will be recalled, had been abandoned in 1940 as a result of pressure from the Catholic hierarchy. Encouraged by this new development, Swift became active in the Party's Fintan Lalor Branch in Dublin's North Central constituency.

At the Party's consultative conference in 1968, Swift presented on behalf of that branch a draft proposal on industrial democracy. The proposal provided for the establishment of industrial democracy in the workplace, to be made operable and safeguarded by complementary legislation that would bring under public control all banking and other financial institutions. Other complementary measures were to provide for the establishing of national and regional planning authorities under the direction and control of national and local government, and with the active participation of the workers directly at job level and through their trade unions and consumer organisations at planning levels.[26] While alternative proposals were presented to the consultative conference, the Fintan Lalor document became the basis for the more detailed draft policy which was prepared later by a subcommittee appointed by the consultative conference.[27] In addition to Swift, this subcommittee comprised Jim Kemmy (Limerick), chairperson, later to become Democratic Socialist Party TD, and later still a Labour TD for a Limerick constituency; K. Halligan; Griff Cashman, a prominent figure in the co-operative movement; Jack Harte, a WUI official who later became a Senator; Jim Quinn, long-serving member of the FWUI'S (now SIPTU'S) executive; and M. A. O'Sullivan (all Dublin); L. Beecher, former branch secretary, ITGWU and J. Doolin (Cork) and M. Johnston (Dundalk).[28] The committee received nine written submissions from committee members and one from Barry Desmond, later to become Labour Party Minister for Health and, later still, an MEP. Dr Noel Browne also gave the subcommittee his views on industrial democracy.[29] It was Swift's draft, however, that was submitted to the Party's 1969 annual conference.[30] Together with other policy statements, some with proposals of a socialist kind, the draft policy was adopted.[31] Despite his authorship of this document, which was retitled 'workers' democracy', Swift was concerned about certain ambiguity in some of its paragraphs, ambiguity possibly brought about in editing by the Party's leadership. He and his subcommittee colleagues had rejected the notion that workers' democracy could be secured by mild reforms or welfare legislation, or by collective bargaining by the trade unions aimed at establishing more consultative machinery or profit sharing in industry or business. It was the subcommittee's conviction that only in a socialist society could effective workers' democracy be achieved.[32]

Industrial democracy had long been a subject of major interest to Swift. As a socialist and trade unionist, he had studied experiments in this field in many countries. On several occasions he had raised the issue in the Irish trade union movement. Thus, at the 1949 ITUC annual conference, he had proposed a motion on behalf of the Bakers' Union calling for workers' participation in management.[33] Nearly twenty years later, at the 1967 ICTU conference, the following motion, proposed by Swift on behalf of the Bakers' Union, had been carried:

> Congress supports the principle and practice of industrial democracy providing for workers' participation in management; and to enable policy on this question to be

formulated at the next Annual Conference, this Congress instructs the Executive Council to examine the question of how best the principle of industrial democracy may be brought into practice in Ireland having regard to:
   (i) experience of its operation in other countries; and
   (ii) the particular context of industrial, commercial and economic life generally in Ireland .[34]

The adoption of these policies by both the ICTU and the Labour Party was followed in 1977 by the enactment of the Worker Participation (State Enterprises) Act, entitling workers of certain state bodies to elect worker directors. This was regarded by Swift as a small step towards the ultimate goal of achieving workers' democracy.

Of the votes cast in the 1969 general election following the adoption of Labour's new policies, the Party secured 225,000 or 17 per cent.[35] This remains the second highest percentage vote (1922 was higher with a vote of 21.3 per cent) ever recorded by the Labour Party in a general election. Thus, in a period of only twelve years Labour's vote had almost doubled, increasing from 112,000 or 9.1 per cent in 1957[36] to 11.7 per cent in 1961,[37] 15.4 per cent in 1965,[38] and 17 per cent in 1969. Even more remarkable was Labour's 1969 performance in Dublin city and county where the Party won 28 per cent of the vote and ten seats in Dáil Éireann.[39] Eight years before that, Labour's Dublin representation had been confined to a single seat.[40] However, Labour's 1969 national vote did not produce extra seats, only eighteen Labour deputies being elected,[41] a drop from the twenty-two who had been returned in the previous election.[42] This perhaps explains why the Party leaders interpreted the results as something less than an outstanding success. But, was there, Swift wondered, another reason for such a negative assessment. Was not the prospect of ministerial office beckoning some of the more prominent Labour deputies? Obstacles to their aspirations were the Party's socialist policies and anti-coalition stance. The arms crisis in 1970, however, provided the pretext for reversing the coalition policy. As for the socialist programme, this was largely ignored by the leadership of the Party. Immediately following the 1973 general election, Labour formed a coalition government with Fine Gael, then the country's most conservative party. As the minority partner in this administration led by the Fine Gael leader, Liam Cosgrave, Labour practically lost its identity. Since then, Labour's support has dwindled dramatically and is currently (June, 1989 general election) little more than half what it was in 1969.[43] Swift, incidentally, while opposed to Labour's participation in such a conservative government, was not opposed in principle to coalition.

The Tánaiste in that 1973 Fine Gael/Labour coalition was the Labour Party leader, Brendan Corish. At the Labour Party's annual conference only four years earlier, he had stated that, in the event of the Party reversing its anti-coalition position, his continued support for socialism would, as a matter of conscience, be from the backbenches.[44]

If this somersault of Corish's failed to provoke a revolt by the Party's socialists, perhaps this was because they expected no better. For Swift, at least, there were even greater concerns than that about Corish. Corish had, after all, on at least one occasion, been disarmingly candid about his allegiances, describing himself as 'A Catholic first, an Irishman second and a socialist third.'[45] It was also Corish who said: '. . . If the Hierarchy gives me any direction with regard to Catholic social teaching or Catholic moral teaching, I accept without qualification in all respects the teaching of the Hierarchy and the Church to which I belong.'[46] Swift was not surprised to learn later that Corish had probably been a member of the Knights of St Columbanus.[47] With his politics owing more to St Vincent de Paul than to Connolly, much less Karl Marx, Corish, it seemed to Swift, was an unlikely socialist leader.

At the 1971 annual conference of the Labour Party, Swift contested the position of chairperson. Other contenders were Roddy Connolly, son of James Connolly, and Michael D. Higgins, later to become Labour TD for the constituency of Galway West. Swift had been encouraged to contest this office by members of the Liaison Committee of the Labour Left, an informal socialist group within the Party that counted among its members Dr Noel Browne, Matt Merrigan, Brendan Scott and Swift. Paul Gillespie, an *Irish Times* journalist and currently the paper's foreign editor, was Swift's election agent. Campaigning on the failure of the party's leadership to promote socialist policies, Swift secured

160 votes, with 213 going to Michael D. Higgins and 383 to Roddy Connolly, the victor.[48]

A severe loss was sustained by the Left in September 1973, with the death, at the age of forty, of Brendan Scott. A secondary schoolteacher by profession, Scott taught in the multi-denominational Sutton Park School in Dublin. Regarded by Swift and many others as one of the finest socialists of his time, Scott was, as well as being an active Labour Party member, a founder of both the Irish Anti-Apartheid Movement and the Ireland–USSR Friendship Society. It was in the role of vice-chairperson of the latter body that he sometimes acted as peace-maker between Frank Edwards and Swift, the society's chief officers, in their turbulent personal relationship. Intelligence, integrity and modesty were among the qualities Swift admired most in Scott. Scott earned the respect of the Irish Left for his tireless commitment to numerous progressive causes and his unceasing efforts to encourage Left unity.

Disillusioned by the Labour leaders' abandonment of socialism, Swift became involved in a new undertaking. In 1973, he was visited in his home by a UCD lecturer and his graduate student, respectively, Fergus D'Arcy and Ken Hannigan. They were interested in founding a society of labour history and thought Swift could help. Swift had been approached with a similar proposition during the late 1940s. On that occasion, a couple of TCD students had visited him to discuss the possibility of securing the records of trade unions and associated organisations for depositing in TCD. These were to be made available to students preparing theses for degrees in the social sciences. Rejecting that narrow approach, Swift had explained that he would not be associated with such a project unless it involved the trade unions, 'the main makers of labour history'.

D'Arcy and Hannigan appeared to share Swift's view and, on 28 June 1973, a preliminary meeting was convened in UCD's Newman House, St Stephen's Green, Dublin. There, it was decided that a labour history society should be formed. A provisional committee, of which Swift was president, was elected to prepare a constitution and to report to an inaugural meeting.[49] Then, on 27 October 1973, again in Newman House, the inaugural meeting of the Irish Labour History Society (ILHS) was held. The representative gathering of academics and trade unionists

included Dr Garret FitzGerald, Minister for Foreign Affairs, and
Senator Michael Mullen, General Secretary of the ITGWU.[50]

In the course of his presidential address to the meeting, Swift
said:

> History is not just the dead past awaiting research. It is
> happening now at this meeting and in all places where
> men and women are living. The history we are making here
> today may become important or significant if the persons
> here assembled and their organisations ponder enough on
> the truth that we as workers are always creating history
> and that the economic relations in our society are in large
> measure determining the moral values operative in our
> society and the kind of history we are passing on to those
> coming after.[51]

Officers elected to the founding committee were: John Swift,
president; Fergus D'Arcy, lecturer, Dept. of Modern History, UCD,
vice-president; Mattie O'Neill, an ITGWU official, secretary; Ken
Hannigan (later to become archivist), Public Records Office (now
the National Archives), Dublin, assistant-secretary; and Gréagóir
Ó Dúghaill, archivist, Public Records Office, Dublin, treasurer.[52]
Swift remained president until 1978 when he was elected unanimously as the first honorary president of the society.[53]

A constitution incorporating the society's objects was adopted
at the inaugural meeting. The objects are:

(A) To promote among the community generally:
 (1) knowledge of Irish Labour History and of Irish people
 in labour history abroad; and (2) appreciation of the
 importance of labour history in programmes of education;
(B) to locate and ensure the preservation of all records relating
 to the current and past experience of Irish working people
 and their organisations;
(C) to build up a collection of all records and reminiscences,
 oral and written of or by persons involved in the experience
 or history referred to above;
(D) to further above objects by promotion of lectures and
 discussions and other means available, including the publication of printed matter on subjects relevant to the purposes of the society.[54]

So far, the society's primary role has been educational. Conferences, lectures, seminars and exhibitions on labour history

themes, held under the organisation's auspices, have been complemented by the society's highly regarded annual journal, *Saothar* and the less academic but equally valuable periodical, *Labour History News*. In addition to stimulating interest in the subject, these educational endeavours have given impetus to the research, writing and publishing of much labour history in recent years. Also of paramount importance in the society's work has been the preservation of records, and here too, a great deal has been achieved. Apart from raising awareness of the importance of locating and safeguarding such material, the society has induced many labour organisations and individuals to deposit their records in the society's archives.

A measure of the society's present standing is the government's recent gifts of a building at Beggar's Bush Barracks, Haddington Road, Dublin, to house a museum of labour history, and grants amounting to £150,000 for the renovation and fitting out of the premises.[55] This assistance, initiated by the former Labour Party Minister for Labour and the Public Service, Ruairí Quinn, was ratified by his successor, Bertie Ahern of Fianna Fáil. On 26 June 1990, in the presence of many distinguished guests from the trade union and academic worlds, the museum was officially opened by the President of Ireland, Dr Patrick Hillery. Other speakers were Chris Kirwan, vice-president, ICTU, and the ILHS president, Francis Devine, who presided.[56]

Neither as president nor honorary president was Swift prepared to be a mere figure-head of the society. Although seventy-seven years old when the organisation was founded, he personally visited the leaders of many trade unions canvassing the corporate affiliation of those bodies. The first to do so was the Bakers' Union, followed soon afterwards by some thirty others including the ICTU, the ITGWU and the WUI. In addition to that, Swift persuaded the Bakers' Union's Dublin No. 1 Branch to place in the society's archives their records dating from 1806.

In 1978, in Mexico City, when representing the ILHS at the first congress of the World Association of Centres for Historical and Social Studies of the Labour Movement, Swift was elected one of several vice-presidents of the international body.[57]

Of the societies that Swift was a founding or prominent member, none has been more successful than the ILHS. A decade after its founding, Francis Devine, the society's vice-president, described Swift's contribution thus:

> John Swift, Founding President, is now Honorary President. Together with Dr Fergus D'Arcy and Ken Hannigan, he helped transform the idea into a vibrant reality. Despite the alleged handicaps of poor health and being over 80, John Swift frequently shames younger members by his constant and informed attendance at meetings where he ruthlessly exposes errors and shortcomings and offers additional information on a variety of labour history themes, often recalling his personal experience of participation in the events under discussion.[58]

Francis Devine probably also penned this earlier anonymous tribute to Swift's role in the society:

> The AGM [ILHS AGM, 1978] in December was noteworthy in particular for the unanimous election of John Swift, founding President of the Society, to the newly-created post of Honorary President. In this way, the Society chose to pay tribute to a remarkable man who more than any other has been responsible for establishing and promoting it.[59]

An important development following Swift's retirement was the emergence of the women's movement. It was a phenomenon he viewed with mixed feelings. He supported, of course, the campaign to eliminate discrimination against women in the workplace. He was supportive, too, of demands by the women's movement for access to contraception, divorce and, in certain circumstances, abortion. Yet, Swift held extremely traditional views on the role of women in society, believing, for instance, that a woman's primary function should be that of wife and mother in the home.

The fact that Swift was born in the late nineteenth century, and lived and worked in a man's world, hardly explains why he should have held such traditional views on this issue. Nor can they be dismissed as the eccentric opinions of someone seeking controversy or attention. These views represented his convictions on the subject over many decades, convictions he never attempted to conceal.

An example of Swift's forthright attitude on women's role in society was evident at the 1988 AGM of the Labour Party's Delia Larkin Branch, to which he had been invited to speak. He was asked what he thought of married women being in the workforce. Although there were present at least five women in that position, he replied without hesitation or embarrassment: 'I don't like it.'

If the early years of Swift's retirement coincided with a period of much change in the South, there were also taking place then significant developments in Northern Ireland. Of special interest to him was the non-sectarian campaign of the Northern Ireland Civil Rights Association (NICRA). While the popular myth persists that the civil rights movement was founded on 5 October 1968, when the RUC baton-charged the famous peaceful demonstration in Derry, NICRA was, in fact, founded in February of the previous year. The groundwork leading to the formation of that organisation was carried out over a period of many years by communists, socialists and trade unionists. These forces, together with some liberals, republicans and independents, were the founders of NICRA. This united group formulated demands for basic democratic rights in Northern Ireland. Specifically, they sought the extension of the franchise in local government elections, or *one man, one vote*, the ending of plural voting, the ending of gerrymandering of the electoral boundaries, the revoking of the Special Powers Act and the ending of discrimination in jobs and housing.[60]

As a result of NICRA's brief but remarkably effective campaign, important concessions were extracted from the unionists and the British Government. Not alone were demands for *one man, one vote* and a cessation of gerrymandering conceded but, through the mass media, particularly television, the undemocratic nature of Northern Ireland was exposed to world view. These events, in turn, helped precipitate the split in the Unionist Party, the abolition of the RUC's Special Force and, indeed, the abolition of the Stormont Assembly.[61]

However, with the rise of the Provisional IRA in the early 1970s, following harassment of the nationalist community by the British Army and local security forces, the civil rights movement was soon eclipsed. The Provisionals, of course, had other priorities which were epitomised in their slogan *Brits Out*. Whatever their objectives, Swift found the Provisionals' sectarian and indiscriminate bombing and shooting campaign repugnant and counter-productive. A decade after they emerged, he said of their campaign: 'I don't like it at all.'[62] Of their politics, he stated on the same occasion: 'They have no political programme that I agree with . . .'[63] Swift was no less severe on the unionist paramilitaries and the British Army. He would like to have seen the British Army withdraw from Northern Ireland but feared this could have resulted in a civil war. While convinced that Britain was primarily responsible for the crisis in the North, Swift laid some of the blame on those promoting sectarianism. Here, he was referring not only to the paramilitaries, the Orange Order and the Ancient Order of Hibernians, but Catholic Church resistance to integrated education. He was heartened, however, that despite strong opposition from the Catholic hierarchy, successful interdenominational schools such as Lagan College had been established in the North.

As one would expect, nothing less than the creation of a 32-county Irish socialist republic would satisfy him. He expressed the view that partition would remain until there was socialism in both parts of Ireland and in Britain.[64] Unity could be achieved, he believed, in a wider European political union, a union that might ultimately render irrelevant the causes of the conflict in Northern Ireland.

That brings us to the question of Ireland's entry to the European Economic Community (now the European Community or EC), which occurred six years after Swift's retirement. This development, in 1973, was opposed vigorously by the Labour Party, Official Sinn Féin, the CPI and the ICTU. Fears of increased unemployment and loss of national sovereignty were the main issues in the campaign. From the beginning, Swift supported Ireland's EC membership. He was well aware, of course, that the community was created to facilitate the trans-national companies and not the ordinary citizens. Nevertheless, he believed that, on balance, Ireland's best interests lay in being a member. He found unconvincing the contention of sections of the Left that unemployment would have been lower here had we not joined. Indeed, he believed the converse to be true, that unemployment would probably have been much worse had we remained outside the EC. On the sovereignty issue, he was well aware that, in exchange for Irish unity, both Eamon de Valera and Seán MacBride were prepared to lead Ireland into NATO.[65] He was conscious, too, that the right wing parties that have dominated Dáil Éireann could not be relied on to defend our neutrality. At the same time he noted that, sixteen years after our EC entry, Ireland was not a member of NATO. The possible future entry to the community of neutral states such as Austria, Cyprus and Sweden, not to mention the countries of Eastern Europe, could, Swift believed, help strengthen Irish neutrality.

But it was neither economic nor sovereignty considerations that influenced his attitude to the EC. Rather it was a desire to see Ireland emerging from its isolation and insularity. With its great heritage of culture and free thought, a heritage that had produced so many outstanding philosophers, composers, writers and artists, Continental Europe, it seemed to Swift, had much to offer Ireland. Ireland's EC membership, he believed, brought us closer to that heritage.

Swift aspired to a united and socialist Europe stretching from the Atlantic to the Urals. Such a Europe, he believed, might comprise a federation of nation states or a unitary state. Neither prospect held any fears for him. In fact, he would have welcomed such a development almost as much as democrats greeted the overthrow of Europe's principalities and dukedoms in favour of nation states in the late nineteenth century.

Some of Swift's retirement was taken up by less momentous matters than the political developments of that era. From the spring of 1972, John and Harriet lived alone, Alice, Grosvenor and I having married between 1967 and 1972. Also that spring, with the birth of the first of their six grandsons and two granddaughters, John and Harriet became grandparents.

In the first decade of his retirement, Swift experienced two serious illnesses. The first, in 1973, when he was seventy-seven, was diagnosed initially in the Soviet Union. The medical authorities there referred him to Dublin's Meath Hospital where his ailment was identified as cancer of the bladder. There followed a course of radium treatment in St Luke's Hospital, Dublin, leading to his complete recovery. Four years later, however, in 1977, he had a slight stroke. This was manifest in a minor speech impediment and balance difficulties which affected his ability to walk. For a while, he also suffered from tremors in his legs, and there were fears that he had contracted Parkinson's disease. Gradually, however, these symptoms disappeared and once again he recovered to full health.

A decade later again, on reaching his early nineties, Swift would sometimes complain that his physical health was deteriorating. His sight and hearing both diminished and his legs became weaker. Despite this he still managed to read a book each week in addition to a daily newspaper. As well as that, he continued to write articles for periodicals and, at the age of ninety-two, completed a full-sized volume of his memoirs. He could still listen with comparative ease to the radio and the television. Conversation was a bigger problem, made more difficult by his refusal to use his hearing aid. Despite these handicaps, he continued to travel often to the city and elsewhere by bus. Evidence that his mind was as clear as ever may be found in his many published writings of that period.

Swift's longevity was not shared by other immediate members of his family. The deaths of his mother and father at fifty-seven and sixty-seven, respectively, were followed by that of his sister, May, who died of a brain haemorrhage in 1953 at the age of fifty.[66] His brother, Paddy, was fifty-five when he died in 1960. Presumably, Paddy's chain-smoking contributed to his untimely death from lung cancer.

For much of his retirement, Swift was the elder statesman of the Irish labour movement. His opinions on events and personalities in labour history and on other issues, were often sought and always generously given. Between 1970 and 1980, Swift was the recipient of several awards, including three from the Soviet Union. The most important of these was the 'Order of Friendship between Peoples' which was conferred on him by the Presidium of the Supreme Soviet, the Soviet parliament, on 26 August 1976, his eightieth birthday. Thus, Swift became the first Irish citizen to receive that Order.[67] The award was presented to him on 4 October by the first Soviet Ambassador to Ireland, Anatoli Kaplin, at a well-attended reception hosted in the ambassador's Dublin residence. Presenting the award, the ambassador said that often it was difficult to build friendships between two nations; that sometimes it was easier to build conflict, but that Swift, with his great influence as a trade union leader, put friendship and peace in the first place to build Irish/

Soviet relations.[68] Swift's acceptance address was reported in the
Irish Times of 5 October 1976:

> Accepting the honour, Mr Swift said that somehow it was
> unifying and a sign of equality to receive an honour on
> one's own birthday rather than on the birthday of some
> personage, but to receive such a great honour from the
> Soviet Union's highest assembly was indeed most unforget-
> table.
>
> Sometimes, he said, honours were given for valour in
> war, but he preferred to be presented with an honour for
> seeking peace and friendship between people.
>
> Mr Swift recalled his trade union life and its essential
> association with peace, not war. He had been in Wormwood
> Scrubs prison for protesting against war when he had heard
> news of the Russian October Revolution in 1917. But from
> his boyhood in Dundalk he had been interested in Wolfe
> Tone and his United Irishmen because of their great play
> with political ideas and the ideas of great writers like Rous-
> seau and Voltaire, rather than with the narrower political
> ideas in Ireland.
>
> And so his interest in the Soviet Union grew with his
> work in Irish trade unions and he visited the Soviet Union
> early in his life. His criterion for judging social progress there
> had been the trade unions. In 1917, the Russian Federated
> Republic had only one million trade unionists. Today there
> were 104 million trade unionists.
>
> As the five-year economic plans advanced so did the
> unions, and so did the working people, he believed. He
> had met Soviet Union leaders and learned of Soviet ideas.
> He had tried to encourage Irish workers to combat those
> who would sow bitterness and hatred against that country.

On the occasion of the thirty-fifth anniversary of its institution,
the World Federation of Trade Unions awarded Swift a gold
medal in 1980 in recognition of his having been a founding
delegate of that body in London in 1945.[69] The presentation was
to have been made in Moscow but, due to ill health, he had been
unable to travel to the Soviet capital. Instead, at a reception
hosted by the ITUC's executive committee in the Congress's
Raglan Road headquarters in Dublin, the presentation was made
by the Belfast trade union leader, Andy Barr. Other guests present

on that occasion included Betty Sinclair,[70] former Secretary, Belfast Trades Council; James Young, General Secretary, Bakers' Union; Francis Devine, Vice-President of the ILHS; and Harriet and I.[71]

In addition to being Irish District Secretary of the National Union of Sheet Metal Workers, Coppersmiths, Heating and Domestic Engineers, Andy Barr was, for many years, an executive council member of the ICTU, and chairman of the CPI. He retired from the last-mentioned post in 1984. When elected President of the ICTU in 1974, Barr became the first CPI member to have held that position.

At a social function held in Leinster House on 6 December 1989, the Labour Party paid tribute to Swift. Among those in attendance on that occasion were Dick Spring and Ruairí Quinn, TDs, Leader and Deputy Leader, respectively; Barry Desmond, MEP; the TDs, Mervyn Taylor, Emmet Stagg and Michael D. Higgins; and the former Labour minister, Justin Keating. Spring, in his address to that gathering, praised Swift's contribution to the labour movement over more than six decades. After being presented with a copy of Marianne Elliott's book, *Wolfe Tone— Prophet of Irish Independence*, Swift, in a brief response, exhorted his Labour colleagues to campaign for a socialist Europe.

Several times since retiring, aspects of Swift's life and work have received attention in the media and elsewhere. On no fewer than five occasions he has been featured in the *Irish Times* column, *An Irishwoman's (or Irishman's) Diary.*[72] Moreover, profiles of Swift by the late Michael McInerney,[73] former political correspondent of the *Irish Times*, and Fintan O'Toole,[74] former arts critic of the *Sunday Tribune*, have appeared in those newspapers. A second *Sunday Tribune* article on Swift was written by the present writer.[75] In addition, an interview of Swift by Anne Harris was published in the September 1980 issue of the Workers' Party journal, *Workers Life*. Swift was the subject, too, of a chapter of Uinseann Mac Eoin's book, *Survivors*, which was first published in 1980.

A six-part ninety-minute serialised interview of Swift by Pádraic Ó Raghallaigh was broadcast by RTE in August and September 1976. This was followed by a television interview of Swift by Una Claffey. Transmitted on 1 July 1985, the eve of the ICTU's annual conference, this comprised an entire edition of RTE's

principal current affairs television programme, *Today Tonight.*
A *Today Tonight* television crew also filmed Swift's ninetieth
birthday party hosted by his family in the ICTU's national headquarters in Dublin. As with his eightieth birthday party, also run
by the family but held elsewhere, the guests were chosen by
Swift from organisations with which he had had associations.
Hence, on both occasions, there were present friends he had
met through the trade union movement, the Secular Society of
Ireland, the Spanish Aid Committee, the Ireland–USSR Society
and the Irish Labour History Society. Special guests at the eightieth
and ninetieth birthday celebrations were the Soviet Ambassadors
to Ireland, respectively, Anatoli Kaplin and Alexie Nesterenko.

Among the unusual gifts received by Swift on his ninetieth
birthday was the previously mentioned police report from Ruairí
Quinn, Minister for Labour and the Public Service. To mark the
same occasion, the Irish Anti-Apartheid Movement conferred on
Swift honorary life membership of that society,[76] while Francis
Devine wrote the following poem in honour of the occasion:

The Privilege

On being first introduced
you stood in a Viennese street,
tipped your trilby and called my wife
Mrs Devine rather than by her name.
I imagined carriages and urchins,
the smell of roasting horse chestnuts
and passing talk in undertones of Larkin,
the one-eyed anti-Christ.

In Mexico you were the mad dog,
tequila disappearing below a pith helmet.
Scarlet melons and hummingbirds,
scented nights and manic mariachi music
seemed ordinary against your twill overcoat
shuffling to the Café Tacuba
to vanquish upstart eurocommunists
and to sing the *Volga Boatman*
to bewildered anarchists from Venezuela.

Cold in your sanitised ward of St Vincent's,
your eyes twinkled as you took me
to filch buns in a dowdy Dundalk bakery.
Under elm trees we discovered Darwin
and things we never understood
but knew enough to shake off the clergy
and pity the itchy collars that lead
the town's wee boys to chapel on Sundays.

When Hilton Hanna came from the US Meatcutters
you swang blue with your Bessie Smith albums;
while sweating on Bewley's night shifts
you insisted the confectioners' chorus *Rigoletto*
and people wondered why their coffee tasted nice.
In Prague at the International Foodworkers
your red haired Irishman spoke Czech,
apologised in Slovak and, accommodating the translators,
explained in perfect Russian
your inability to pronounce Irish.

In suburban Dundrum the postman scans
Soviet Weekly opening your neatly painted gate.
Your family worries that your night time
appointment with the revolution may be your last.
I am encouraged to discourage you
but long to hear your correct the Ambassador,
lambast a neutered Labour leadership
and defy their discountenance
as you lap them all again on the rutted May Day round.
I even enjoy your irascible dressings down
accepting them as part of the privilege.

Although not preoccupied with the past, Swift could enjoy
the occasional trip down memory lane. Very often around the
time of his birthday he would visit his native Dundalk where he
spent his happy and interesting childhood. Its principal streets
had changed little since he left the town about 1912. On these
excursions, he would be accompanied by the present writer
and, occasionally, by some other family members. Only he and
I were present the year we visited the Convent of Mercy where,
more than eighty years earlier, he had attended the kindergarten

there. We were received with great hospitality by the nuns who brought us on a tour of the school and the chapel before treating us to tea and cake in their parlour. To our great relief, not once did they mention religion!

A bizarre revelation awaited Swift on our visit to Dundalk in May 1986. At the Irish Christian Brothers school which he had attended after leaving the kindergarten, he enquired if there were any elderly people in the town who might have recollections of the Dundalk of his childhood. After being referred to Paddy Cooper, a former lay teacher of the school, we wondered if he could possibly be a relative of John's uncle and aunt, John and Mary Cooper. It turned out that Paddy and his twin sister, Lily Cooper, with whom he lives, were indeed the nephew and niece of his uncle and aunt. But Lily Cooper had a greater surprise than that in store. She revealed something John had completely forgotten: that 75 years earlier, he had stood as her godfather!

A Life Celebrated

Towards the end of 1989, after living there for more than forty years, John and Harriet sold their Dundrum home. By then, their feeble physical condition had reached the stage where, even with assistance from their family, and from a part-time home help, they were no longer able to cope. From around the time of his ninety-third birthday, a few months earlier, having virtually lost the ability to walk, John had been more or less house-bound. Harriet's health, too, had been gradually failing and, on several occasions, in the late 1980s, she had been admitted to hospital. For a while, Harriet and John had considered remaining in their bungalow and employing a full-time housekeeper, but that option had had little appeal for John.

Having worked in the Royal Hospital, Donnybrook, before her marriage, and having been a short-term patient there in the summer of 1989, Harriet convinced John that they should seek accommodation in that institution. Only Harriet secured a place, however, as there were no vacancies for men. Instead, John went to live with his daughter and son-in-law, Alice and Michael Robinson, in their home in Portrane, Co. Dublin. From John's viewpoint, this arrangement was not altogether satisfactory for, although appreciative of Alice and Michael's hospitality and kindness, he felt isolated in this remote part of north County Dublin. He also missed Harriet greatly and, with his hosts not having a car, and he being unable to use public transport, his visits to Harriet were less frequent than he would have wished.

On 17 February 1990, following Michael's transfer to Cork, John left Portrane and moved into the Florence Garden Nursing Home, 5 Florence Terrace, Bray, Co. Wicklow, where he had a comfortable bedroom to himself, with a quiet sitting room nearby. This establishment was partly owned and run by Marie

Woods, who shared with John an interest in reading and music, as well as radical politics. For these reasons, this nursing home seemed an ideal abode for John, at least until he could join Harriet in the Royal Hospital.

Yet, being separated from Harriet continued to cause him much anguish, as, indeed, did the loss of his home, and he would half-jocosely describe himself as an itinerant. In this period following the sale of his house, he would yearn for Sunday when he would spend the day with his sons and their families, visiting Harriet in the afternoon.

A fortnight or so after entering the nursing home, on 6 March, John became ill, complaining of a pain in his left foot and leg. After receiving medical treatment in the home, he was admitted to St Columcille's Hospital, Loughlinstown, Co. Dublin, on 19 March, and, later the same day, to St Vincent's Hospital, where his condition was diagnosed as a clot in his foot. He underwent an operation the following morning but, because of his advanced years, did not leave the theatre until around 6.00 p.m. While the operation itself was described as a success, the medical staff cautioned against any premature optimism about his recovery. Visiting the hospital an hour or so later, I found him beginning to shake off the effects of the anaesthetic. His eyes opened briefly as he strove to remove the oxygen mask from his face. Later again, at about 8.30 p.m., Grosvenor and his wife, Gill, found John in an agitated state, still attempting to remove the oxygen mask. Quite lucid by that stage, he asked to be raised up in the bed. Before departing, following a brief visit, Grosvenor indicated his intention to return the following day. Squeezing Grosvenor's hand, John told him to look after himself before saying goodbye. At 11 p.m., a telephone enquiry to the hospital about John's condition was deferred due to a crisis in the ward. John, apparently, had become increasingly active and agitated to such an extent that he had been given a tranquilliser. Five minutes later, however, at 11 p.m., John died from heart failure. Thus, on Tuesday 20 March 1990, at the age of ninety-three, John's long and active life finally came to an end.[1]

In accordance with his wishes, John's death and funeral service were of a non-religious character. He had stipulated this himself in his will in 1951: 'I request that when I die there shall be no religious ceremony of any kind at my funeral.' The absence of a similar provision in his final will, made shortly before his demise, is significant only in that he had already indicated to me the type of non-religious ceremony he desired, and he was confident that his wishes would be fulfilled.

So, on Friday 23 March, at 2.00 p.m. in Glasnevin Crematorium, Dublin. John's secular and socialist funeral service was held.[2] Immediately before that, the family had gathered in the morgue of St Vincent's Hospital to pay their private respects. On arrival at the crematorium gates, the cortège halted briefly while the coffin, draped in the red flag and blue starry plough, was raised on to the shoulders of the pallbearers: the trade unionists, Francis Devine, John Kane[3] and Fergus White;[4] John's two eldest grandchildren, David and Justin Swift; and myself and Grosvenor. Slowly then, through the crowd that had assembled, the coffin was carried into the crematorium.

Despite the sadness of the occasion, it had been decided that the ceremony should take the form of a celebration of his life, with tributes being interspersed with some of his favourite music and verse. Master of ceremonies was Martin Sheil, executive committee member of the Ireland–USSR Society and President of SIPTU's Dublin No. 19 Branch. Sheil, in his opening address of welcome, referred to Swift's unique contribution to the Ireland–USSR Society, particularly his fostering of trade union contacts between those two countries. Next to speak was Francis Devine, president of the Irish Labour History Society, and tutor with SIPTU. In the course of a wide-ranging tribute to Swift's life and work, Devine declared:

> John Swift's sudden death has occasioned sadness and shock. It is perhaps strange that the loss of a man born in 1896 should provoke surprise among a generation of people in 1990. It is, of course, a tribute to John Swift's accepted indestructibility. His presence at socialist and labour movement gatherings was constant, shaming many younger comrades with his commitment, indefatigable energy and boundless optisim in the face of adversity. But let no one have the misapprehension that John Swift's honoured place in Irish labour ranks was simply a function of his longevity. His life should be celebrated for its quality and we should be grateful that age allowed that quality such lengthy and splendid expression . . .[5]

Further tributes were paid by Peter Cassells, General Secretary of the Irish Congress of Trade Unions, who highlighted Swift's pioneering work in the field of industrial democracy; and Michael O'Riordan, Chairman of the Communist Party of Ireland, who described Swift as a person of outstanding integrity. O'Riordan also praised Swift's consistent defence of the Soviet Union, in good times and bad, and his efforts on behalf of Republican Spain. In a moving and final tribute, Michael D. Higgins, Labour TD for Galway West, said of Swift:

> . . . I salute him for what he did in the 1930s above all else. I salute him for the authenticity of his life. I salute him for integrity. I salute him for completeness and, above all, in these times, too, I salute him for his solidarity—with fellow workers through the trade union movement, with those who gave their lives to change this world, who recognised the impulse of humanity and who saw that the assertion of this humanity knew no national boundaries.[6]

Seven weeks after his death, with messages of sympathy still arriving from many parts of the world, Harriet Swift died in the Royal Hospital, Donnybrook. Her debility had prevented her attending his funeral. Always concerned for his welfare, she was unable to come to terms with his demise. With her main purpose in life now gone, she became quite listless and quickly lost the will to live. She died of heart failure on 9 May 1990, at the age of seventy-eight.

Her well-attended funeral service, preceded by a private family ceremony in the hospital, was held two days later in Taney Church of Ireland Parish Church, Dundrum. Harriet was interred in Shanganagh Cemetery, Shankill, Co. Dublin. A mere six days earlier, John's ashes had been buried in the same grave.

Appraisal

What was Swift's view of the progress of labour during his lifetime? On the political front, though he was, naturally, disappointed that socialism had not been established in Ireland, he remained convinced that socialism would come and that the determining influence in that would be external rather than internal. The advance of socialism in Ireland, he believed, would be part of a wider European trend and not an isolated occurrence on this island.

Viewing the progress of socialism internationally, Swift derived much satisfaction from the fact that, within his lifetime, more than a third of the world became socialist. This occurred in the period between the Bolshevik Revolution in 1917, when Swift was twenty-one, and the mid-1970s, when he was eighty, when capitalism was overthrown in South Vietnam.

Against that, however, in the last years of his life, sweeping changes were occurring in the Soviet Union and elsewhere in Eastern Europe. Earlier still, there had been the rise in Poland of the 'independent' trade union, Solidarity. No doubt, Solidarity's self-declared independence referred to the absence of links between itself and the communist Polish United Workers' Party. But, was Solidarity independent of the Vatican and its Polish pope? Swift had his doubts. With many of its more prominent leaders, notably Lech Walesa, constantly in the company of Catholic clerics, and Catholic symbols prevalent at many of its meetings, Swift considered Solidarity to be blatantly sectarian. More than anything else, he perceived it as a manifestation of Polish Catholicism and nationalism, made worse by the centuries-old antagonisms between Poland and Russia.

While these recent developments in Poland could be easily disregarded by Swift, other happenings in Eastern Europe were more difficult to dismiss, particularly the far-reaching events in the Soviet Union. Before considering Swift's reaction to such matters, let us first remind ourselves of his political position. Although he considered Hegel the finest of all the philosophers, he described his own philosophy of life as socialism.[1] As a Marxist, his objective was not simply the reform of capitalism, but rather, its complete abolition and replacement by socialism. This, he made clear when describing himself as 'a socialist, and not a social democrat'.[2] At the same time, he believed that, in capitalist societies, socialists should strive to improve the conditions of workers.

This, then, was Swift's position when Mikhail Gorbachev came to power in the Soviet Union. His initial reaction to the new Soviet leader and his policies of *perestroika* and *glasnost* was one of caution. This was not a question of clinging to outmoded ideas or defending the indefensible. Actually, Swift welcomed many of the initiatives taken by the new Soviet leadership, not least those curbing bureaucracy and corruption. He was enthusiastic, too, about the extension of freedom of expression, an area he had privately regarded as a shortcoming in that state.[3] He also recognised the need for some economic reforms. On the other hand, he was concerned that the reforms in the USSR, particularly in the economic and social spheres, could possibly destabilise socialism and democracy. To put it another way, he feared that, in attempting to rectify its problems, the USSR might throw out the baby with the bath water. That baby, for Swift, represented the very corner-stone of a socialist society, where the right to work was guaranteed; where education and health services were comprehensive and free; where transport services, housing and fuel were available at low cost; where culture was encouraged and generously supported; and where industrial democracy was prevalent in every enterprise. In this regard, Swift, though perplexed by the uncertain future of Soviet socialism, was not altogether pessimistic:

> If we are to assess the degree of democracy in a society in the extent to which the people participate in decision-making in matters in which they are mutually involved, we will have to rate the degree of democracy in the Soviet Union as high, that is, in the important field of the Soviet Union's economic activities. In my several visits to the

Soviet Union I have seen how the workers participate in decision-making in the economic life, at the different levels from the planning commissions to the enterprise committees in the workplace. I believe it works much the same in the other socialist countries.

It seems to me likely that whatever changes are taking place in the Soviet Union and in others of the Warsaw Pact countries, the experiments in worker participation in economic direction and management will remain.[4]

A consequence of recent reforms in some of the Warsaw Pact states has been the resurgence of nationalism and religion. Taken together, Swift saw this as a potentially lethal concoction, capable of causing much damage to socialism. Of particular concern to him was the outbreak of sectarianism and ethnic violence in several socialist republics. That, he feared, could be the springboard for challenging the secular nature of those states.

The likely outcome of all that was happening in Eastern Europe when Swift died was anything but clear. Should this turn out to be capitalism, or some dressed-up version of capitalism, we can be certain that it would not have secured his allegiance. It is unlikely that he would have identified with the present clamour for a market economy in those countries. He had seen the failure of such economies in other states in the West, including Ireland, where the consequences had been substantial and almost constant emigration, and a dole queue in 1990, of close to a quarter of a million. To Swift, the ultimate test for socialism in Eastern Europe would have been based, not on labels or slogans, for which he had little time, but on whether those states could retain their present social services and their democracy in the workplace.

As for the response of Western governments to events in Eastern Europe, Swift considered these hypocritical and fake. The real objective of the West, he contended, was the opening up of new markets for Western goods and services. Western exhortations for democracy in the East he found quite incredulous, especially coming from the US, which had supported corrupt and undemocratic regimes throughout the world, most notably in South-East Asia, the Middle East and Central and South America. There was little Western enthusiasm for democracy, Swift noted, when Allende's democratically elected Marxist government in

Chile was overthrown by the American CIA. Nor was there a Western whimper when tens of thousands of Chileans were subsequently murdered by the pro-Western dictators who seized power in that state. Equally shocking to Swift was the West's backing for the notorious Pol Pot led Khmer Rouge in Kampuchea, following the extermination by that force of some three million Kampucheans. He considered the ambivalent attitude of the West to apartheid in South Africa, opportunist and hypocritical. Leaving aside the discriminatory treatment of ethnic minorities in the US, he saw little prospect of the likes of America, West Germany and Britain seriously challenging white supremacy in South Africa when these very same powers had substantial investments there. In all these examples, the West's objective, it seemed to Swift, was one of self-interest and had nothing to do with democracy.

Whatever the set-backs in Eastern Europe, Swift, in his final years, remained optimistic about the future of socialism in that continent. Apart from any socialism that could be salvaged in Eastern Europe, elements of that ideology, he noted, already existed in the West. Here, he was referring particularly to industrial democracy and the welfare state. The former was to be found in such places as West Germany, France and Scandinavia, while the latter existed, in some form or other, in every Western European democracy. The welfare state originated, of course, not in Great Britain, as many believe, but in Bismarck's Germany in the 1880s, where, paradoxically, social security schemes were introduced to stem the rise of socialism. Swift observed with interest that, despite ten years of Thatcher's Tory rule, the British welfare state remained largely intact, albeit badly bruised through inadequate funding.

Central to Swift's optimistic view of socialism was what he regarded as the very real prospect of European unity. In such a united Europe, it seemed to him, the electorate's attention would focus on economic and social policies rather than on more traditional parochial issues. That, he felt, would present the Left with the challenge of political power. He was convinced that that challenge would be met.

There remains one final reason for Swift's optimism for the future of socialism. Capitalism's Achilles heel, he believed, was its inherent immorality, manifested in its exploitation of man by man and its insatiable greed for private profit. Such a system, it seemed to Swift, would always be unstable. Socialism, on the other hand, whatever its failings in practice, was based on sound moral grounds which would eventually see its triumph over capitalism.

Assessing the performance of labour's industrial wing during his lifetime, Swift was conscious of what he regarded as the non-political nature of the Irish trade union movement. That lack of politics, he felt, was the movement's greatest weakness.

He was disappointed, too, with the lack of cultural interests shown by Irish trade unionists. Nevertheless, he derived much satisfaction from the phenomenal growth in union membership since the mid-1940s, when he was first elected to the ITUC's executive. In that period of less than half a century, the affiliated membership of congress unions increased by almost half a million, from 189,000 in 1944[5] to 670,000 in 1988.[6]

Swift was proud, too, of the Irish trade union movement's achievements in bringing about improved working conditions. A century ago, in 1890, his own father worked a seven-day week of more than 100 hours, mostly at night. There were no paid holidays or other fringe benefits. The great fight then of the unions was for the six-day, 60-hour week. When Swift retired in 1967, the 40-hour, 5-day week was all but universal with most workers being entitled to a minimum of three weeks' annual holidays with pay. Furthermore, many workers by then had a range or other benefits such as pension and sick pay schemes. The credit for this progress, Swift believed, belonged to the trade union movement: 'For whatever advances have been made over the half century [up to 1967] political parties are liable to claim credit. But for those of us who have had to deal with the resolutions of the unions and of Congress over the years, we know it is the pressure of the organised workers that has brought things this far.'[7]

In considering Swift's contribution to the trade union movement, it has to be stated that the assessment of trade union leaders is a rather hazardous exercise, if only because trade unions are democratic organisations in which decisions are made collectively. Besides, the achievements of a trade union are frequently shared by the entire movement. The increase from two to three weeks' paid holidays in the 1960s, for example, was secured by virtually the whole movement, as was the earlier phased reduction in the working week from forty-eight to forty hours. True, a single union may occasionally make a break-through on some issue or other, but this is more likely to relate to the industrial strength of that union than any negotiating skill a particular official may possess.

Under the Bakers' Union's rules, Swift, as General Secretary, was not entitled to vote at NEC meetings. Against that, however, as the organisation's chief official, he enjoyed considerable influence in the union, particularly at NEC level.

With regard to Swift's ability as a union official or, at least, as a negotiator, we have the opinions of two colleagues with whom he worked on the joint union bakery committee. The first of these was Christopher Noonan, National Treasurer of the Bakers' Union, who described Swift as 'a great negotiator'.[8] Conor O'Brien, a branch secretary of the ITGWU, declared that he considered Swift 'one of the greatest negotiators of his time'.[9] For an employer's view, we can turn to the former Director-General of the Federated Union of Employers (now the Federation of Irish Employers), Dan McAuley: 'I got to know John well in the 1960s, during negotiations in the Bakery Industry. He was an extremely capable and competent general secretary of the Union and represented his members with skill and ability . . .'[10]

Having declared, with justification, that Swift's career as a union official is often neglected, Francis Devine went on to offer his own assessment:

> Under his leadership, membership of the IBCAWAU grew substantially from 2,400 in 1936 to 5,349 in 1967. He tirelessly travelled the country in pursuit of members' claims, all by public transport as he never drove. Wages and conditions improved and Swift enjoyed a fine reputation, among both members and employers, as an able negotiator. Swift's concern for detail, ability to assimilate and synopsise information, his meticulous eye and research, allied to a good unflappable 'presence' at the negotiating table made him a formidable opponent . . .[11]

The Bakers' Union, of course, had formed their own impressions of Swift's trade union career. In a lengthy tribute to him at its 1966 national delegate conference [Swift's final conference before retiring as General Secretary], Peter Flanagan, National

Treasurer, and Secretary, Dublin No. 1 Branch, declared: '. . . There can be but few careers in the world trade union movement to equal in attainment and distinction that of our General Secretary's. Coming from a very small union, and a small country, he has reached a position of eminence in the world movement that is usually reserved for the officials of very large unions in countries exercising strong influence in world affairs . . . '[12]

Another to remark upon Swift's internationalism was the ICTU's General Secretary, Peter Cassells: '. . . John Swift's extensive international involvement was in keeping with his broad vision of the role of trade unions at home and abroad. His abiding interest in extending the cultural horizons and enriching the lives of workers and their families placed him firmly in that noble tradition epitomised by Seán O'Casey when he said it was important not just to put bread on the table, but a rose as well.'[13]

In an obituary by the IUF, Swift was described as a 'firm internationalist'.[14] Highlighting that aspect of Swift, the IUF's General Secretary, Dan Gallin, said: 'John Swift was among the great figures of the Irish labour movement. His principal qualities were integrity and courage; in the IUF we also valued his deep commitment to internationalism. By the time he served as IUF President, he had accumulated a vast amount of culture, knowledge and experience which served the international well at a crucial time in its development. As long as he was active in the IUF, he helped strengthen its self-reliance, its militancy and its determination always to support those in the front line of the struggle.'[15]

A wider assessment of Swift's legacy to the labour movement would surely acknowledge his distinctive contribution in the field of culture and education. Of particular relevance here would be his pioneering initiatives in co-founding the Dublin Bakery School, the People's College and the Irish Labour History Society. Were these among the factors that prompted Michael O'Halloran, the ICTU's Education and Training Officer and former Bakers' Union member, to observe that Swift 'believed in the all-round development of the person'?[16]

Regarding Swift's broader contribution to society, Michael McInerney once said that Swift had created the tangible and the intangible.[17] Presumably, the former referred to his well-chronicled achievements in the labour movement. Less identifiable is the intangible; but here, perhaps, McInerney was referring to a wider stage, to Swift's crusade against reaction. That reaction ranged from Catholic triumphalism in his own country to apartheid in South Africa, and fascism, in all its manifestations, to American aggression in Vietnam. In mentioning the intangible it is likely that McInerney was mindful, too, of Swift's advocacy of a socialist and secular state where social justice, tolerance and rational thought would prevail. McInerney would also have been aware of the hostile environment in which Swift pursued these broader objectives. So, too, were Brendan Scott and others when they declared that Owen Sheehy Skeffington, Mai Keating, Noel Browne and John Swift could always be found in the high, lonely places, championing the just causes made dangerous by the evasive retreat of others.[18] It was possibly such considerations that elicited this judgment of Swift by Donal Nevin, on the occasion of Swift's ninetieth birthday: 'John Swift has never been a camp follower of the obsolete or of history, but has always maintained a position a bit ahead of his time. He was a trend setter who knew what it was like to swim against the tide. He had survived and has frequently been found to have been correct.'[19]

Another evaluation of Swift has been offered by Francis Devine: '. . . He was, so often, a solitary voice in the wilderness. Many of the causes he espoused came to be accepted as the norm. Much of Swift's heresy in the 1930s to 1950s was fast becoming orthodoxy in the 1970s and 1980s. The courage to have pioneered so many causes was little understood by a later generation that took freedom of thought and expression for granted. . .'[20]

A more explicit version of those themes of Devine's came from Michael D. Higgins, TD. Contending that Swift's life had been 'lived with authenticity on the Left', Higgins went on to say:

> . . . We must never forget . . . that darkest moment in our own history in the 1930s when even books were dangerous; when the largest church gate collection since O'Connell was gathered to send ambulances to Franco. It was in that environment and in that atmosphere that John Swift stood with courage and said: 'We must take our stand against fascism.'

He lived at a time when the Republic was betrayed. In his founding with Owen Sheehy Skeffington of the Secular Society, he showed his belief in the civic republic. It was he who said: 'We need no transcendent directions to tell us how to express our humanity to each other . . .'[21]

Complementing these assessments of Swift is this tribute by Justin Keating, on the occasion of Swift's death: '. . . With truth, dying, he could say that all his life and all his strength had been given to the noblest cause in the world—the liberation of mankind.'[22] Some fifteen years earlier, similar sentiments had been expressed by Michael McInerney: '. . . His record is one of daring endeavour with an inspiring record of service to his fellow men, perhaps the best criterion of the genuine socialist.'[23]

No greater tribute could be paid to John Swift.

Notes

CHAPTER 1 (1–15)

1. Edward MacLysaght, *Irish Families*, Dublin, 1972, 302.
2. Little Britain Street Bakers' Society, roll of members, 1820 to 1869.
3. National Federal Bakers' Union, report of executive for quarter ending 30 June 1890.
4. ibid, report of founding meeting, November 1889.
5. Operative Bakers of Ireland National Federal Union, report of first delegate meeting, 1890.
6. *Dundalk Democrat*, 21 June 1890.
7. Operative Bakers of Ireland National Federal Union, op cit.
8. *Dundalk Democrat*, 27 October 1894.
9. *Dundalk Examiner*, 27 September 1890.
10. ibid, 13 December 1890.
11. ibid.
12. *Tempest's Annual*, 1890.
13. ibid.
14. *Dundalk Democrat*, 14 June 1890.
15. National Federal Bakers' Union, report of executive for quarter ending 30 June 1890; Operative Bakers of Ireland National Federal Union, op cit; *Dundalk Democrat*, 21 June 1890.
16. *Dundalk Democrat*, 21 June 1890.
17. The term 'Union' in verse 2, line 1, refers, of course, to the Workhouse or Poor-house and not to the Bakers' Union.
18. Interview with John Swift, 1 January 1989.
19. *Dundalk Democrat*, 21 February 1891.
20. ibid, 12 March 1892.
21. ibid, 27 October 1894.
22. ibid, 18 August 1894.
23. ibid, 5 September 1896.
24. *Education Times*, 21 November 1974.
25. See *Irish Times*, 2 August 1982.
26. *Education Times*, 21 November 1974.
27. ibid.
28. *Dundalk Democrat*, 6 June 1891; 25 May 1901; 1 July 1911.
29. ibid, 16 October 1909.
30. ibid, 20 October 1900.
31. ibid, 5 September 1908.
32. ibid, 22 October 1904.
33. ibid, 3 March 1905.
34. *Tempest's Centenary Annual*, 1959, 41.
35. *Dundalk Democrat*, 30 August 1890; 20 September 1890.

36. The account of John Swift's childhood in Dundalk is based mainly on a series of interviews with him in 1986.

CHAPTER 2 (16–22)

1. John Swift, *History of the Dublin Bakers & Others,* Dublin, 1948, 305–18.
2. ibid, 305–18.
3. *Irish Times,* 14 March 1977, interview with John Swift, 1986.
4. ITGWU, *Fifty Years of Liberty Hall,* Dublin, 1959, 37.
5. ibid, 30–50; C. Desmond Greaves, *The Irish Transport and General Workers Union—The Formative Years, 1909–1923,* Dublin, 1982, 95–126.
6. Greaves, op cit, 91, 276.
7. Interview with John Swift, 1986.
8. John Swift, 'Trade Union Militancy Versus the Establishment', *Irish Socialist,* November 1985.
9. Interview with John Swift, 1986.
10. ibid.
11. ibid.
12. ibid.
13. F.S.L. Lyons, *Ireland Since the Famine,* London, 1971, 1973 ed, 311.
14. ibid, 330.
15. ibid.
16. The account of John Swift's experiences in Dublin between late 1912 and mid-1915 is based mainly on a series of interviews with him in 1986.

CHAPTER 3 (23–28)

1. South Dublin Union, Indoor Admissions Register, 1913.
2. ibid.
3. The account of John Swift's experiences in the South Dublin Union is based mainly on his article published in the *Irish Socialist* in May 1985.
4. The account of John Swift's experiences during the 1916 Rebellion and of his views of that and related events are based mainly on an interview with him in 1986.
5. The account of John Swift's experiences in Rathmines Bakery, Johnston, Mooney & O'Brien's and Bewley's, and joining the Bakers' Union, is based mainly on an interview with him in 1986.
6. Irish Bakers' Amalgamated Union, Dublin Branch, minutes of executive committee meeting, 16 November 1916.
7. ibid, 16 January 1917.

CHAPTER 4 (29–40)

1. British House of Commons, Parliamentary Debates, vol XCVIII, cols 810–811, 24 October 1917.
2. ibid, vol C, col 217, 4 December 1917.
3. ibid, vol C, col 1163, 12 December 1917.

4. ibid, vol C, cols 1977–1978, 19 December 1917.
5. Information given to John Swift by Christopher Noonan.
6. Interview with John Swift, 1986.
7. ibid.
8. The account of John Swift's experiences in the lead works and his subsequent arrest and imprisonment is based mainly on an interview with him in 1986.

CHAPTER 5 (41–48)

1. Alice Swift's death certificate states, incorrectly, that she was fifty-five when she died. Her baptism certificate certifies that she was born on 2 January 1861. Since she died on 15 November 1918, she was then, in fact, fifty-seven.
2. The account of John Swift's experiences in the British Army in France, Belgium and Germany between 1917 and 1919 is based mainly on an interview with him in 1986.

CHAPTER 6 (49–54)

1. Uinseann Mac Eoin, *Survivors*, Dublin, 1980, 71–2.
2. Patrick Swift's death certificate states, incorrectly, that he was sixty-eight when he died. His baptismal certificate certifies that he was born on 8 September 1858. Since he died on 15 February 1926, he was then, in fact, sixty-seven.
3. Interview with John Swift, 1986.
4. The account of John Swift's experiences during the periods of the War of Independence and the Civil War is based mainly on an interview with him in 1986.

CHAPTER 7 (55–61)

1. Interview with John Swift, 1986. The earliest evidence of John Swift's membership of the Bakers' Union is an entry in a cash book of the IBNAU's Dublin Branch. The entry, dated 26 August 1916, states: New—John Swift—2/6.
2. John Swift, *History of the Dublin Bakers and Others,* Dublin, 1948, 324.
3. ibid, 296.
4. John Swift, 'The Bakers' Records', *Saothar* 3, 1977, 4.
5. Boot Lane Bakers' Society, roll of members (1806–1891) which starts as a transcript of enrolments from 1806, made in 1838 by the society's secretary at that time, and his copy of the heading of the original document: 'This Society of Bakers commenced in Boot Lane, May 14th. 1789, for the support of the Sick and Burial of Deceased of Sd [said] Society.' The number of former members readmitted from 1806 onwards suggests that the Boot Lane Society's claim to have commenced in 1789 is probably authentic.

6. Boot Lane Bakers' Society, roll of members (1806–1891).
7. ibid.
8. ibid.
9. ibid.
10. Bridge Street Bakers' Society, minutes of general meeting, 22 September 1860.
11. ibid, 14 December 1862.
12. ibid, 31 January 1869.
13. John Swift, 'The Bakers' Records', op cit, 3.
14. Sydney and Beatrice Webb, *The History of Trades Unionism*, Longman, Green's second ed, 1896, appendix on the assumed connection between the Trade Unions and the Guilds in Dublin.
15. John Swift, quoted, *Irish Times*, 23 February 1976.
16. John Swift, 'The Bakers' Records', op cit, 1.
17. Transcript of a Memoranda Roll of the Exchequer, 13 and 14 Elizabeth, M. 108, in the Thrift Abstracts, National Archives, Dublin.
18. Dublin Operative Bakers' Friendly Society, or Friendly Brothers of St Anne, New Rules and Regulations, originally certified 29 January 1834; revised and amended January 1875.
19. Bridge Street Bakers' Society, apprentice indenture form.
20. IBCAWAU, apprentice indenture form used since the establishment of the Dublin Bakery School in 1935.
21. Christopher Noonan, quoted, *Irish Times*, 14 March 1977.
22. Interview with John Swift, 1986.
23. Information from Owen Curran.
24. Information from Fergus Whelan.
25. Little Britain Street Bakers' Society, roll of members (1820–1845 and 1845–1869).
26. ibid.
27. John Swift, *History of the Dublin Bakers and Others*, 231.
28. National Federal Bakers' Union, report for quarter ending 30 June 1890.
29. IBNAU, Dublin Branch, ledger recording payments of members' union dues.
30. John Swift, *History of the Dublin Bakers and Others*, 305–18; Christopher Noonan, op cit.
31. John Swift, *History of the Dublin Bakers and Others*, 324.
32. ibid.
33. IBCAWAU, minutes of executive meeting, 13 August 1918.
34. John Swift, *History of the Dublin Bakers and Others*, 332.
35. ibid.
36. Christopher Noonan, op cit.
37. Interview with John Swift, 1986.
38. John Swift, *History of the Dublin Bakers and Others*, 324.
39. ibid.
40. ibid, 324–32.
41. CSO, Consumer Price Index, 1914 to 1924.
42. John Swift, *History of the Dublin Bakers and Others*, 324–33.

43. ibid, 324–33.
44. Information from Owen Curran. An article on the records of the Irish Graphical Society (until 1970, the Dublin Typographical Provident Society), was published in *Saothar* 9, 1983, 111–15.
45. Interview with John Swift, 16 April 1989.
46. ibid, 1986.
47. IBCAWAU, Dublin No. 1 Branch, minutes of AGM, 8 July 1934.
48. ibid, 20 June 1930.
49. ibid, 8 July 1934.

CHAPTER 8 (62–73)

1. IBCAWAU, Dublin Branch, minutes of AGM, 10 July 1927.
2. ibid, 24 June 1928.
3. ibid, 14 July 1929.
4. IBCAWAU, foreword on history of national union, 15, published with agenda of union's national delegate meeting, 1968.
5. John Swift, *History of the Dublin Bakers and Others,* Dublin, 1948, 333.
6. Information from Owen Curran.
7. CSO, Consumer Price Index, average annual index, 1925 and 1933.
8. IBCAWAU, Dublin No. 1 Branch, minutes of AGMs, 14 July 1929 and 29 June 1930.
9. ibid, management committee meeting, 4 December 1929.
10. ibid, 15 January 1930.
11. For information on Hanna Sheehy Skeffington see Leah Levenson, and Jerry Natterstad, *Hanna Sheehy Skeffington: Irish Feminist,* New York, 1986.
12. Swift, op cit, 346.
13. IBCAWAU, Dublin No.1 Branch, minutes of adjourned general meeting, 22 January 1933.
14. IBCAWAU, Dublin No. 1 Branch, minutes of adjourned AGM, 15 July 1934.
15. IBCAWAU, Dublin No.1 Branch, minutes of special general meeting, 18 October 1936.
16. The *nom de plume,* Bolivar, was chosen by John Swift, not as a corruption of Jonathan Swift's *Gulliver,* but as a tribute to the South American revolutionary leader, Simon Bolivar, who, seemingly, was a free-thinker.
17. For information on Sam Anthony, see John O'Dowd, *The Dublin Bakery School, 1935–1985,* Dublin, 1985, 3; John Swift, 'Sam Anthony', an appreciation, *Irish Times,* 31 July 1985.
18. John O'Dowd, *The Dublin Bakery School, 1935–1985,* Dublin, 1985, 15.
19. John Swift, *History of the Dublin Bakers and Others,* Dublin, 1948, 344–49.
20. IBCAWAU, Dublin No. 1 Branch, minutes of AGM, 20 June 1930.
21. ibid, 5 July 1931.
22. IBCAWAU, Dublin No. 1 Branch, minutes of special general meeting, 15 January 1933.

23. IBCAWAU, Dublin No. 1 Branch, minutes of adjourned general meeting, 22 January 1933.
24. IBCAWAU, Dublin No. 1 Branch, minutes of special general meeting, 24 November 1935.
25. ibid.
26. IBCAWAU, Dublin No. 1 Branch, minutes of AGMs, 20 June 1930; 5 July 1931.
27. IBCAWAU, report of conference, 26–27 August 1936.

CHAPTER 9 (74–82)

1. Originally a member of the CPI, Michael McInerney later joined the Labour Party. Apart from his writings for newspapers, he was the author of several books, including his biography, *Peadar O'Donnell: Irish Social Rebel,* Dublin, 1974.
2. *Irish Times,* 11 September 1986.
3. ibid.
4. An obituary and an appreciation of Paddy Stephenson was published in *An Leabharlann,* Library Association of Ireland, vol 18, no 2, June 1960.
5. *Irish Times,* 30 October 1982.
6. C.S. Andrews, *Man of No Property,* Dublin, 1982, 40.
7. ibid, 40.
8. Although it was stated, falsely, in *Hibernia,* 19 February 1971, that John Swift had been a member of Clann na Poblachta, he was never, in fact, a member of any political party other than the Labour Party.
9. Interview with John Swift, August 1986.
10. *Workers' Life,* September 1980.
11. See, for example, *Irish Socialist,* May 1985; January 1986.
12. RTE, *Today Tonight,* 1 July 1985.
13. *Communist Party of Ireland—Outline History,* Dublin, 1975, 8. Larkin's Irish Worker (not Workers') League was named after his paper, the *Irish Worker.* This information was supplied on 24 July 1989 by Michael O'Riordan who had heard it from Johnny Nolan.
14. *Communist Party of Ireland,* op cit, 8.
15. ibid.
16. C. Desmond Greaves, *The Irish Transport and General Workers Union—The Formative Years, 1909–1923,* Dublin, 1982, 137, 317.
17. ibid, 116, 321.
18. ibid, 321; Emmet Larkin, *James Larkin: Irish Labour Leader, 1876–1947,* 1989 ed, 280–82; Donal Nevin, 'The Birth of the Workers' Union', *Obair,* no 1, May 1984, 3–4.

CHAPTER 10 (83–95)

1. J.H. Whyte, *Church & State in Modern Ireland—1923–1970,* Dublin, 1971, 71.
2. *Irish Catholic,* 23 December 1933.
3. *Standard,* 25 September 1934.
4. *Irish Catholic,* 24 August 1935.

5. *Standard*, 18 May 1934.
6. ibid, 23 February 1934.
7. *Irish Catholic Directory*, 1933.
8. Michael O'Riordan, *Connolly Column*, Dublin, 1979, photograph between 64 and 65.
9. *Standard*, 8 January 1937.
10. CSO, Live Register of Unemployed, total live register, 1930 to 1936.
11. CSO, estimated net emigration, 1937.
12. John Swift, 'The Contemporary Club—a Refuge for Free-thinkers', *Irish Socialist*, October 1984.
13. *Communist Party of Ireland, Outline History*, Dublin, 1975, 19.
14. ibid.
15. *Irish Catholic*, 17 June 1933.
16. ibid.
17. For information on Peadar O'Donnell see George Gilmore, *The Republican Congress*, 1934, Dublin, n.d., 1970?; Michael McInerney, *Peadar O'Donnell—Irish Social Rebel*, Dublin, 1974; Uinseann Mac Eoin, *Survivors*, Dublin, 1980, 1980 ed, 21–34; Richard English, 'Peadar O'Donnell: Socialism and the Republic, 1925–1937', *Saothar* 14, 1989; *Irish Times*, 14 May 1986.
18. George Gilmore was one of three brothers who were prominent, radical republicans, and close associates of Peadar O'Donnell. George Gilmore is the author of *The Republican Congress, 1934*, Dublin, n.d., 1970?
19. F.S.L. Lyons, *Ireland Since the Famine*, London, 1971, 1973 ed, 502.
20. John Swift, 'Report of Commission on Vocational Organisation (and its times, 1930–1940s)', *Saothar* 1, 1975, 54–63.
21. ibid.
22. Whyte, op cit, 80–81.
23. *Irish Catholic Directory*, 1939.
24. *Irish Times*, 2 July 1987.
25. Swift, op cit, 55.
26. John Swift, 'The Corporate State Fascism Irish-style', *Irish Socialist*, November 1984.
27. John Swift, 'Report of Commission', op cit, 60.
28. Whyte, op cit, 82–4.
29. *Standard*, 21 April 1939.
30. Whyte, op cit, 82–4.
31. *Standard*, 28 January 1944.
32. *Irish Catholic Directory*, 1936.
33. IBCAWAU, Dublin No. 1 Branch, minutes of AGM, 1 July 1933.

CHAPTER 11 (96–104)

1. For information on The Republican Congress see George Gilmore, *The Republican Congress, 1934*, Dublin, n.d. 1970?
2. Uinseann Mac Eoin, *Survivors,* Dublin, 1989, 73.
3. *Irish Press,* 17 January 1934.
4. ibid.

5. J.H. Whyte, *Church and State in Modern Ireland—1923–1970*, Dublin, 1971, 21.
6. Interview with Andrée Sheehy Skeffington, 17 November 1986.
7. In Uinseann Mac Eoin's book, *Survivors*, John Swift is described, inaccurately, as a pacifist. Confusion about this probably derives from Swift's association with pacifists during World War I.
8. Sheehy Skeffington, op cit.
9. *Irish Press*, 17 January 1934.
10. ibid.
11. Five sons of Lily Geraghty became prominent trade unionists. Seán, the eldest, is secretary of what was, until recently, the press branch of the Electrical, Electronic, Telecommunications and Plumbing Union (EEPTU), in London, which is now a branch of the Graphical, Paper and Media Union (GPMU). Tom is an employee of the Dublin Fire Brigade. Formerly a member of the FWUI's executive, he is now an NEC member of SIPTU. Shay, originally an ATGWU shop steward in Urney's Chocolates, Tallaght, Co. Dublin, later became a full-time official of that union. Des was a national official of the ITGWU before being appointed to a similar position in SIPTU. Hugh, a shop steward in CIE's Inchicore Works in Dublin, is chairperson of the Dublin District Committee of the Amalgamated Engineering Union (AEU).
12. *Standard*, 20 January 1934.
13. *Irish Catholic*, 20 January 1934.
14. ibid.
15. *Standard*, 25 September 1936.
16. ibid, 16 October 1936.
17. ibid, 30 October 1936.
18. ibid, 19 March 1937.
19. *Irish Catholic Directory*, 1938.
20. Michael O'Riordan, *Connolly Column*, Dublin, 1979, 41.
21. ibid, 33.
22. Emmet Larkin, *James Larkin—Irish Labour Leader*, London, 1965, 298.
23. O'Riordan, op cit, 162–5.
24. ibid, 100.
25. John Swift, 'The Contemporary Club—a Refuge for Free-thinkers', *Irish Socialist*, October 1984.
26. For further information on Bobbie Edwards see, 'Bobbie Edwards', *Irish Socialist*, December 1988.
27. For further information on Frank Edwards see, Mac Eoin, op cit, 1–20; Manus O'Riordan, *Portrait of an Irish Anti-Fascist: Frank Edwards 1907–1983*, Morgan Freiheit, New York, 18 September 1983, reproduced by Labour History Workshop, Dublin 1984; 'Frank Edwards Dies in Dublin', *Irish Times*, 8 June 1983; 'Tributes paid to Mr Frank Edwards', *Irish Times*, 10 June 1983.
28. *Irish Catholic Directory*, 1936.
29. Mac Eoin, op cit, 14.
30. An engineer by profession, Robert Tweedy was a pioneer in the development of the Irish peat industry.

31. Interview with John Swift, June 1987.
32. See 'Terence (Terry) Flanagan', an appreciation, *Irish Times*, 10 September 1990.
33. O'Riordan, op cit, 41.

CHAPTER 12 (105–110)

1. Peter Kemp, *The Strauss Family—Portrait of a Musical Dynasty*, Tunbridge Wells, Kent, 1985, 15–16.
2. The account of John Swift's European tour in 1938 is based mainly on interviews with John Swift, 3 November 1987, 6 December 1987; articles he wrote under the pseudonym 'Bolivar's Half Hour' which were published in *The Bakery Trade's Journal*, vol 3, no 9, October 1938; vol 4 no 2, April–June 1939. *The Bakery Trade's Journal* was a publication of the Irish Bakers' Confectioners' & Allied Workers' Amalgamated Union.
3. The account of John Swift's 1939 visit to Europe is based mainly on interviews with John Swift, 1986 and 30 December 1987.

CHAPTER 13 (111–119)

1. DTUC, annual report, 1936–1937.
2. DTUC, minutes of AGMs, 1936–1946.
3. ibid, 1937–1942.
4. ITUC, annual report, 1941–1942, 121–8.
5. Séamus Cody, John O'Dowd, Peter Rigney, *The Parliament of Labour—100 years of Dublin Council of Trade Unions*, Dublin, 1986, 171–2.
6. Charles McCarthy, *Trade Unions in Ireland—1894–1960*, Dublin, 1977, 142–63.
7. ibid.
8. ibid.
9. DTUC, minutes of council meetings, 20 May 1941 and 3 June 1941.
10. DTUC, annual reports, 1933/4 to 1940/1.
11. DTUC, Council of Action Standing Commitee, minutes of meetings, 6 June 1941 and 16 June 1941.
12. Police report, 23 June 1941.
13. DTUC, Council of Action Standing Committee, minutes of meeting, 30 June 1941.
14. ibid.
15. ibid.
16. Cody, O'Dowd, Rigney, op cit, 176; interview with Andrée Sheehy Skeffington, 17 November 1986.
17. Andrée Sheehy Skeffington, op cit.
18. DTUC, Council of Action Standing Committee, minutes of meeting, 26 June 1941.
19. ITUC, report of special conference, 23 October 1941.
20. ibid, 26 March 1942.

21. Archie Jackson was a member of the Amalgamated Society of Wood-
    workers (ASW) which was later incorporated into the Union of
    Construction Allied Trades and Technicians (UCATT). From 1941 to
    1943, he was president of the DTUC, immediately preceding Larkin,
    Sen. in that office. Swift and Jackson were colleagues on the DTUC
    executive in the early 1940s, Swift serving as vice-president to
    Jackson's presidency 1942–1943. Jackson was also a part-time lay
    preacher of one of the smaller Protestant churches. Considering him to
    be both a man of principle and a staunch trade unionist, Swift had a
    high regard for Jackson.
22. Walter Carpenter, a member of the ASW, served as president of the
    DTUC (1948–1949), and the ITUC (1958–1959). His father, also Walter,
    was the non-Jewish secretary of the International Tailors', Machinists'
    and Pressers' Trade Union which was founded by Jewish clothing
    workers in Dublin, in 1908. In 1921, having been secretary of its
    antecedent, the Socialist Party of Ireland, Carpenter, Sen. became the
    first secretary of the Communist Party of Ireland (CPI). Two years later,
    he presided at the first congress of the CPI. (The above information on
    Carpenter, Sen. is taken from Manus O'Riordan, 'The International
    Tailors', Machinists' and Pressers' Union', unpublished document, 1987.)
23. Cody, O'Dowd, Rigney, op cit, 177.
24. *Irish Times*, 22 August 1942.
25. J. Anthony Gaughan, *Thomas Johnson*, Dublin, 1980, 377.
26. ibid, 377.
27. ibid, 377.
28. *Communist Party of Ireland—Outline History*, Dublin, 1975, 20, 29;
    McCarthy, op cit, 256–7.
29. *Communist Party of Ireland*, op cit, 29.
30. ibid.
31. IBCAWAU, report of national delegate meeting, 1–3 September 1943;
    'Toganrog' may, in fact, have been 'Tíre na nÓg', the error possibly
    deriving from Swift's ignorance of Irish.
32. DTUC, minutes of executive committee meetings, 2 April 1942, 4
    March 1943 and 15 March 1945.
33. John Swift, 'Keeping to the Line of Least Persistence!', *Irish Socialist*,
    April 1984.
34. The account of the DTUC's executive committee meetings is based
    mainly on an article by John Swift published in the *Irish Socialist* in
    April 1984; interviews with John Swift, 16 March 1986, 8 February 1988.
    See also John Swift, quoted, *Irish Times*, 1 October 1988.

CHAPTER 14 (120–38)

1. IBCAWAU, minutes of NEC meeting, 6–8 March 1945.
2. Interview with John Swift, 10 September 1988.
3. ibid.
4. Séamus Cody, John O'Dowd, Peter Rigney, *The Parliament of Labour—
   100 Years of the Dublin Council of Trade Unions*, Dublin, 1986, 154.

5. Charles McCarthy, *Trade Unions in Ireland, 1894 to 1960*, Dublin, 1986, 253–4.
6. J. Anthony Gaughan, *Thomas Johnson*, Dublin, 1980, 377.
7. ibid, 378.
8. *Standard*, 4 February 1944.
9. Gaughan, op cit, 379.
10. ibid.
11. ILP and TUC, report of annual congress, 1918, 9.
12. *Communist Party of Ireland—Outline History*, Dublin, 1975, 31.
13. *Standard*, 17 March 1944.
14. *Communist Party of Ireland*, op cit, 31.
15. *Standard*, 17 March 1944.
16. ibid, 28 April 1944.
17. ibid; *The Brú* (The Larkin Unemployed Centre), May 1990, 6.
18. Interview with John de Courcy Ireland, 21 April 1990; *The Brú*, op cit, 6.
19. Interview with John de Courcy Ireland, 21 April 1990.
20. *Standard*, 28 April 1944.
21. Labour Party, annual reports, 1940–1941; interview with Joe Deasy, 26 July 1989.
22. Interview with Joe Deasy, 26 July 1989.
23. Interview with Andrée Sheehy Skeffington, 17 November 1986.
24. ibid.
25. McCarthy, op cit, 258.
26. *Standard*, 27 October 1944.
27. Evelyn Bolster, *The Knights of St. Columbanus,* Dublin, 1979, 98.
28. Gaughan, op cit, 379.
29. ibid, 381.
30. *Standard*, 18 July 1947.
31. ITUC, annual report, 1944/5.
32. ITUC, annual reports, 1936/7 to 1958/9; ICTU, annual reports, 1959 to 1966/7.
33. ITUC, annual report, 1944/5.
34. ibid, 1943/4, 106.
35. *Review*, May 1945.
36. IBCAWAU, general secretary's report of executive proceedings to national delegate meeting, 10–12 April 1946.
37. *Review*, May 1945.
38. ITUC, annual report, 1944/5, 122.
39. *Reynolds News*, 7 July 1946.
40. ITUC, annual report, 1945/6.
41. Gaughan, op cit, 385.
42. IBCAWAU, minutes of NEC meeting, 11 March 1947.
43. McCarthy, op cit, 292.
44. DTUC, minutes of executive committee meeting, 30 January 1947.
45. ITUC, annual report, 1944/5, 51.
46. There is no record of this delegation or their report in the ITUC annual reports. This may be a consequence of the split in the ITUC which disrupted the general secretaryship of that body. References to the

delegation may be found in *Irish Times*, 21 August 1980; *Irish Press*, 24 August 1980; *World Trade Union Movement*, no 9, 1980, 5; no 11, 1980, 23; *Irish Socialist*, February 1981.

47. ITUC, annual report, 1945/6.
48. *Irish Times*, 2 September 1970.
49. ITUC, annual report, 1958/9; ICTU report, 1959.
50. Provisional United Trade Union Organisation, second report of committee, 1956/7.
51. Labour Party, annual report, 1969.
52. *Liberty*, May–June and July–August, 1989.
53. *Newsline* (SIPTU), vol 1, no 1, May 1990, 4.
54. ITUC, annual report, 1948/9, 55; interview with Donal Nevin, 25 August 1989. Nevin expressed his belief that John Swift was the principal progenitor of the People's College.
55. John Swift, 'The Launching of the People's College', *Irish Socialist*, February 1985; Ellen Hazelkorn, 'The Social and Political Views of Louie Bennett, 1870–1956', *Saothar* 13, 1988, 32–44. See also 'Memorial to Louie Bennett', *Irish Times*, 26 September 1958.
56. John Swift, 'The Launching of the People's College', op cit.
57. Ruaidhrí Roberts, Dardis Clarke, *The Story of the People's College*, Dublin, 1986, 25.
58. John Swift, 'How Larkin Died on his Knees', *Irish Socialist*, January 1985; John Swift, 'The Launching of the People's College', op cit; 'Growth from Strength', unpublished report of the working party to advise the Jesuit Provincial on the future of the College of Industrial Relations, 1 May 1983, 13.
59. *Growth from Strength*, op cit, 18.
60. ibid, 13.
61. ibid, 20.
62. ITUC, annual report, 1953/4, 143.
63. Interview with John Swift, 19 August 1989.
64. NCIR, Prospectus 1985/6; Roberts, Clarke, op cit, 123. In 1985, there were twenty trade union corporate members of the NCIR. The same year, the number of unions affiliated to the People's College was twenty-two.
65. John Swift, 'The Launching of the People's College, op cit.
66. John Swift, 'We Need a School of Socialism', *Irish Socialist*, July 1970.
67. Letter, Fr Tom Morrissey, SJ, director NCIR, to John Swift, 25 March 1988; letter, John Swift to Fr Tom Morrissey, SJ, undated, but written on 31 March 1988.
68. *Liberty*, May 1983.
69. ITUC, annual report, 1948/9, 53.
70. Interview with John Swift, 14 June 1987; see article on career of Donal Nevin in *Irish Times*, 20 January 1989.
71. DTUC minutes of executive committee meeting, 30 January 1947.
72. Emmet Larkin, *James Larkin, Irish Labour Leader*, London, 1965, 1989 ed, 9.
73. *Irish Socialist*, January 1985.

74. John Swift, 'Larkin's New Clothes', *Irish Socialist*, December 1984; John Swift, 'How Larkin died on his knees', *Irish Socialist*, January 1985.
75. *Standard*, 7 February 1947.
76. John Swift, 'How Larkin died on his knees', op cit.
77. ibid.
78. ITCU annual report, 1946/7, 109-110.
79. Emmet Larkin, op cit, 194–5.
80. ibid, 290–91.
81. *Standard*, 17 January 1941.
82. ibid, 20 February 1942.
83. *Communist Party of Ireland*, op cit, 29.
84. ibid, 30.
85. John Swift, 'Learning to Work with Jim Larkin', *Irish Socialist*, June 1984.
86. John Swift, 'The De-Politicisation of Big Jim Larkin', *Irish Socialist*, September 1984.
87. John Swift, 'How Great was de Valera?', *Irish Socialist*, July 1984.

CHAPTER 15 (139–152)

1. IBCAWAU, report of national delegate meeting, 1–4 September 1943.
2. IBCAWAU, Dublin No. 1 Branch, minutes of AGM, 4 July 1943.
3. ibid, minutes of special general meeting, 11 April 1943.
4. ibid, 10 May 1943.
5. ibid, 11 April 1943.
6. ibid.
7. ibid.
8. IBCAWAU, Dublin No. 1 Branch, minutes of special meeting, 11 April 1943.
9. ibid, Dublin No. 1 Branch, minutes of AGM, 4 July 1943.
10. Interview with John Swift, June 1986.
11. ibid.
12. ibid.
13. IBCAWAU, minutes of NEC meeting, 2–3 June 1943.
14. IBCAWAU, report of national delegate meeting, 1943.
15. ibid, 1946.
16. ibid.
17. ibid.
18. John Swift, 'How the Bakers' Library Came to be "Blessed"!', *Irish Socialist*, April 1986.
19. IBCAWAU, report of national delegate meeting, 1946.
20. John Swift, 'How the Bakers' Library Came to be "Blessed"!', op cit.
21. IBCAWAU, Dublin No. 1 Branch, report of special committee to investigate matters in connection with Four Provinces House, 7 March 1950.
22. IBCAWAU, Dublin No. 1 Branch, minutes of special general meeting, 14 May 1944.
23. ibid.
24. IBCAWAU, minutes of RMC meeting, 26 February 1946.

25. John Swift, 'How the Bakers' Library Came to be "Blessed"!', op cit.
26. Interview with Johnny Devlin, 7 August 1990.
27. IBCAWAU, minutes of NEC meeting, 11–14 December 1946.
28. IBCAWAU, Dublin No. 1 Branch, report of special committee to invest-
    igate matters in connection with Four Provinces House, 7 March 1950.
29. IBCAWAU, minutes of NEC meeting, 6–8 March 1945.
30. *Sunday Tribune*, 25 November 1984.
31. *Standard,* 13 June 1947; John Swift, 'How the Bakers' Library Came to
    be "Blessed"!', op cit.
32. IBCAWAU, minutes of NEC meeting, 2–5 June 1947.
33. ibid.
34. *Standard,* 13 June 1947.
35. IBCAWAU, minutes of NEC meeting, 19–21 August 1947.
36. *Standard,* 1 August 1947.
37. IBCAWAU, minutes of NEC meeting, 15 April 1948.
38. IBCAWAU, minutes of RMC meeting, 22–23 October 1947.
39. IBCAWAU, minutes of NEC meeting, 19–21 August 1947.
40. IBCAWAU, minutes of RMC meeting, 22–23 October 1947.
41. *Standard,* 3 June 1949.
42. IBCAWAU, minutes of RMC meeting, 29 August 1946.
43. *Standard,* 5 February 1954.
44. IBCAWAU, minutes of NEC meeting, 2–4 December 1947.
45. IBCAWAU, report of national delegate meeting, 1–4 September 1948.
46. Interviews with John Swift, 9 August 1987; Michael O'Reagan, 31 May
    1989.
47. ibid.
48. Interview with Michael O'Reagan, 31 May 1989.
49. IBCAWAU, report of national delegate meeting, 1–4 September 1948.
50. IBCAWAU, minutes of NEC meeting, 25–27 May 1946.
51. ibid, 9–10 November 1948.
52. IBCAWAU, minutes of RMC meeting, 18 October 1948.
53. IBCAWAU, minutes of NEC meeting, 9–10 November 1948.
54. John Swift, 'How the Bakers' Library Came to be "Blessed"!', op cit.
55. Interview with John Swift, 7 February 1988.
56. IBCAWAU, minutes of NEC meeting, 9–10 November 1948.
57. The officers were Johnny Byrne and Christopher Noonan, president
    and secretary, respectively, of the Dublin No. 1 Branch; and Cecil and
    James Bradbury, president and secretary, respectively, of the Dublin
    No. 2 Branch.
58. Interviews with John Swift, 9 August 1987; Michael O'Halloran, 14
    October 1987. It was some time after it occurred that Swift first learnt
    of this event from Cecil Bradbury, a member of the delegation.
    Bradbury's account was corroborated by Michael O' Halloran who had
    heard it from Christopher Noonan, another member of the delegation.
59. *Sunday Tribune*, 25 November 1984.
60. *Standard,* 24 December 1948; IBCAWAU, minutes of RMC meeting, 20
    December 1948; *Irish Catholic Directory,* 1950. The *Standard* and the
    Irish Catholic Directory state that the dedication of Four Provinces

House was at the request of the IBCAWAU's NEC. There is no evidence in the union's records to support this claim.

61. IBCAWAU, minutes of RMC meeting, 16–17 January 1946.
62. ibid.
63. ibid, 15 November 1949.
64. IBCAWAU, Dublin No. 1 Branch, report of special committee to investigate matters in connection with Four Provinces House, 7 March 1950, and reply by the NEC to the more important points in the report.
65. ibid.
66. ibid.
67. ibid.
68. ibid.
69. ibid.
70. ibid.
71. *Sunday Tribune*, 13 March 1988.
72. Anne Haverty, 'Labour History's Hidden Murals', *Irish Times*, 14 March 1984; Robert Ballagh, 'The Bakers' Cultural Initiative', *Obair*, no 2, January 1985; Deirdre McQuillan, 'Going to the Wall', *Sunday Tribune* (*Colour Tribune*), 19 July 1987; Letter, John Swift to Patrick Shanley, general secretary, BFWAU, 22 August 1987; Deirdre McQuillan, 'Unique Murals Destroyed in Dublin Demolition', *Sunday Tribune*, 3 April 1988; Frank McDonald, 'Murals Destroyed For Want of £20,000', *Irish Times*, 4 April 1988; for further information on Four Provinces House and the Bakers' Union's cultural activities, see John Swift, *History of the Dublin Bakers and Others*, Dublin, 1948, 344–9; Michael McInerney, 'A Lifetime in the service of Labour', profile of John Swift, *Irish Times*, 31 July 1975; RTE, audio interview of John Swift by Pádraic Ó Raghallaigh, part 3, first broadcast on 24 August 1976; *Workers' Life*, September 1980, 14–15; Uinseann Mac Eoin, *Survivors*, Dublin, 1980, 1980 ed, 74; Eileen O'Brien, *An Irishwoman's Diary*, *Irish Times*, 5 September 1983; John Swift, *Labour Education*, unpublished paper read at conference on worker education, under the auspices of the Irish Society for Worker Education, 12 May 1984; Fintan O'Toole, 'Swift and Sure', interview of John Swift, *Sunday Tribune*, 25 November 1984; Una Claffey, 'The State of the Unions Then and Now', *RTE Guide*, 28 June 1985; RTE, *Today Tonight*, television interview of John Swift by Una Claffey, transmitted, 1 July 1985; John O'Dowd, *The Dublin Bakery School, 1935–1985*, Dublin, 1985; John Swift, 'How the Bakers' Library Came to be "Blessed"!', *Irish Socialist*, April 1986; ILHS, *The Parliament of Labour: 100 Years of the Dublin Council of Trade Unions*, exhibition catalogue, 1986; audio interview of John Swift by John P. Swift, 1986; John Swift, 'A Trade Union's Last Art Collection', *Sunday Tribune*, 26 July 1987; John P. Swift, 'Irish Labour's Living History', *Sunday Tribune* (*Colour Tribune*), 23 August 1987; *Sunday Tribune*, 13 March 1988; Francis Devine, '"A Dangerous Agitator": John Swift, 1896–1990, Socialist, Trade Unionist, Secularist, Internationalist, Labour Historian', *Saothar* 15, 1990, 8–9, 14–15.

CHAPTER 16 (153–163)

1. IBCAWAU, Dublin No. 1 Branch, minutes of adjourned general meeting, 11 November 1945, mention a membership figure of 1,100 for Dublin No. 1 Branch. Figures for Dublin No. 2 Branch are not available for this period, but were probably close to 300 members.
2. IBCAWAU, minutes of special NEC meeting, 8–10 May 1951, mention a figure of 4,410 as the total union membership at the end of 1950.
3. Interviews with Luke MacKeogh, 7 August 1987; Michael O'Halloran, 14 October 1987.
4. St Joseph's Young Priests' Society, Constitution.
5. *Standard,* 24 April 1939.
6. St Joseph's Young Priests' Society, collection book, 1949–1950.
7. *Irish Catholic Directory,* 1936.
8. *Standard,* 11 June 1948.
9. IBCAWAU, Dublin No. 1 Branch, minutes of adjourned general meeting, 11 November 1945, mention a membership figure of 1,100.
10. *Standard,* 8 July 1938.
11. *Irish Catholic Directory,* 1945.
12. Interviews with Luke MacKeogh, 7 August 1987; Michael O'Halloran, 14 October 1987.
13. Mary Jones, *These Obstreperous Lassies, A History of the Irish Women Workers' Union,* Dublin, 1988, 6.
14. *Standard,* 9 May 1952.
15. Registry of Friendly Societies, file T409, vol 3, MPGWU.
16. *Irish Catholic Directory,* 1955.
17. *Liberty,* May 1965.
18. IBCAWAU, minutes of NEC meeting, 21–24 November 1950.
19. *Standard,* 27 October 1950.
20. *Irish Catholic Directory,* 1951.
21. Noel Browne, *Against the Tide,* Dublin, 1986, 175.
22. Dáil Éireann, Parliamentary Debates, vol 125, col 951, 17 April 1951.
23. ibid, vol 125, col 668, 12 April 1951.
24. Browne, op cit, 163–5, 175–7.
25. *Irish Catholic Directory,* 1951.
26. ibid.
27. ibid, 1950.
28. See Evanne Kulmurray, 'Joe Deasy: The Evolution of an Irish Marxist, 1941–1950', *Saothar* 13, 1988, 112–19.
29. *Irish Workers' Voice,* April 1951; *Standard,* 17 October 1952, 14 November 1952, 21 November 1952, 19 December 1952; *Communist Party of Ireland—Outline History,* Dublin, 1975, 54.
30. *Standard,* 4 September 1953 and 9 October 1953.
31. ibid, 14 May 1954.
32. ibid, 21 May 1954.
33. IBCAWAU, report of national delegate meeting, 5–7 May 1954.
34. ibid, 8–10 May 1956.
35. ibid, 5–7 May 1954 and 8–10 May 1956.
36. ibid, 8–10 May 1956.

37. IBCAWAU, minutes of NEC meeting, 28–30 August 1956.
38. Registry of Friendly Societies, file T245, vol 3, Bakery and Food Workers' Amalgamated Union.

CHAPTER 17 (164–172)

1. ITUC, annual report, 1957/8.
2. IBCAWAU, report of national delegate conference, 1936.
3. Interview with John Swift, 3 August 1980.
4. ibid.
5. *Irish Times,* 31 July 1975.
6. Interview with John Swift, 11 September 1988.
7. *Irish Times,* 31 July 1975.
8. IBCAWAU, minutes of special NEC meeting, 23 July 1946.
9. Interview with John Swift, 11 September 1988.
10. IUF, *News Bulletin,* June–July 1967, 5.
11. *Irish Times,* 31 July 1975.
12. IBCAWAU, minutes of NEC meeting, 21–22 May 1963; the other members of the Bakers' Union's delegation to the USSR were Cecil Bradbury and John Cullinane.
13. Dublin Trades and Labour Council, Report of Irish Labour Delegation (appointed on the invitation of the All-Russia Trades Union Council) 1929. See also Michael O'Riordan, *Pages from History on Irish-Soviet Relations,* Dublin, n.d., 1977?, 3–6.
14. IBCAWAU, minutes of NEC meeting, 21–22 May 1963.
15. *Evening Press,* 26 July 1963 and 30 July 1963.
16. IBCAWAU, minutes of NEC meeting, 11–12 September 1963.
17. ibid, 21–22 February 1967; 2 June 1967; *Evening Herald,* 25 April 1967.
18. *Irish Times,* 8 November 1967.
19. ICTU, annual report, 1988, 273–7.
20. John Swift, 'Impressions in the USA', unpublished article, March 1988.
21. Michael McInerney, 'Grand Old Man of US Radicals', *Irish Times,* 4 September 1975; Bill Leahy, 'Maverick Leader Dies in Chicago', *Irish Times,* 19 September 1980; John Swift, 'Pat Gorman, an appreciation', *Saothar* 7, 1981, 7–8.
22. John Swift, 'Impressions in the USA', unpublished article, March 1988.
23. ibid.
24. ibid.
25. ibid.
26. *Irish Times,* 4 November 1965.
27. *Irish Times,* 31 July 1975.
28. *Irish Times,* 4–5 November 1965.
29. See IUF's *News Bulletin,* no 3, 1980 for tribute to Nätscher by Swift.
30. Interview with John Swift, 3 August 1980.
31. IBCAWAU, minutes of NEC meeting, 3–4 June 1964.
32. IUF, general secretary's report to fifteenth congress, 1967, XIa/7.
33. *Irish Independent,* 29 May 1967.
34. *Irish Times,* 24 May 1967.

CHAPTER 18 (173–183)

1. See *Bakery World*, March 1987, for tribute to Flanagan by Swift.
2. John's marriage certificate states incorrectly that he was forty-four. Both his baptism and birth certificates certify that he was born on 26 August 1896. Since he married on 26 September 1941, he was, in fact, forty-five.
3. Uinseann Mac Eoin, *Survivors*, Dublin, 1980, 14.
4. Interview with George Jeffares, 30 July 1990.

CHAPTER 19 (184–207)

1. IBCAWAU, agenda of national delegate conference, 1968, with foreword on history of the union, 23.
2. ibid, 26.
3. Sceim na gCeardchumann (literally, trade union scheme) which originated in Cork was a broad left-wing cultural association. Among the activities of this body were the promotion of the Irish language and traditional music and the organisation of workshops on industrial democracy.
4. IBCAWAU, minutes of NEC meeting, 26–27 September 1961; interview with John Swift, 19 August 1989.
5. *Irish Press*, 17 February 1949; *Irish Times*, 5 March 1949; *Irish Independent*, 15 April 1949.
6. IBCAWAU, general secretary's report to national delegate conference, 1966, 78; Interview with Ken Hannigan, 10 August 1989.
7. Francis Devine, "'A Dangerous Agitator'": John Swift, 1896–1990, Socialist, Trade Unionist, Secularist, Internationalist, Labour Historian', *Saothar* 15, 1990, 16.
8. CSO, Live Register of Unemployed, 1989.
9. CSO, estimated net emigration, 1951–1971.
10. J.H. Whyte, *Church and State in Modern Ireland—1923–1970*, Dublin, 1971, 351.
11. *Ireland–USSR, 21st Anniversary,* Ireland/USSR Society, 1987, 4.
12. ibid.
13. ibid.
14. ibid.
15. Interview with Michael O'Riordan, 24 July 1989.
16. *Communist Party of Ireland —Outline History,* Dublin, 1975, 33–4.
17. Information from Eric Fleming, 26 July 1989.
18. Information from Sean Garland, 1 August 1989.
19. Information from Marion Boushell, 2 August 1989.
20. Labour Party, annual report, 1967.
21. C. Desmond Greaves, *The Life and Times of James Connolly*, London, 1961; Samuel Levenson, *James Connolly, a Biography*, London, 1973.
22. Levenson, op cit, 113.
23. ibid, 321.
24. ibid, 321–2.

25. John Swift, election address contesting position of chairperson of the Labour Party at the Party's annual conference, 26–28 February 1971.
26. ibid.
27. ibid.
28. Labour Party, report, recommendations and draft policy document of subcommittee on industrial democracy.
29. ibid.
30. Swift, op cit.
31. ibid.
32. *Irish Socialist,* February 1969.
33. ITUC, annual report, 1948/9, 101–103.
34. ITUC, annual report, 1966/7, 195–205.
35. Labour Party, annual report, 1969.
36. ibid, 1956/7.
37. ibid, 1961/2.
38. ibid, 1969.
39. ibid.
40. ibid, 1961/2.
41. ibid, 1969.
42. ibid.
43. *Irish Times,* 19 June 1989.
44. ibid, 25 January 1969.
45. John Horgan, *Labour: The Price of Power,* Dublin, 1986, 33; Michael Gallagher, *The Irish Labour Party in Transition, 1957–82,* Manchester and Dublin, 1982, 42.
46. Gallagher, op cit, 42.
47. Evelyn Bolster, *The Knights of St. Columbanus,* Dublin, 1979, 96.
48. Labour Party, certificate of ballot..
49. Memorandum of meeting held on 28 June 1973, to consider the formation of a society for Irish labour history.
50. ILHS, letter, dated January 1974, from Matt O'Neill, secretary, to the general secretary of each trade union with corporate affiliation appeal.
51. ILHS, president's address to inaugural meeting, 27 October 1973.
52. ILHS, letter, dated January 1974, op cit.
53. *Saothar* 5, 1979, 3.
54. *Saothar* 1, 1 May 1975.
55. *Labour History News,* no 4, summer 1988, 10–11; ILHS, annual report, 1988.
56. *Labour History News,* no 6, summer 1990, 5.
57. John Swift, conference report, 'Founding Congress of the World Association of Centres for Historical and Social Studies of the Labour Movement, 27 February–3 March 1978, Mexico City', *Saothar* 5, May 1979, 92–3.
58. *Workers Life,* September 1983.
59. *Saothar* 5, 1979, 3.
60. *Communist Party of Ireland—Outline History,* op cit, 45.
61. ibid.
62. *Evening Herald,* 16 September 1980.

63. ibid.
64. ibid.
65. Noel Browne, *Against the Tide*, Dublin, 1986, 136–7.
66. May Swift's death certificate states, incorrectly, that she was forty-seven when she died. Her baptism and birth certificates certify that she was born on 29 May 1903. Since she died on 19 June 1953, she was then, in fact, fifty.
67. *Irish Socialist*, November 1976.
68. *Irish Times*, 5 October 1976.
69. ibid, 21 August 1980.
70. For further information on Betty Sinclair, see Hazel Morrissey, 'Betty Sinclair: A Woman's Fight for Socialism, 1910–1981', *Saothar 9*, 1983, 121–31.
71. *Irish Socialist*, February 1981.
72. *Irish Times*, 23 February 1976, 2 August 1982, 5 September 1983, 11 September 1986, 1 October 1988.
73. ibid, 31 July 1975.
74. *Sunday Tribune*, 25 November 1984.
75. ibid, (*Colour Tribune*), 23 August 1987.
76. Letter, John Swift to Kadar Asmal, chairman, IAAM, 10 September 1986.

CHAPTER 20 (208–211)

1. *Evening Press, Irish Independent, Irish Press, Irish Times*, 22 March 1990.
2. *Irish Times*, 24 March 1990.
3. Since the mid-1970s, John Kane has been branch secretary of the Dublin No. 2 Branch, SIPTU (ITGWU up to December 1989). Prior to its disbandment in December 1989, Kane was also for many years secretary of the ITGWU's Dublin District Council. It was on Kane's initiative that Swift delivered the annual memorial lecture to the council on 24 November 1987. Kane, it was, too, who described Swift as the doyen of the trade union movement.
4. Fergus White, a socialist, is the son of Swift's first cousin, Paddy White. A printer by trade, Fergus is a member of the Graphical Paper and Media Union.
5. Extracts from Francis Devine's funeral tribute were published in *Newsline* (SIPTU), vol 1, no 1, May 1990, 20. The full text appeared in *Labour History News*, no 6, summer 1990, 21–2.
6. Michael D. Higgins's funeral tribute was published in full as an appreciation in the *Irish Times*, 16 April 1990.

CHAPTER 21 (212–220)

1. RTE, *Donncha on Sunday* (Donncha O Dulaing), radio programme devoted to the golden jubilee of the Dublin Bakery School, including interview with John Swift, broadcast 24 March 1985.
2. *Jerusalem Post*, 1 July 1965.

3. Swift revealed this reservation of Soviet life to a small number of socialist friends. He refrained from criticising the USSR publicly, arguing that that state had more than its share of enemies.

4. John Swift, 'Political Drift', *Irish Times,* 6 October 1989.

5. ITUC, annual report, 1943/4, 6–20.

6. ICTU, annual report, 1987/8, 1.

7. John Swift, 'The March of Organised Labour', *Irish Times,* 9 August 1973.

8. Christopher Noonan, quoted, *Irish Times,* 14 March 1977.

9. *Liberty,* October 1983.

10. Letter, Dan J. McAuley to Harriet Swift, 27 March 1990.

11. Francis Devine, ' "A Dangerous Agitator": John Swift, 1896–1990, Socialist, Trade Unionist, Secularist, Internationalist, Labour Historian', *Saothar* 15, 1990, 13.

12. Peter Flanagan, 'Retirement of General Secretary', IBCAWAU, general secretary's report to national delegate conference, 1966.

13. Peter Cassells, 'Tribute to John Swift', ICTU, press release, 21 March 1990.

14. IUF, *News Bulletin,* vol 60, no 1–2, 1990, 10.

15. Dan Gallin, IUF, *News Bulletin,* vol 60, no 1–2, 1990, 10..

16. Michael O'Halloran, quoted, *Irish Times,* 29 November 1984.

17. Michael McInerney, 'A Lifetime in the Service of Labour' (a profile of John Swift), *Irish Times,* 31 July 1975.

18. *Irish Times,* 12 February 1973.

19. Donal Nevin, quoted, *Irish Times,* 11 September 1986.

20. Devine, op cit, 17.

21. Michael D. Higgins, funeral tribute to Swift, 23 March 1990, which was published in full as an appreciation in the *Irish Times,* 16 April 1990.

22. Justin Keating, 'Justin Keating column', *Evening Herald,* 27 March 1990.

23. McInerney, op cit.

Bibliography

SELECT PUBLISHED WRITINGS
Articles (A), Book (B), Letters (L), Papers (P) and Speeches (S) of John Swift

B *History of the Dublin Bakers and Others*, Dublin, 1948.
A 'The Trade Union Split: Who Benefits?', *Review*, May 1945.
A 'Must End TU Split to Fight for Free and United Ireland', *Reynolds News*, 7 July 1946.
A 'European Journey'—1, *Irish Times*, 29 September 1951.
A 'European Journey'—2, *Irish Times*, 1 October 1951.
A 'European Journey'—3, *Irish Times*, 2 October 1951.
A 'European Journey'—4, *Irish Times*, 3 October 1951.
A 'European Journey'—5, *Irish Times*, 4 October 1951.
A 'Progress Towards Unity in Trade Union Movement', *Irish Times* (supplement), 1 January 1958.
A 'Ill Fares the Land', *Irish Times*, 18 August 1958.
A 'Progress Towards Trade Union Unity', *Irish Times* (supplement), 1 January 1959.
A 'German Labour's Line, Policy Making of the Non-Political', *Irish Times*, 22 October 1962.
A 'German Labour's Line, Sharing in Management', *Irish Times*, 23 October 1962.
A 'An example for all Lovers of the Melodies of Moore', *Irish Press*, 23 November 1962.
A 'The USSR Revisited—1, Moscow Skyline Dominated by Temples of Secular Aspiration, Soviets have given the People Palaces', *Irish Times*, 27 November 1963.
A 'The USSR Revisited—2, Leningrad's War Background Dramatises Peace Desires, Trade Unions Influence Cultural Life', *Irish Times*, 28 November 1963.
A 'The Messianic Mission of Israel, An Example of Co-operation', *Irish Times*, 4 November 1965.
A 'Israel Surrounded by Her Enemies, Where Past, Present and Future Merge', *Irish Times*, 5 November 1965.
A 'Ireland Celebrates its Independence', IUF *News Bulletin*, July/August 1966.
A 'How Labour Relations Work in Russia'—1, *Irish Times*, 7 November 1967.
A 'How Labour Relations Work In Russia—2, A Choice of Systems', *Irish Times*, 8 November, 1967.
A 'Looking for Connolly and the Dread of Finding Him', *Irish Times*, 23 July 1968.

A 'Looking for Connolly—2, Labour and the Development of the State', *Irish Times*, 24 July 1968.

A 'Industrial Democracy: A Reply' (to Michael O'Riordan), *Irish Socialist*, February 1969.

P 'Baker of the Year', Competition Sponsored by the Irish Flour Millers' Association, *Irish Independent*, 4 June 1969.

A 'Irish Trade Unionism in the Seventies', *Irish Democrat*, February 1970.

S 'We Need a School of Socialism', *Irish Socialist*, July 1970.

A 'International Trade Unions—1, Workers of the World', *Irish Times*, 2 September 1970.

A 'International Trade Unions—2, Bargaining with Cartels', *Irish Times*, 3 September 1970.

A 'The First Land Tax Man', *Irish Times*, 3 November 1970.

A 'Commemorating Hegel', *Irish Times*, 6 November 1970.

A 'Vocationalism Last Time', *Irish Times*, 12 January 1971.

A 'State Aid to the ICTU', *Irish Times*, 29 January 1971.

A 'Labour and Workers' Democracy—1, Connolly Revised', *Irish Times*, 22 February 1971.

A 'Labour and Workers' Democracy—2, The Silence on Socialism', *Irish Times*, 23 February 1971.

A 'The Political Strike', *Irish Times*, 12 April 1971.

A 'Sources of Irish Secularism'—1, *Irish Times*, 14 May 1971.

A 'Sources of Irish Secularism'—2, *Irish Times*, 15 May 1971.

A 'Thoughts about the Congress', *Irish Times*, 21 July 1971.

A 'Thoughts about the Congress', *Irish Times*, 23 July 1971.

A 'Defenders of the Clyde', *Irish Times*, 14 September 1971.

A 'For Want of a Quorum', *Irish Times*, 20 October 1971.

A 'Labour and Constitution', *Irish Times*, 26 July 1972.

A 'Workers in Miami'—1, *Irish Times*, 10 October 1972.

A 'Workers in Miami'—2, *Irish Times*, 11 October 1972.

A 'Ireland's Soviet Friends', *Irish Times*, 8 November 1972.

A 'The March of Organised Labour', *Irish Times*, 9 August 1973.

A 'A Protestant Streak in the Gap of the North', *Education Times*, 21 November 1974.

P 'Industrial Democracy West and East', CSEU *Review*, May/June 1975.

A 'Report of Commission on Vocational Organisation (and its Times, 1930–1940s)', *Saothar* 1, 1 May 1975, 54–63.

A 'Irish Labour History Society Has High Educational Potential', *Education Times*, 15 May 1975.

A 'Early Societies of Journeymen Bakers in Waterford', *Munster Express*, 30 January 1976.

A 'Waterford Bakers' Societies', 1822–89, *Decies* (Old Waterford Society) No. 3, October 1976, 7.

A 'Soviet Pricing Policy', *Irish Socialist*, January 1977.

S 'The Bakers' Records', *Saothar* 3, 1977, 1–5.

A 'Irish Labour and Russian Revolution', *United Irishman*, November 1977.

A 'Irish Labour and Russian Revolution', *United Irishman*, December 1977.

A 'The Irish TU Movement and the October Revolution'—1, *Liberty,* October 1977.

A 'The Irish TU Movement and the October Revolution'—2, *Liberty,* November 1977.

A 'Remembering de Valera, My First Impressions', *Irish Socialist,* September 1982.

A 'De Valera Centenary, A Man too Remote from the Workers', *Irish Socialist,* October 1982.

A 'De Valera Centenary, Ambiguity a Hallmark of his Character', *Irish Socialist,* November 1982.

A 'Memories of Mortished', *Liberty,* May 1983.

A 'The "Holy" Crusade for the Corporate State', *Irish Socialist,* May 1983.

A 'A Decade of Irish Labour History', *Irish Socialist,* June 1983.

L 'Pius Memories', *Sunday Tribune,* 21 August 1983.

L 'Noel Browne and the Defects in our Education System', *Sunday Tribune,* 29 January 1984.

A 'John Swift Remembers Larkin, Keeping to the Line of Least Persistence!', *Irish Socialist,* April 1984.

L 'Coughing in Concert', *Irish Times,* 24 April 1984.

A 'Remembering Jim Larkin', *Irish Socialist,* May 1984.

A 'Learning to Work with Jim Larkin', *Irish Socialist,* June 1984.

A 'How Great Was de Valera?' *Irish Socialist,* July 1984.

A 'The De-Politicisation of Big Jim Larkin', *Irish Socialist,* September 1984.

A 'The Contemporary Club a Refuge for Free-Thinkers', *Irish Socialist,* October 1984.

A 'The Corporate State—Fascism Irish-Style', *Irish Socialist,* November 1984.

A 'Larkin's New Clothes', *Irish Socialist,* December 1984.

A 'How Larkin Died on His Knees', *Irish Socialist,* January 1985.

A 'The Launching of the People's College', *Irish Socialist,* February 1985.

A 'The Cult of Management', *Irish Socialist,* March 1985.

A 'Who or Where is Management?', *Irish Socialist,* April 1985.

A 'Life in the Poor House in Early 20th Century', *Irish Socialist,* May 1985.

A 'Life in the Poor House', *Irish Socialist,* June 1985.

A 'The Fight for the Sixty-Hour Week', *Irish Socialist,* July 1985.

A 'The Fight to Make the Unions Turn to a Political Direction', *Irish Socialist,* September 1985.

A 'The October Revolution in Russia and the Irish Labour Party', *Irish Socialist,* October 1985.

A 'Trade Union Militancy Versus the Establishment', *Irish Socialist,* November 1985.

A 'Union Establishments Turn Political', *Irish Socialist,* December 1985.

A 'The Rich Grow Richer and the Poor Stay Poor', *Irish Socialist,* January 1986.

A '"Social Partnership" is Just a Form of Class Collaboration', *Irish Socialist,* March 1986.

A 'How the Bakers' Library Came to be "Blessed"!', *Irish Socialist,* April 1986.

A 'The Mystique of Numbers and the Pace of Life', *Irish Socialist*, April 1987.

L 'A Trade Union's Lost Art Collection', *Sunday Tribune*, 26 July 1987.

A 'Reflections on a Birthday Honour', *Irish Socialist*, August 1987.

A 'Opinion Polls are Used to Manipulate Our Democracy', *Irish Socialist*, December 1987.

A 'Advertising the Opium of the Late Capitalist Era', *Irish Socialist*, April 1988.

A 'Looking Back at 60 Years of Trade Union Membership', *Irish Socialist*, May 1988.

L 'Political Drift', *Irish Times*, 6 October 1989.

SELECT UNPUBLISHED WRITINGS
Manuscripts (M), Articles (A), Papers (P) and Speeches
(S) of John Swift, in the possession of John P. Swift.

M 'Obituaries', July 1984.

M 'Told in Toberona—One Man's Labour History', February 1989.

P 'Social Principles', early 1930s.

A 'Role of the Trade Unions in Poland', 3 May 1963.

A 'Commemorating Soviet Revolution—Some Likely Durables', 1967.

P 'Some Notes on the History and Development of the Trade Union Movement in Ireland', 6 August 1968.

P 'Who are the Bankers? Where the Source of Banking Power?', c. late 1960s.

A 'The Talk About Natural Law'—1, *c*.1970.

A The Talk About Natural Law'—2, *c*.1970.

A 'The French and their Funerals', 1970 or 1971.

A 'Revolt on the Clyde', August 1971.

A 'The Rise of the Irish Workers', *c*.1970s.

A 'Party Drifts Backwards in Politics', mid-1970s.

A 'Early Operative Bakers' Societies in Dublin', 1976.

A 'Early Societies of Journeymen Bakers in Waterford', 1976.

P 'The Soviet Trade Unions—Some Notes on their History, Structure and Functions' (paper prepared for members of a People's College group who visited the USSR in 1977), 20 June 1977.

P 'The Great October Revolution—Irish Labour's Reaction' (paper read to ILHS's annual seminar, November 1977), 10 November 1977.

A 'Women's Liberation and the Equality Agency', 1983.

P 'Labour Education' (paper read to 'Conference on worker education', under the auspices of the Irish Society for Worker Education), 12 May 1984.

S 'Birthday Party' (speech on the occasion of his ninetieth birthday), 26 August 1986.

P '70th Anniversary of Russian Revolution 1917—Irish Labour's Reaction to Revolution—Reaction Today' (paper read to public meeting held under the auspices of the Ireland–USSR Society), 17 November 1987.

A 'Literature of the T-Shirt', 1 January 1988.

A 'Impressions in the USA', March 1988.
A 'The New is Such We Sigh for the Old', March 1988.

LABOUR RECORDS

A Bakery and Food Workers' Amalgamated Union and its antecedents
(i) National Union
National Federal Bakers' Union, report of founding meeting, 1889.
Operative Bakers' of Ireland National Federal Union, report of first delegate meeting, 1890.
National Federal Bakers' Union, report of executive for quarter ending 30 June 1890.
Irish Bakers' National Amalgamated Union, minutes of NEC, 1913–1918.
IBCAWAU, minutes of NEC, 1918–1967.
IBCAWAU, minutes of resident council, 1930–1938.
IBCAWAU, reports of delegate meetings, 1936–1966.
IBCAWAU, minutes of resident management committee, 1943–1967.
IBCAWAU, general secretary's reports to delegate meetings, 1946–1968.
IBCAWAU, Dublin No. 1 Branch, report of special committee to investigate matters in connection with Four Provinces House, 7 March 1950, and reply by the NEC to the more important points in the report.
IBCAWAU, foreword on history of national union published with agenda of union's national delegate conference, 1968.
IBCAWAU, rule book.

(ii) Dublin Union(s)
Boot Lane Bakers' Society, role of members, 1806–1891.
Little Britain Street Bakers' Society, or Guild of Saints Clement and Anne, Role of members, 1820–1869.
Bridge Street Bakers' Society, or Dublin Operative Bakers' Friendly Society, or Friendly Brothers of St Anne, minutes of general meetings, 22 September 1860, 14 December 1862, 31 January 1869.
Bridge Street Bakers' Society, new rules and regulations, originally certified 29 January 1834; revised and amended January 1875.
Bridge Street Bakers' Society, apprentice indenture form.
IBNAU, Dublin Branch, ledger recording payments of members dues, 1913–1918.
IBNAU, Dublin Branch, minutes of executive committee meetings, 1912–1918.
IBCAWAU, Dublin Branch (Dublin No. 1 Branch from 1928), minutes of executive committee meetings, 1918–1952.
IBCAWAU, Dublin Branch (Dublin No. 1 Branch from 1928), minutes of management committee meetings, 1920–1952.
IBCAWAU, Dublin Branch (Dublin No. 1 Branch from 1928), minutes of general meetings, 1923–1959.
IBCAWAU, Dublin No. 1 Branch, apprentice indenture form, 1935.

B   Dublin Trades Union Council (DTUC)
    DTUC, minutes of council meetings, 1929–1946.
    DTUC, annual reports, 1933/4 to 1945/6.
    DTUC, minutes of executive committee meetings, 1941–1947.
    DTUC, minutes of Council of Action's Standing Committee, 2 June 1941
    to 24 July 1941.

C   International Union of Food and Allied Workers' Associations (IUF)
    IUF, general secretary's report to fifteenth congress, 1967.
    IUF, programme of fifteenth congress, May 1967.
    IUF, minutes of fifteenth congress, Dublin, 28–30 May 1967.

D   Irish Congress of Trade Unions (ICTU) and its antecedents.
    ITUC, annual reports, 1934/5–1958/9.
    CIU, annual reports, 1945–1959.
    PUTUO, second report of the committee, June 1956–July 1957.
    ICTU, annual reports, 1959–1989.

E   Irish Labour History Society (ILHS)
    Letter, undated, from Fergus A. D'Arcy, inviting persons to attend meeting
    on 28 June 1973 'to consider the possibility of forming such a society'
    [for the study of Irish labour history].
    ILHS, provisional committee, minutes of meetings 28 June; 11, 25 July;
    8, 22 August; 12, 19 September 1973.
    ILHS, notice, 19 September 1973 of inaugural meeting, 27 October 1973.
    ILHS, agenda of inaugural meeting, 27 October 1973.
    ILHS, president's address to inaugural meeting, 27 October 1973.
    ILHS, letter, dated January 1974, from Matt O'Neill, secretary, to the
    general secretary of each trade union with corporate affiliation appeal.
    ILHS, annual reports, 1988, 1989.

F   Labour Party
    Labour Party, annual reports, 1930/1–1987/9.
    Labour Party, report, recommendations and draft policy document of
    subcommittee on industrial democracy, 1968.
    Labour Party, election address of John Swift for the election of party
    chairman at the Party's annual conference, 26–28 February 1971.
    Labour Party, certificate of ballot for chairman, vice-chairman and
    financial secretary at 1971 annual conference.

G   Marine Port and General Workers' Union (MPGWU) and its antecedents
    MPGWU, rule book.

    LABOUR AND REPUBLICAN PERIODICALS AND PUBLICATIONS

A   Civil Service Executive Union (CSEU)
    Review, November/December 1973; November/December 1974; May/
    June, November/December 1975; March/April 1977; November/Decem-
    ber 1980; January/February 1981.

B Communist Party of Ireland (CPI) and its antecedents
   Review, May 1945.
   Irish Workers' Weekly, 5, 19 October; 14 December 1940; 30 August 1941.
   Irish Workers' Voice, April 1951.
   Irish Socialist, May 1961 to September/October 1989.
   Unity, 31 March 1990.

C Connolly Association
   Irish Democrat, October 1968; January 1970.

D Dublin Trade Union Council (DTUC)
   Workers' Action, 1 May 1942.

E International Union of Food and Allied Workers' Associations (IUF)
   News Bulletin, July/August 1966; June/July 1967; no 3, 1980; no 1–2,
   1986; no 1–2, 3–4, 1990.

F Irish Bakers' Confectioners' and Allied Workers' Amalgamated Union
   (IBCAWAU)
   Bakery Trade's Journal, 1936–1947.

G Irish Congress of Trade Unions (ICTU) and its antecedents
   ITUC, *Congress Bulletin*, 1955.
   ICTU, *Congress News*, July 1990, no 2.

H Irish Labour History Society (ILHS)
   Saothar 1, 1975, to 15, 1990.
   Obair, no 1, May 1984; no 2, January 1985.
   Irish Labour History News, no 1, summer 1986.
   Labour History News, no 2, autumn 1986–no 6, summer 1990.
   *The Parliament of Labour, 100 years of the Dublin Council of Trade
   Unions*, ILHS catalogue of exhibition, 7 October–31 December 1986, in
   the Dublin Civic Museum.

I Irish Transport and General Workers' Union (ITGWU)
   Liberty, 1972–1984.
   Liberty News, 1984–1989.

J People's College
   Newsletter, November 1988.

K Services, Industrial, Professional and Technical Union (SIPTU)
   Newsline, 1990.

L Workers' Party and its antecedents
   United Irishman, November, December 1977.
   Workers' Life, September 1980; September 1983.

M World Federation of Trade Unions (WFTU)
   World Trade Union Movement, no 9, 1980; no 11, 1980.

PARLIAMENTARY DEBATES

British House of Commons, Parliamentary Debates, vol XCVIII, cols 810–11, 24 October 1917; vol C, col 217, 4 December 1917; vol C, col 1163, 12 December 1917; vol C, cols 1977–1978, 19 December 1917.

Dáil Éireann, Parliamentary Debates, vol 125, col 668, 12 April 1951; vol 125, col 951, 17 April 1951.

OTHER REPORTS AND RECORDS

CSO, consumer price index, 1914–1989.
CSO, estimated net migration, 1927–1986.
CSO, live register of unemployment, total live register, 1923–1986.
College of Industrial Relations, 'Growth from Strength', unpublished report of the working party to advise the Jesuit Provincial on the future of the College of Industrial Relations, 1 May 1983.
College of Industrial Relations, prospectus 1985/6.
Police Report, 23 June 1941.
St Joseph's Young Priests' Society, certificate of membership.
St Joseph's Young Priests' Society, collection book, 1949–1950.
St Joseph's Young Priests' Society, constitution.
South Dublin Union, indoor admissions register, 1913.

INTERVIEWS

In addition to extensive interviews with John Swift between 1980 and 1990, and less extensive ones during the same period with Harriet Swift, Alice Robinson (nee Swift) and Grosvenor Swift, the following were also interviewed by John P. Swift:
Joe Deasy, 26 July 1989.
Dr John De Courcy Ireland, 7 September 1989; 21 April 1990.
Johnny Devlin, 7 August 1990.
Ken Hannigan, 10 August 1989.
Dr George Jeffares, 30 July 1990.
Luke MacKeogh, 7 August 1987.
Donal Nevin, 25 August 1989.
Michael O'Halloran, 14 October 1987.
Michael O'Regan, 31 May 1989.
Michael O'Riordan, 24 July 1989.
Andrée Sheehy Skeffington, 17 November 1986.

SELECT PUBLISHED WRITINGS ABOUT JOHN SWIFT AND
HIS LIFE AND TIMES.

Anon, 'Union Pays Tributes to Secretary', *Irish Times*, 4 June 1964.

Anon, 'Union Elects First Irish President', *Irish Independent*, 4 June 1964.

Anon, 'Tributes to Union Man', *Irish Press*, 4 June 1964.

Anon, 'Food Workers' Union Barometer of Wealth', *Jerusalem Post*, 1 July 1965.

Anon, 'Soviet Ambassador Presents Order to Irish Trade Unionist', *Irish Times*, 5 October 1976.

Anon, 'Socialist Veteran Dies', *Irish Independent*, March 22, 1990.

Anon, 'Funeral of Mr John Swift', *Irish Times*, March 24, 1990.

Anon, 'Late Mr John Swift', *Dundalk Democrat*, 31 March 1990.

Anon, 'Farewell to John Swift', *Unity*, 31 March 1990.

John Armstrong, 'Special Branch Files as a Birthday Present', *Irish Times*, 29 August 1986.

Michael Barber, 'Russian Honour for Irishman', *Irish Press*, 27 August 1976.

Paddy Bergin, 'An Unusual Celebration', *Labour History News*, no 2, autumn 1986.

Nigel Brown, 'An Irishman's Diary', *Irish Times*, 11 September 1986.

Coleman Cassidy, 'Death of a Trade Union Leader', *Irish Press*, 22 March 1990.

Coleman Cassidy, 'Death of Union Leader' *Evening Press*, 22 March 1990.

Una Claffey, *Today Tonight Special*, 'The State of the Unions Then and Now', *RTE Guide*, 28 June 1985.

Fergal Costello,? (Anon) 'Soviet Honour', *Irish Socialist*, November 1976.

Mary Cummins, 'Embassy Toasts October Revolution', *Irish Times*, 7 November 1984.

Francis Devine, 'John Swift, 1896–1990', *Newsline*, vol 1, no 1, May 1990, 20.

Francis Devine, 'John Swift 1896–1990', *Labour History News*, no 6, summer 1990, 21.

Francis Devine, '"A Dangerous Agitator": John Swift, 1896–1990, Socialist, Trade Unionist, Secularist, Internationalist, Labour Historian', *Saothar* 15, 1990, 7–19.

Oliver Donohue, ? (Anon) 'John Swift', ICTU *Congress News*, July 1990, no 2, 8.

Ronan Farren, 'The 20s—and What Makes One Man Different', *Evening Herald*, 16 September 1980.

Dan Gallin,? (Anon) 'John Swift', IUF *News Bulletin*, vol 60, no 1–2, 1990, 10.

Anne Harris, 'Bakers Dozen', *Workers' Life*, September 1980.

Anne Haverty, 'Labour History's Hidden Murals', *Irish Times*, 14 March 1984.

Michael D. Higgins, (MDH) 'John Swift—An Appreciation', *Irish Times*, 16 April 1990.

Justin Keating, *Evening Herald*, 27 March 1990.

Micheál Mac Aonghusa, 'John Swift 1896–1990', *Anois*, 1 April 1990.

Uinseann Mac Eoin, *Survivors*, Dublin, 1980, 56–74.

Andreas McEntee, 'John, 92, Still Fighting', 'Dubliner's Diary', *Evening Press*, 20 September 1988.

Michael McInerney, ? (Anon) (untitled) *Irish Times*, 24 May 1967.

Michael McInerney, 'A Lifetime in the Service of Labour', *Irish Times*, 31 July 1975.

Deirdre McQuillan, 'Unique Murals Destroyed in Dublin Demolition', *Sunday Tribune*, 3 April 1988.

Seamus Martin, 'Union Leader Mr John Swift Dies', *Irish Times*, 22 March 1990.

Gill Nesbitt, 'An Irishwoman's Diary', *Irish Times*, 1 October 1988.

Eileen O'Brien ('Candida'), 'An Irishwoman's Diary', *Irish Times*, 23 February 1976.

Eileen O'Brien, 'An Irishwoman's Diary', *Irish Times*, 2 August 1982.

Eileen O'Brien, 'An Irishwoman's Diary', *Irish Times*, 5 September 1983.

Pádraic Ó Raghallaigh, (Anon)? 'Workers' Champion', *RTE Guide*, 6 August 1976.

Fintan O'Toole, 'Swift and Sure', *Sunday Tribune*, 25 November 1984.

John P. Swift, (Anon) 'Presentation to John Swift', *Irish Socialist*, February 1981.

John P. Swift, 'Irish Labour's Living History', *Sunday Tribune* (*Colour Tribune*), 23 August 1987.

Brian Trench,? (Anon) '90 Not Out', *Sunday Tribune*, 24 August 1986.

AUDIO AND AUDIO/VISUAL RECORDS OF JOHN SWIFT AND HIS LIFE AND TIMES

Audio interview of John Swift by Ken Hannigan, 1975.

RTE, audio interview of John Swift by Pádraic Ó Raghallaigh, broadcast in six episodes on 10, 17, 24, 31 August; 7, 14 September 1976; rebroadcast in April and May 1990.

Audio interview of John Swift by Uinseann Mac Eoin, c.1976.

RTE, 'Awaiting the Revolution—75 years of the Irish Transport and General Workers' Union', television documentary, transmitted 1984.

RTE, 'Donncha on Sunday' (Donncha O Dulaing), radio programme marking the golden jubilee of the Dublin Bakery School, broadcast on 24 March 1985.

RTE *Today Tonight*, television interview of John Swift by Una Claffey, transmitted 1 July 1985.

Audio interviews of John Swift by John P. Swift 1986–1988.

NATIONAL AND LOCAL NEWSPAPERS AND PERIODICALS

Anois, 1 April 1990.

Bakery World, October 1975; January/February 1981; March 1987; May 1990.

Cork Examiner, 6 June 1969.

Decies (Old Waterford Society), no 3, October 1976.

Dublin Evening Mail, 16 February 1961.

Dundalk Democrat, 1887–1913; 31 March 1990.
Dundalk Examiner, 1887–1894.
Education, vol 3, no 5, n.d., late 1980s?
Education Times, 21 November 1974; 15 May 1975.
Evening Herald, 22 August 1946; 16 February, 1 June, 1961; 11 January 1974; 16 September 1980; 25 July 1988; 27 March 1990.
Evening Press, 26, 30 July 1963; 8 November 1975; 20 September 1988; 22 March 1990.
Hibernia, 19 February 1971; 21 March 1975.
Irish Catholic, 1930–1960.
Irish Catholic Directory, 1930–1962.
Irish Independent, 15 April 1949; 29 August 1962; 4 June 1964; 29 September 1966; 29 May 1967; 18 January 1969; 24 April 1988; 8 November 1989; 22 March 1990.
Irish Press, 28, 29, 30 March 1933; 17 January 1934; 5, 6 July, 22, 26, 27 August 1946; 9 September 1947; 17 February 1949; 2 September 1959; 23 November 1962; 4 June 1964; 29 May 1967; 18 January 1969; 27 August, 5 October 1976; 29 January 1977; 24 August 1980; 30 September, 8, 14 October 1982; 22 March 1990.
Irish Times, 26 March, 22 August 1942; 29 September, 1, 2, 3, 4 October 1951; 1 January, 18 May, 18 August, 26 September 1958; 1 January 1959; 1 September 1960; 29 August, 22, 23 October 1962; 27, 28 November 1963; 4 June 1964; 4, 5 November 1965; 24 May, 7, 8 November 1967; 23, 24 July 1968; 25 January, 24 March 1969; 20 July, 2, 3 September, 3, 6 November 1970; 12, 22, 29 January, 22, 23 February, 14 March, 12 April, 14, 15, 31 May, 21, 23, 31 July, 14 September, 20 October 1971; 26 July, 9 August, 10, 11 October, 8 November 1972; 12 February, 9 August 1973; 31 July, 4 September 1975; 23, 24 February, 24 March, 5 July, 5, 10 October, 1976; 14 March, 23 September 1977; 21 August, 13, 19, 29 September 1980; 9 September 1981; 2 August, 17 September, 30 October 1982; 30 April, 8, 10 June, 5 September 1983; 14 March, 24 April, 4 May, 7, 29 November 1984; 29 April, 8 June, 31 July 1985; 9 January, 14 May, 7 June, 14, 15, 16, 17, 18 July, 29 August, 4, 11 September, 15 November 1986; 6, 29, 30 June, 1, 2, 4, 30, 31 July 1987; 14 March, 4, 25 April, 17 September, 1, 14 October, 7 November 1988; 20 January, 25 February, 6 March, 19 June, 6, 13 October, 8 November 1989; 22, 24 March, 16 April, 10 September 1990.
Jerusalem Post, 1 July 1965.
Leabharlann (Library Association of Ireland) vol 18, no 2, June 1960.
Reynolds News, 7 July 1946.
RTE Guide, 6 August 1976; 28 August 1985.
Standard, 1930–1959.
Sunday Independent, 19 July 1970; 7 September 1986.
Sunday Press, 19 July 1970; 24 August 1980.
Sunday Tribune, 21 August 1983; 29 January, 25 November 1984; 24 August, 16 November 1986; 19, 26 July, 23 August 1987; 13 March, 3 April 1988.
Tempest's Annual, 1887–1913.
Tempest's Centenary Annual, 1959.

SELECT BOOKS AND ARTICLES

C.S. Andrews, *Man of No Property*, Dublin, 1982.

Robert Ballagh, 'The Bakers' Cultural Initiative', *Obair* no 2, January 1985, 7.

David Boulton, *Objection Overruled*, London, 1967.

Andrew Boyd, *The Rise of the Irish Trade Unions*, Dublin, 1972.

Kenneth D. Browne, 'Larkin and the Strikes of 1913: Their Place in British History', *Saothar* 9, 1983, 89–99.

Noel Browne, *Against the Tide*, Dublin, 1986.

Seamus Cody, 'May Day in Dublin, 1890 to the Present', *Saothar* 5, May 1979.

Seamus Cody, 'The Remarkable Patrick Daly', *Obair*, no 2, January 1985, 10–11.

Seamus Cody, 'Dublin Trades Council and the 1913 Lock-Out', *Irish Labour History News*, no 1, summer 1986, 6–9.

Seamus Cody, John O'Dowd, Peter Rigney, *The Parliament of Labour— 100 Years of the Dublin Council of Trade Unions*, Dublin, 1986.

Communist Party of Ireland—Outline History, Dublin, 1975.

Seán Cronin, 'The Rise and Fall of the Socialist Labor Party of North America', *Saothar* 3, 1977, 21–33.

Mel Doyle, 'The Dublin Guilds and Journeymen's Clubs', *Saothar* 3, 1977, 6–14.

Eighty Years of the ITGWU, Dublin, 1979.

Richard English, 'Peadar O'Donnell: 'Socialism and the Republic 1925–37 ', *Saothar* 14, 1989, 47–58.

Tony Farmer, *The Legendary Lofty Clattery Cafe—Bewley's of Ireland*, Dublin, 1986.

ITGWU *Fifty Years of Liberty Hall*, Dublin, 1959.

Clara Foucault-Mohammed, 'Workers in History—The Dublin Bakers: From the Guilds to Geneva', *Labour and Education* (ILO) no 73, 1988/4.

Michael Gallagher, *The Irish Labour Party in Transition 1957–82*, Dublin and Manchester, 1982.

J. Anthony Gaughan, *Thomas Johnson*, Dublin, 1980.

Luke Gibbons, 'Labour and Local History: the Case of Jim Gralton, 1886–1945', *Saothar* 14, 1989, 85–94.

George Gilmore, *The Republican Congress, 1934*, Dublin, n.d., 1970?

C. Desmond Greaves, *The Life and Times of James Connolly*, London, 1961.

C. Desmond Greaves, *The Irish Transport and General Workers' Union: The Formative Years, 1909–1923*, Dublin, 1982.

Ken Hannigan, 'British Based Unions in Ireland: Building Workers and the Split in Congress', *Saothar* 7, 1981, 40–49.

Ellen Hazelkorn, 'The Social and Political Views of Louie Bennett, 1870–1956', *Saothar* 13, 1988, 32–44.

John Horgan, *Labour: The Price of Power*, Dublin, 1986.

T.A. Jackson, *Ireland Her Own—An Outline History of the Irish Struggle*, London, 1947.

Mary Jones, *These Obstreperous Lassies, A History of the Irish Women Workers' Union*, Dublin, 1988.

Peter Kemp, *The Strauss Family—Portrait of a Musical Dynasty*, Tunbridge Wells, Kent, 1985.

Dermot Keogh, 'William Martin Murphy and the Origins of the 1913 Lock-Out', *Saothar* 4, 1978, 15–34.

Emmet Larkin, *James Larkin—Irish Labour Leader, 1876–1947*, London, 1965.

J.J. Lee, 'Aspects of Corporatist Thought in Ireland: The Commission on Vocational Organisation, 1939-1943' in A. Cosgrove and D. McCarthy (eds), *Studies in Irish History: Presented to R. Dudley Edwards*, Dublin, 1979, 324–46

Samuel Levenson, *James Connolly*, London, 1973.

F.S.L. Lyons, *Ireland Since the Famine*, London, 1971.

Uinseann Mac Eoin, *Survivors*, Dublin, 1980.

Edward MacLysaght, *Irish Families*, Dublin, 1972.

Charles McCarthy, *Trade Unions in Ireland, 1894–1960*, Dublin, 1977.

Charles McCarthy, 'The Impact of Larkinism on the Irish Working Class', *Saothar* 4, 1978, 54–6.

Michael McInerney, *Peadar O'Donnell: Irish Social Rebel*, Dublin, 1974.

Michael McInerney, 'Grand Old Man of US Labour Radicals', *Irish Times*, 14 September 1975.

Michael McInerney, 'Larkin: the Name Scrawled in Rage', *Irish Times*, 20 January 1976.

Enda McKay, 'Changing with the Tide: The Irish Labour Party, 1927–1933', *Saothar* 11, 1986, 27–38.

Miceál McKeown, *A Sketchbook of Dundalk—Past and Present*, Dundalk, 1988.

Matt Merrigan, *Eagle or Cuckoo? The Story of the ATGWU in Ireland*, Dublin, 1989.

Mike Milotte, *Communism in Modern Ireland*, Dublin, 1984.

Bill Moran, '1913, Jim Larkin and the British labour Movement', *Saothar* 4, 1978, 35–49.

Hazel Morrissey, *Betty Sinclair—A Woman's Fight for Socialism*, Belfast, 1983.

Hazel Morrissey, 'Against Enormous Odds, Betty Sinclair', *Labour History News*, no 3, spring 1987, 11–12.

Donal Nevin, 'Radical Movements in the Twenties and Thirties' (Thomas Davis Lectures—Secret Societies in Ireland' no 15; broadcast RTE radio, 24 January 1971).

Donal Nevin, 'The Birth of the Workers' Union', *Obair*, May 1984, 3–4.

Donal Nevin, 'The Founding of the Irish Congress of Trade Unions', *Labour History News*, no 5, autumn 1989.

James Newsinger, 'As Catholic as the Pope: James Connolly and the Roman Catholic Church in Ireland', *Saothar* 11, 1986, 7–18.

D.R. O'Connor Lysaght, 'The Rake's Progress of a Syndicalist: The Political Career of William O'Brien, Irish Labour Leader', *Saothar* 9, 1983, 48–62.

John O'Dowd, *The Dublin Bakery School, 1935-1985*, Dublin, 1985.

John O'Dowd, 'Dublin Bakery School's Fiftieth Anniversary', *Obair*, no 2, 1985, 5.

Manus O'Riordan, 'Larkin in America', *Saothar* 4, 1978, 50–53.

Manus O'Riordan, 'Portrait of an Irish Anti-Fascist: Frank Edwards, 1907–1983', *Morgen Freiheit,* New York, 1983, reproduced by Labour History Workshop, Dublin, 1984.

Manus O'Riordan, *The International Tailors', Machinists' and Pressers' Union,* unpublished document, 1987.

Michael O'Riordan, *Pages from History on Irish–Soviet Relations,* Dublin, 1977.

Michael O'Riordan, *Connolly Column,* Dublin, 1979.

Michael O'Riordan, 'Ireland's International Heroes: The Story of the Men Who Fought for the Spanish Republic', *Obair,* no 2, 1985, 4–6.

Hugh Oram, *Bewley's,* Dublin, 1978.

Henry Patterson, 'James Larkin and the Belfast Dockers' and Carters' Strike of 1907', *Saothar* 4, 1978, 8–14.

Bob Purdie, *Politics in the Streets: The Origins of the Civil Rights Movement in Northern Ireland,* Belfast, 1990.

Ruaidhrí Roberts, Dardis Clarke, *The Story of the People's College,* Dublin, 1986.

Séamas Sheils, 'Seventy-five Years of the ITGWU', *Obair,* May 1984, 9–11.

Eric Taplin, 'James Larkin, Liverpool and the National Union of Dock Labourers: The Apprenticeship of a Revolutionary', *Saothar* 4, 1978, 1–7.

Sydney Webb and Beatrice Webb, *The History of Trade Unionism,* London and New York, 1894.

Noel Ward, *The INTO and the Catholic Church, 1930–1955* (M.A., UCD, 1987) unpublished thesis.

Victor, Whitmarsh, *Memories of Dundalk,* Dundalk, 1977.

Victor Whitmarsh, *Old Dundalk,* Dundalk, 1988.

J.H. Whyte, *Church and State in Modern Ireland, 1923–1970,* Dublin, 1971.

James Wickham, 'The New Irish Working Class', *Saothar* 6, 1980, 81–8.

Index